CONFESSIONS OF STOCK MARKET WIZARDS

CONFESSIONS OF STOCK MARKET WIZARDS

DOYENS OF INDIAN INVESTING ON THEIR BIGGEST LEARNINGS

SAFIR ANAND

HARPER
BUSINESS

An Imprint of HarperCollins *Publishers*

First published in India by Harper Business 2025
An imprint of HarperCollins *Publishers*
4th Floor, Tower A, Building No. 10, DLF Cyber City,
DLF Phase II, Gurugram, Haryana – 122002
www.harpercollins.co.in

4 6 8 10 9 7 5 3

Copyright © Safir Anand 2025

P-ISBN: 978-93-6569-995-1
E-ISBN: 978-93-6569-638-7

The views and opinions expressed in this book are the author's own and the facts are as reported by him, and the publishers are not in any way liable for the same.

None of the content in this book is intended to be a substitute for professional financial advice and should not be relied on as financial advice. Always seek the guidance of your financial advisor with any questions you may have regarding your finances.

Safir Anand asserts the moral right
to be identified as the author of this work.

All rights reserved. No part of this publication may be reproduced, stored in a retrieval system, or transmitted, in any form or by any means, electronic, mechanical, photocopying, recording or otherwise, without the prior permission of the publishers.

Typeset in 11.5/15 Garamond Premier Pro at
HarperCollins *Publishers* India

Printed and bound at
Thomson Press (India) Ltd

This book is produced from independently certified FSC® paper
to ensure responsible forest management.

*To the pursuit of knowledge and the empowerment of
the investing community through equity*

The detailed notes and references pertaining to this book are available on the HarperCollins *Publishers* India website. Scan this QR code to access the same.

Contents

Preface	ix
1. Samir Arora: The maverick of the market	1
2. Sanjoy Bhattacharya: The unstoppable leader of market complexities	13
3. Vikas Khemani: The financial architect on a quest for hidden gems	35
4. Devina Mehra: The data-driven equity crusader	46
5. Manish Bhandari: The strategic visionary and value hunter	57
6. Raamdeo Agrawal: The luminary with an eye for long-term success	69
7. Atul Suri: The insight strategist and market alchemist	76
8. Sankaran Naren: The anatomy of an investment mistake—lessons from the school of hard knocks	88
9. Vijay Kedia: The melodic rationalist with a legacy of success	99
10. Ayush Mittal: The young fin-tech trailblazer	107
11. Gautam Trivedi: The global strategist with an Indian twist	119
12. Ravi Dharamshi: The guardian of marketing fundamentals	130
13. E.A. Sundaram: The philosopher of wealth and wisdom	140

14. Jyoti Jaipuria: The investment pioneer and deep diver — 152
15. Viraj Mehta: The rising innovator with an unconventional approach — 163
16. Prashant Khemka: The experienced portfolio navigator — 171
17. Sunil Singhania: The market whisperer with a passion for trends — 182
18. K. Sarath Reddy: The daredevil with a strategic edge — 193
19. Amisha Vora: The limitless data-driven leader — 207
20. Madhusudan Kela: The investing mastermind with a heart of gold — 222
21. Ramesh Damani: The lessons on mistakes and the role of humility from a true blue-blooded veteran — 235
22. Punita Kumar-Sinha: The champion of breaking investment barriers — 242
23. Sanjay Bakshi: The wisdom-infused educator — 246
24. Rajeev Thakkar: The unshakable sustainable strategist — 253
25. Satya Prakash Mittal: The revolutionary architect of India's financial landscape — 264
26. Hiren Ved: The dynamic force behind India's wealth transformation — 281

Conclusion — 287
Notes and References — 303

Preface

WHILE many books and writings appear on the successes of investors and fund managers, and much is taught even in academics on how to identify companies and value them, it has always intrigued me why the subject of risk management and mistakes is not formally taught, whether in context of life in general or—as an extension—in context of markets, and much of it is learnt by experience. There are hardly any books on selling, and the confessions about the goof-ups or the pitfalls avoided, even by luck.

Despite making good returns in the market by owning some stocks, if you end up making too many costly mistakes with few others, the net effect of your return could be embarrassing. Almost similar to building a body but ignoring the warning signs of trouble, until it's too late to revive.

Thus, I set up writing this book, and what better than to reach out to some of the finest fund managers of the country, laden with experiences of all sorts, dealing with client infusion of funds at the peak or pull-out at the bottom, and how their psychology was tested across the ups and downs of market and in decision-making.

Much to my joy, twenty-six of them I handpicked and have learnt from agreed to be part of the book.

This book carries the wisdom of many mistakes and the teachings they brought to the table.

I would like to thank each of the fund managers for being so generous and open with their sharing, which I hope makes you—the reader—a better thinker.

I would also like to thank HarperCollins for their support, from loving the concept of the book to its execution.

Thanks to Sehr Anand for supporting me in getting the book completed.

Mr Market has always been a teacher, even if I was at the receiving end of it—thank you.

I hope you enjoy this book as much as I did while putting it together. Some of the fund managers called it an awakening of sorts while telling and highlighting their confessions, which were never perceived the way this book has made them think of and relay.

CHAPTER 1

Samir Arora

The maverick of the market

THIS is a chapter about the prolific Samir Arora, a technocrat, whose professional path of many decades demonstrates a blend of calculated moves and intuitive insights. It also shows that despite being so seasoned, he never claims to know it all, and through his interviews and tweets, repeatedly shares his learnings and mistakes.

In his early days, his educational path began at IIT-Delhi, leading him to IIM Calcutta, and eventually to the mecca of finance, the Wharton School of the University of Pennsylvania. Many may not be able to crack IIT, IIM and Wharton but Samir's learning curve suggests the mistake that some people make in undermining the importance of good education towards learning. Mind you, education, as it will later play out in this chapter, does not limit itself to institutes. It includes reading books (Samir is a prolific reader of books on many subjects), reading newspapers, magazines and journals and revisiting experiences of the past towards thinking ahead.

I asked Samir if his journey is characterized by early realizations of misaligned choices, and he answered with an affirmative. He shared with me how he ramped up an entire realigned path by taking well-thought-out decisions on moving from engineering to finance and eventually, to growth investing.

Since this chapter is all about mistakes, it's important to consider Samir's early realizations. According to *Merriam-Webster*, a mistake is 'to blunder in the choice of'. In Samir's case, he didn't make a mistake in the literal sense; rather, he had the gift of realization—one of them concerned his initial academic choice. While in school (he had opted for physics, chemistry, maths and accounts for maximum flexibility), Samir hoped to become a chartered accountant someday, but went on to study at IIT only because he passed the Joint Entrance Examination and 'no one refuses an IIT admission'. Despite coming third in his mechanical engineering course at IIT-Delhi, he knew that his passion lay elsewhere. The only way to correct this was to study some more; this took him to IIM Calcutta where he was the class topper and discovered a keen interest in business and finance.

Since there were little to zero investment jobs in the 1980s India, his first job was in financial planning at a Delhi-based corporate.

After working for three years in two corporates, Samir again recognized the misalignment between the investment jobs he was really seeking and the financial planning work that he was doing—he viewed it as an opportunity rather than a setback and applied to select US universities for admission to their finance programmes to again study his way out of his predicament. Point to be noted: Misalignment and retrospection on it could be an opportunity for course correction. It is up to us to reorient our perspective and fix our trajectory, be it education, sports, choice or the market.

Many a times, in markets, a decision to buy or sell a stock is taken as if the decision was right. Our ego blocks us from revisiting the decision and introspecting on facts. Facts change and so should evaluation. It is far more difficult for a fund manager to reverse a decision, given he can be questioned by his investors. But Samir remains open to the idea that it is the outcome of the decision that will decide the right and wrong, not the ego of being adamant.

Samir's journey is a lesson in intuition; it is a great tool for making choices. The mistake many of us make is, we don't probe our intuitive powers. Intuition comes with a level of what we are exposed to. Even when we sleep, we think basis what resides within us. However, intuition needs the passion to analyse. Here, Samir uses his analytical-thinking capability to full advantage. For example, when he headed Alliance, I remember, he was one of the earliest investors in HDFC Bank/Kotak Bank, Bharti, IT companies and Trent/Pantaloon. His ability to link the opportunity in India for these companies decades back to the analysis of how these sectors had done in countries such as the USA and Korea/China had guided his intuitive faith in these companies. They ended up as multibaggers.

Samir also used his intuitive capability to full use in the case of HDFC Bank, a stock where he made some 500x returns, and continues to be invested even today in his fund, Helios. When asked why he chose HDFC Bank in the mid-1990s, Samir's logic was: private sector taking on public sector with high-quality management, technology, service orientation and limited political interference. Not only did he make a great return for his investors through HDFC bank, he maximized the returns by investing in several companies where private sector similarly took on public sector companies, such as Kotak, Bharti, Zee, and insurance companies.

Sometimes, we make the mistake of being fixated on one outcome in a company, not realizing that there may be multiple opportunities resonating from our thoughts in other companies, which may benefit from a 'shift'. I asked Samir if he had considered the price-to-earnings (P/E) ratio in Bharti Airtel when investing during its initial public offering (IPO) in 2002, when it was one of the top holdings in only one mutual fund—the Samir Arora–managed Alliance funds. He said he looked at the 'size of opportunity' and its comparison with China for his conviction in Bharti around its IPO. Most investors are too fixated on only a few valuation tools. However, valuation tools for companies disrupting sectors cannot be the same as those for established, well-known incumbents in these sectors. Recently, Samir applied the same thinking in his investment in Zomato, a company his fund entered early, resulting in great returns. This led me to a new realization—financial metrics are not static. Optically, while they are important tools, a loss-making company burning cash may be creating a huge opportunity, where once it creates a business model, there could be a monopoly kind of earning and move from loss-making to cash-generation.

Samir left me with one more learning here. A good decision is not a one-day move. I have often heard his interviews on TV and seen some of his fund disclosures. Akin to revisiting decisions, he believes a stock's journey could be long, and hence, does not suffer from the mistake of 'price anchoring' bias. Rather, he focuses on where the puck can go.

Samir's strength lies in intuitively staying away from a course that could lead to blunders. His journey is also a lesson on the importance of education. It is unlikely that Samir would have reached the heights he has without the education he received.

The investment sector and Samir's journey

Samir's story is a testament to the power of intuition and the courage to admit when you're wrong. He is often quoted as saying, 'No one knows anything about anything beyond a point'. Samir does not believe in 'all or nothing'; reasoned decision-making is his mantra. Those who know him vouch for his ability to laugh at his mistakes and course correct. For Samir, in the unpredictable world of investing, mistakes aren't failures—they're just plot twists in a thrilling financial adventure.

A mistake some of us make is that of overconfidence and sticking to wrong decisions, stubbornly believing them to be right. As Samir says, 'it could be right' but 'it could be wrong'. Being open to any possibility allows one to reverse a decision if it is wrong or have the patience to wait if it is right.

Talking to Samir, one quickly learns that in the rollercoaster world of investment, mistakes are as common as a Sunday breakfast of chhole bhature in a Punjabi household. As a seasoned investor with a great sense of humour, Samir understands that even the best-laid plans can sometimes go hilariously wrong. When tracing his journey, it becomes clear that he embraces mistakes much like a comedian embraces a heckler—sure, it's not ideal, but it's all part of the show. Samir believes that every blunder is a golden opportunity to learn and grow, as long as you don't pull the same stunt twice. Think of it as a game of Whack-a-Mole: you might miss on the first swing, but you'll get better at whacking those pesky mistakes over time. By catching his errors early and correcting them with a chuckle, Samir ensures each mistake becomes a stepping stone to smarter, more savvy investment decisions in the future. After all, what's the point of a mistake if you can't laugh at it and learn from it? And that reference to chhole bhature wasn't without reason—that's Samir's comfort food of sorts!

Samir's journey teaches us that life is meant to be enjoyed and learnt from. Being too rigid prevents us from learning. He gives his mind a reward for getting it right and laughter for getting it wrong.

I asked him that wrong can still erode return, so how does he cope with this. His answer to me was a full chapter of learning.

'Conviction is higher in rejection that in acceptance.' It is easier to know what is bad than to know what is good. As an example, you may not like sugar and may reject eating it without much thought. The decision is fast and well–thought-of from health or other reasons. However, to choose between Chinese and Indian food will need more fact scoring. To choose between these will require some view on 'which restaurant', 'which dish', 'what did you eat in the meal before', and other such factors.

Investment decisions (and, perhaps, those in life, generally) should start with eliminating obvious mistakes. Potential obvious mistakes that can be avoided are buying into 'known bad managements', 'high valuations', and 'weak balance sheet', among others. Instead of choosing good and strong factors (which are more difficult to define), focus on elimination. The journey of investing does not end in a day; it blossoms through continuous learning and analysing facts over time.

Samir further explains that one day of market underperformance or outperformance does not matter. However, repeated underperformance needs you to probe more.

Samir's investment career has been as carefully crafted as a gourmet recipe, complete with a generous dash of realizations for that extra flavour. He knew early on that aiming for perfection in the volatile financial markets is like trying to catch smoke with a butterfly net. Samir believes that to do very well in the long term, you must do well over different periods, which is why the Helios Mutual Fund advertisements use the tagline 'Har term ke liye' (For every term). He emphasizes that you will win the bout in boxing if you don't get a knock-out, and hence, you should focus on avoiding that than believing you will always hit the best jab.

He tries to build a strategy that can handle a few speed-breakers without sending everything into a tailspin. His secret sauce? Diversifying his portfolio, employing top-notch risk-management techniques, and keeping his brain sharp and well-fed with the latest market insights. By weaving room for mistakes into his master plan, Samir has created a resilient, adaptive investment approach that can dance gracefully to the market's unpredictable rhythms.

Another learning from Samir is based on Darwin's principle of 'survival of the fittest'. He believes that to be in the run for returns you must survive and let the good market days reward you. Hence, he is open to change, even switching his favoured sectors into non-ownership over time.

Let us look at an example from the IT sector.

In the pre-2000 era, Samir was like an oracle on technology and media stocks, spotting undervalued gems before they became the belle of the ball. With a keen eye on the American markets, he recognized India's IT potential and was one of the early adopters of this 'next big thing'. Spotting winners like Infosys and Satyam, among others, was his forte, and he understood early on that IT stocks were about to take off like a rocket.

This rewarded his Alliance fund immensely. It was the best-performing fund for nearly a decade.

After he moved on from Alliance, Samir went all-in and launched Helios Capital in 1998.

Helios Capital's fortunes soared over the next two decades, thanks to Samir's shrewd bets, including the more recent ones of Varun Beverages (10x) and Zomato (5x), and also along the way shorting stocks like Idea Cellular and Satyam Computers. The key point to note here is that although in the Alliance days his returns had come from the IT sector, in Helios days, the returns came from a diverse group of sectors and companies.

Samir became a legend in Indian fund management, with his easy-going candour and friendly advice, making him a favourite on business news channels and earning him a significant Twitter following. However, Samir's journey was not all smooth sailing. There were plenty of banana peels along the way, and he's the first to admit that some slips were due to a nasty bout of overconfidence, a common ailment among investors. The global financial crisis was a particularly rude wake-up call for many investors, including Samir.

From running a large overweight position in IT stocks in the 1990s to maintaining a market-weight position for the next two decades, Samir reduced his sector weight to near zero in mid-2022 when he observed issues such as pricing concerns, slow recruitment, layoffs, valuation challenges and rising US interest rates. Typically, investors who have made money in a particular sector become comfortable with those and are unwilling to go outside their comfort zone. Samir has shown flexibility to change stocks and sectors, and has even switched from 'being long a stock for a long period to being short the same stock' in a day or two, many times in his career.

TV interviewers often ask him if he plans to return to the IT sector. He says that flexibility is never compromised, and if a stock does not meet his criteria of rejection, facts will decide its acceptance. He adds that he has often gone from 'being long for a long time' to 'being short' without any emotional attachment.

The mistake many investors make is the attachment bias. What worked for us is assumed to be for perpetuity. Samir does not believe in this approach. He often points out that even Warren Buffett does not say 'our favourite holding period is forever', clarifying that it is 'forever' only if the companies do well. Therefore, Samir advocates remaining invested in the market at all times and adjusting the proportion of investments and stocks when companies face challenges.

Frank admissions

After three decades in the investment world, Samir has turned countless mistakes into valuable lessons, gaining profound insights into both stocks and sound decision-making. He believes that picking stocks requires a calm mind, asserting, 'good decisions come from mental peace'. Despite his esteemed position, Samir remains candid and unpretentious, enjoying simple pleasures like bhujiya, vacationing in London and listening to Arijit Singh. His views on wealth creation have evolved, and he now advocates a balanced life as a foundation for prudent investment decisions.

Samir cautions against emotional investing, emphasizing that personal and professional satisfaction are crucial to avoid high-risk mistakes driven by frustration. His journey, marked by successes—many of which stemmed from realizing and learning from mistakes—underscores the importance of mental peace and emotional stability in achieving professional success in finance.

I asked Samir how he maximizes returns. He makes an insightful distinction between companies that offer 'high confidence in reasonable returns' and those that offer 'reasonable confidence in high returns'. Interestingly, there is no category of 'high confidence in high returns' for that would lead to concentration and violate his other strong principle of 'no one knows anything about anything, beyond a point'. The first goal, always, is to survive in investments—'to survive is to win'. He, therefore, follows a diversified portfolio of both categories so as to get more alpha and yet not suffer a serious 'knock out' if anything goes wrong. This balances his mind and return, both.

He reminds me of how the late legend Rakesh Jhunjhunwala ran a separate trading portfolio and a separate investing portfolio. It's almost like Daniel Kahneman and his award-winning *Thinking, Fast and Slow*—have a different mindset for different companies in your portfolio.

When Samir sells something that later moves up or buys something that does not, he certainly considers it a part of life: 'As long as you have more winners than losers, it is enough; you can't get this right 100 per cent.'

Samir is keenly aware of the dangers of overconfidence. He warns that an investor is only as good as their most recent performance or last investment decision.

Reflecting on his career, Samir candidly shares instances where overconfidence and poor analysis led to significant mistakes. One notable blunder occurred in 2008, when he remained fully invested for much of the year, believing that Indian companies were insulated from the global financial crisis and that the Indian market and its economy would not be affected by global events. Before 2008, Samir used to collect only figures of bulls, but since then, his office has figures and paintings of both bulls and bears to remind him and the team that one needs to be always open minded.

Samir firmly believes that while mistakes are inevitable, they must always serve as valuable learning experiences. He cautions, however, that when a decision made with high confidence goes wrong, it can severely impact an investor's morale. This recognition of the fine line between confidence and overconfidence is a cornerstone of Samir's investment philosophy.

His outlook on India reflects his ability to see the bigger picture and maintain a long-term perspective as against short-term bullishness. He is generally bullish on the India growth story (but post 2008 wants to always question this thesis with an open mind). This confidence in India's economic potential is supported by his unique dual exposure to both the US and Indian markets, which enables him to differentiate between the macro and micro strengths of these economic powerhouses. Samir's optimism about India also stems from his deep understanding of the country's economic fundamentals and growth prospects. He acknowledges that mistakes are made by every country and the people at the helm of its affairs. Similarly, personal frustrations exist in every country, but an equity investor's natural inclination is towards optimism about the market they invest in.

This positive outlook is not about being blindly confident but is based on a comprehensive analysis of India's economic trajectory and potential. The key to Samir's success lies in balancing the confidence which he has gained from his own, and possibly others', mistakes, with prudence. His extensive experience has taught him to be wary of overconfidence while maintaining a bullish outlook on promising markets like India. By learning from past mistakes and keeping a level-headed approach, Samir continues to navigate the complexities of the investment world effectively. His mantra emphasizes the importance of mental peace and emotional stability in making sound investment decisions. Overconfidence can lead to reckless decisions, while a balanced, well-informed approach can pave the way for sustained success. Samir's insights offer valuable lessons for investors, highlighting the importance of patience, humility, continuous learning, and an optimistic albeit cautious approach on the future.

The fallacy of learning from others

When asked about the possibility of learning from others' mistakes without having to commit them, Samir chuckles at the idea that we can learn everything we need from others or from books—he calls it the 'great study buddy fallacy'.

According to Samir, real learning happens when you're in the thick of it, having your skin exposed, feeling the heat and making your own mistakes. One of his most eye-opening experiences was during the 2008 financial crisis, when he had a lightbulb moment about the interconnectedness of global markets. It was like discovering that your quiet neighbour's wild parties actually shake your house too. He realized that despite the miles between them, global economic conditions could give India a good shake as well.

This epiphany hammered home the importance of not living in financial silos and recognizing the global nature of markets. So, forget the armchair theories—Samir says it's all about getting out there and learning from your own financial bumps and bruises.

Samir knows that while some mistakes can be spotted a mile away, not all can be dodged. He says avoiding companies with known poor management, terrible financial histories, or wildly overvalued stocks is like steering clear of the questionable shrimp at a buffet—smart but not foolproof. His approach is refreshingly pragmatic: he estimates that about 30 per cent of companies will flop like a bad movie sequel, and the goal is to keep that percentage as low as possible. Striving for perfection or a spotless record is a sure way to become overly cautious, which can prevent you from cashing in on potential blockbusters.

Then there's FOMO—the fear of missing out—the stock market's annoying little gremlin that strikes everyone at some point. Samir has a humorous take on it: worrying about missed opportunities is as pointless as fretting over a missed dessert at an all-you-can-eat buffet. The market is full of potential winners, so missing one good stock is not a big deal; there are plenty more where that came from. This laid-back attitude helps keep the investment journey balanced and less stressful.

Samir emphasizes that mistakes are simply part of the ride in the investing amusement park. Education, experience and exposure can reduce the number and severity of mistakes but cannot eliminate them entirely. Early investing blunders are like the embarrassing haircuts of our youth—inevitable and part of the learning process. While some errors, such as falling for get-rich-quick schemes or making low-probability bets, can be minimized with better education and analysis, the reality is that everyone stumbles. The key is to laugh it off, learn from it and keep moving forward.

Good can be bad, and bad can be good, depending on where you are standing

According to Samir, the best ways to avoid obvious mistakes in investing are quite straightforward. First, steer clear of companies run like a circus—poor management is a red flag that shouldn't be ignored. Next, keep an eye out for overvalued stocks and industries; nobody wants to pay champagne prices for beer. Accept that some mistakes are inevitable—like dropping your phone; it's bound to happen, but hopefully not too often. Focus on not repeating those blunders and try to keep the duds in your portfolio to a minimum. Remember, personal experience is invaluable—there's no better teacher than getting your own hands dirty in the market. Stay calm to avoid emotional investing; think of yourself as the Zen master of stocks. This mindset will help you ride out the market's rollercoaster without losing your lunch—or your shirt.

Today, Samir stands tall as a seasoned investor, shaped in part by the many mistakes he made early in his career. As the mastermind behind Helios Capital, Samir has fine-tuned his investment philosophy to focus on high-quality companies with sustainable business models and significant growth potential. His investment strategy resembles a Sherlock Holmes mystery—rooted in meticulous analysis of company fundamentals, a keen eye for market dynamics, and a cautious yet sunny outlook on risk.

Samir ends our interview by discussing his most recent mistake—not entering the fund-management space earlier with portfolio-management services (PMS), alternative investment funds (AIF) or mutual fund offerings. For too long, Samir operated in India solely as a foreign portfolio investment (FPI) fund manager, but he is now also the promoter of the fast-growing Helios Mutual Funds. From being a co-borrower (with his father) of a Rs 50,000 loan from HDFC Ltd (along with a top-up loan of Rs 15,000) in the 1980s, Samir has come a long way in both his personal and professional life.

His takeaways on investing mistakes after a thirty-year track record are: one, mistakes are part of the game and a cost of doing business, every investor has to pay this tuition fee to the market; two, do not make the same mistake twice; three, 'elimination investing', which is the Helios philosophy, is not about eliminating mistakes entirely but rather striving to reduce their frequency; and four, you need a diversified portfolio so that no single mistake takes you out of the game or causes seriously harm.

Samir champions the virtues of long-term investing, advocating for patience and discipline like a financial Zen master. He prioritizes good corporate governance and top-notch management, ensuring he invests in companies with ethical leaders who can steer the ship without hitting an iceberg. His mantra 'no one knows anything about anything beyond a point', encourages embracing mistakes—because, let's face it, even the best investors trip up now and then. Samir's journey shows that with a mix of humility, humour and a solid game plan, you can navigate the wild world of investing without losing your cool—or your money.

CHAPTER 2

SANJOY BHATTACHARYA

The unstoppable leader of market complexities

As I start this chapter, I have a confession to make. Much of my investment thinking, shaped over years of my own mistakes and learning, has been course-corrected by reading about a few individuals or listening to the interviews they have given. There is much to learn by observing how some of the great people think and behave. Sanjoy Bhattacharya is certainly on my list. Even though he keeps a low profile, his presentations at the FLAME University Investment Lab and CFA Institute have been both entertaining and instructive.

When I began investing, I saw cheapness as a proxy for value, and low P/E stocks seemed immensely attractive. I naively believed that once earnings growth became more visible, the P/E ratio would magically rise. After experiencing some losses and considerable confusion about whether value investing made sense, I happened to meet Sanjoy for the first time. To my (un)pleasant surprise, I discovered that we were fellow travellers seeking answers to the same questions. One of the first things that struck me was his insistence on owning a business that could use capital efficiently and grow consistently over time. This notion was corroborated by the first company that he ever bought—Asian Paints—in 1983. He explained that his reason for buying it was simply because a close friend had joined the company through campus recruitment at IIM. An early success that subsequently multiplied 560 times over twenty-one years—Infosys Technologies—was due to three individuals (each of whom had worked in IT services) passionately endorsing the business and being greatly impressed by the founders. Sanjoy's epiphany was complete after an hour-long meeting with N.S. Raghavan.

Sanjoy occasionally reminds me of O. Henry's masterpiece, *The Last Leaf*, where Johnsy, a poor young woman, is critically ill due to pneumonia. She believes that when the ivy vine on the wall outside her window would lose all its leaves, she would die too. However, her neighbour, Behrman, an artist, tricks her by painting a leaf on the wall. Johnsy recovers.

One of the traits that a fair few are struck by is his enduring passion to learn and be acquainted with new ideas. He is happiest reading a book that opens his mind to unexplored concepts and theories. Quite often, the ideas do not bear a direct link with the mechanics of investing but instead present a unique and powerful framework for building a rational perspective at variance with conventional wisdom. His current interests include behavioural finance, complex systems and intuition. The books that have had a profound influence on his thinking include *Margin of Safety* by Seth Klarman, *A Zebra in Lion Country* by Ralph Wanger, *Value Investing* by James Montier, *The Zurich Axioms* by Max Gunther and *Winning the Loser's Game* by Charles Ellis.

He identifies small- and mid-cap stocks by doing what he knows best—reading exhaustively about their management teams and founder, financial statements, cash flows and competitive strategy. Our conversations are often characterized by comments such as '*Shri Anand, yeh promoter ke bare mein aap kya jante ho*' (Mr Anand, please elaborate on how much you know about the promoter)?

His obsessive focus on the character and integrity of the top-management team is quite unusual among Indian investors. Equally, he is a firm believer that 'leopards never change their spots' and intent matters just as much as execution. Instead of being enchanted by a wonderful story and letting the imagination wander, his constant refrain is 'what can go seriously wrong?' His belief in the primacy of a truly resilient balance sheet and rational capital allocation, as opposed to earnings growth and an intricate tapestry of forecasts is what has kept him out of trouble over the last four decades.

In many ways, the key elements of his investment approach have been shaped by his extended stint as a credit analyst at CRISIL and ICRA which allowed him to explore more than 350 companies in excruciating detail. The constant emphasis on downside risk rather than the ability to visualize a glorious future in all its splendour reflect the travails of his initial journey commencing in the mid-eighties and fundamental (Bengali!) aversion to losing money. On the rare occasion when the check-list is completed to his full satisfaction, you can sense tremendous joy akin to a eureka moment. For his close friends, this is typically articulated as: '*Isko to dabaa ke khareedna chahiye, zoron se*' (One should buy this and make a significant portfolio allocation).

Over the years, what stands out are a couple of fundamental beliefs: Don't let noise distract or blind you to what can go wrong. Try and figure out the business in depth and understand the agenda of the owners. Focus on understanding the business, its competition and the quality of its accounting as a proxy for the integrity of top management. If you come up trumps, ensure you make a meaningful commitment because such opportunities are rare!

Another unusual habit, which most of us eschew, is to determine a sensible entry point (initial buying price). Much like the fisherman who waits for the fish to bite the bait, Sanjoy is of the old-school view that patience and discipline pay and that the extra margin may well lead to better returns. Thus he has already trained his mind and model towards 'buying right' and not 'right-away buying'. I asked him, what if the company runs up? He says there are many fish in the pond. One that runs away does not mean others won't bite. And if the fish is worth its weight in gold, you may always be attracted towards it if the going gets better.

Sanjoy is a truly long-term investor. Though, of late, he is less convinced about the merits of an unvarnished buy-and-hold philosophy, this may be more to do with VUCA. If there are fundamental changes likely to affect future cash flows, he is clear that an objective re-evaluation should be the basis for action rather than the comfort of having owned a stock for years (aka Coca-Cola, Washington Post).

Not a great believer in analyst forecasts or management meetings, his primary motivation is an objective assessment of current performance and what the future portends on a sustainable basis. A favourite quote is: 'You never ask the barber whether you need a haircut.'

He is perfectly willing to hold stocks that offer predictable low double-digit (10–15 per cent) growth, provided the valuations remain reasonable (ITC, Infosys, Hawkins Cooker and Coromandel International are examples) in order to promote the power of compounding as opposed to paying tax on an immediate gain. When he first started out, STCG and LTCG had huge holding-period differences. As he is fond of saying, 'selling is the dark continent of investing'. If, along the journey, a company underperforms, he enjoys tracking its business more than its stock price, focussing on behavioural science and intrinsic value rather than the market's mood.

He thus shares, an individual managing his own fund is better placed than a fund in the pursuit of small- and mid-cap ideas until they are adequately discovered by institutional research. The market seems abnormal to the extent that more people put in money in funds at highs and pull out at lows—contrary to all norms of sensible investing. If there are many fish in a pond, I ask him how does he know which one will yield the best returns? He answers, 'I don't! I try and catch more fish'. In effect, he believes in owning a diversified pool of companies with a decent allocation and waiting for Father Time to do the rest.

The guru in him awakens to the joy of sharing knowledge. A blessing inherited from his illustrious father, Professor Santosh Kumar Bhattacharyya, who taught at IIM Ahmedabad from 1964 to 1977 and then retired to set up his own consultancy firm, Management Structure and Systems, in Mumbai. Dr Bhattacharya was also part of the visiting faculty at Harvard Business School and Stanford Research Institute. Later, he worked briefly in consulting with McKinsey & Co in New York and had a well-deserved reputation as a dedicated teacher and an outstanding consultant.

There is a strong resemblance between father and son, and most certainly a love for teaching and sharing what they know. Sanjoy acknowledges that his basic values and intellectual motivation have been hugely influenced by his father and suggests that his father was a truly remarkable investor as well! His first and only broker, Raamdeo Agarwal, willingly bears testament to this observation. Sanjoy says that his father gets full credit for inculcating discipline and rigour and promoting a desire to continually expand one's intellectual boundaries. Rather glumly, he concedes that he is far from having mastered accounting in the manner that his father would have liked to see. Clearly, there is life beyond your genes!

Sanjoy has immense respect and gratitude for all those who have helped him learn and move forward. I must admit, rarely have I seen such modesty and openness, and if there were awards for being brutally honest as an investor, Sanjoy would have won, hands down.

He says, 'In your youth, if you grow up in an environment like I did, in IIM Ahmedabad, where my dad was a professor and taught accounting, you learn about business at the dinner table. Very few would have had the immense good fortune to spend time with legends such as Holck Larsen and R.K. Talwar in their early teens.' Being a teacher's son has its own rewards and blessings!

He regrets not having studied engineering as an undergraduate. However, as if embracing a mistake as an opportunity, he comments: 'But equally, I feel extremely lucky that my undergraduate degree was in statistics. That put a practical framework in my head, which has stayed till date, and which meant that I could possibly think in ways that allowed me to figure the odds better than most. Further, a majority of my 'decisions are close to reality because of my initial training in statistics and I would say also, what they call the effect of the Holy Trinity.'[1]

While I am still mulling over what he just shared, he almost jumps out of his chair to say, 'I made friends with Raamdeo (Agrawal) early when I did not know a damn about investing.' In the mid-eighties, he was exposed to several very smart investors. Despite having sharp differences with some of them subsequently, there is no question about how they changed his perspective on markets.

He also acknowledges Pradip Shah's (the first managing director of CRISIL) massive imprimatur in terms of thinking sensibly about business and assessing risk. As a young impressionable analyst, Sanjoy was fascinated by how Shah helped him think sensibly by gently focusing on the obvious flaws. Whether it was relating the financial statements to the context of the business, making sense of the notes to accounts or unravelling the implications of contingent liabilities, Shah was a wonderful mentor. Perhaps the single most important and lasting contribution of Shah was to help in building a framework that objectively assessed the capabilities of a senior management team in a truly comprehensive manner. Much of this education was by way of personal example and judgement!

Finding the fine line between being practical and being objective in judging character and competence is the best lesson Sanjoy learnt from his mentor. Shah was equally a wonderful institution-builder and highly supportive of his young team, encouraging them not be afraid of making mistakes. His only request was not to repeat previous errors. Quite often, he explained how the received wisdom might be misleading. As an example, he emphasized the overwhelming importance of cash flow in determining credit quality, and illustrated why collateral was often of limited value. Finally, he was unswerving in his support of the professional conduct of his younger colleagues in dealing with clients, particularly in hostile circumstances. This required not only immense personal courage but also the faith and trust that he reposed in individuals who were meticulous, of high integrity and hardworking.

Sanjoy is convinced that having great role models has a tremendous impact on one's value systems, thought process and willingness to embrace risk. He believes that he was extremely fortunate to work with a truly amazing group at HDFC Asset Management, where he realized the importance of process and its relationship to outcomes vividly. He recalls that most of the people were younger than him but incredibly smart, which enabled him to learn a lot from them (note: no ego). His most fundamental lesson at HDFC AMC was the importance of upholding and demonstrating the commitment to fiduciary responsibility as an investment manager. To this day, he is puzzled but incredibly grateful that Deepak Parekh, the renowned icon who transformed HDFC into one of India's most-respected financial institutions through his strategic foresight and leadership, entrusted him with the responsibility of leading the investment team.

Deep-diving further into mistakes, Sanjoy is of the view that 'a realization will surface depending on the nature of the mistake, and that is the interesting thing about investing'. As an analogy to bridge, a game in which Sanjoy participates even in national tournaments, he says, 'The feedback loop is instant—you play a hand, you see the result, you go one down and you know that instead of taking a finesse, had you played for a squeeze, you would have a superior result. So, there is an instant feedback loop, which takes you all of thirty seconds, when you have an analytical mind.'

In investing, he adds that the feedback loop can be complicated because market sentiment, macroeconomic factors or significant events can dramatically impact results, which could sometimes be vastly different from the performance and outlook for the business. There could be multiple interacting variables which need to be isolated and understood prior to understanding the outcome, and that is not easy. Sometimes, it can take years to figure out what went wrong.

In fact, on occasion, the best fund managers offer excuses like, 'I was right but too early' or 'If I had been given more time' or 'Others have made even worse mistakes' or 'Why are you judging me on a sample of one irrespective of all the other great things that I have done?' Sanjoy believes these are pitiable excuses that reflect a lack of accountability and unwarranted ego.

He goes on to say, 'There are many challenges arising from volatility and uncertainty that are extremely difficult to figure out. There are multiple variables at work, and you do not know which variable causes how much damage and when it will get sorted out. There are other mistakes wherein you make an assumption about a company, and the assumption is simply wrong, and you need to cut the ego out of the process. Though people presume that I am quite smart, this happens to me quite frequently.'

He adds, 'But what I have learnt is that just as gains compound on the upside, losses compound on the downside. I have learnt to limit the damage as I make the mistakes. It is not that I do not make them, I do not wait for them to compound. I have become better at spotting the mistakes of assumption, if my hypothesis or premise for owning the stock is no longer valid.'

He offers a real-life example that was unclear at the time of discussion but eventually turned out well. He bought a stock that may well be a mistake waiting to happen: 'When the going isn't bad, it is difficult to state the mistake. But, when you look at data, it seems difficult for me to comprehend why people don't own this stock. The company I am referring to is Godfrey Philips, which I bought recently around Rs 2,050. There are some interesting things about Godfrey Philips. Over a 10–15 year period, GPIL's profits have compounded faster than ITC. During this period, GPIL has maintained a market share of 12–13 per cent. It's profits in the first quarter (FY 2023–24) were Rs 250 crore, including a charge of Rs 67 crore. Sales volume growth of Godfrey Philips has been identical to ITC, but there is a Modi-promoter factor (the company is promoted by late Mr K.K. Modi, Ms Bina Modi and family) shining on the sky. So, if ITC commands a higher P/E, the expert argument is that ITC's cigarette business is just as cheap but the other businesses, such as FMCG, food, hotels, paper—which yield less—cause the damage. That being the case, it is a no-brainer to buy ITC rather than GPIL! Whether investing in Godfrey was a mistake or not, I am not willing to comment at this moment. However, based on data, earning, cash flows, sustainability of those cash flows, margins, on every single ground, Godfrey scores.

'However, ITC's brands appear far more powerful than Godfrey Philips'. Apart from Marlboro, GPIL cigarette brands are far weaker than ITC. However, over the past few years, especially 15–20 years, Godfrey Philips has given returns superior to ITC.

'The first thing about investing is to stay focused on the facts. It is true that there has been capital misallocation and a number of misadventures with trading at GPIL. Not that ITC stands out as a saint in terms of capital allocation. I don't know. All I am saying is my feedback loop in learning whether Godfrey Philips is a mistake or not will be quick. He will not take long to figure it out.'

(As I write this chapter, the Godfrey Philips stock has tripled in less than a year from the point Sanjoy bought. The joys of evidence-based investing appear to be staggering!)

I go on further to ask Sanjoy about the first step taken by him towards admission of his mistake and the steps of rectification that follow.

He answers, 'It depends on the nature of the mistake. There is no fixed answer to this question. More the onset of complex circumstances leading to the mistakes, typically longer it will take to act to rectify it. For example, if you have made a simple judgement of having bought a high-class company at an obscene valuation and you can identify the same, that shouldn't take you long to get out. The only hindrance in your way is *ego* and a bias to hold on to what you have advocated as ideal'.

Even when you identify a great business, it does not mean that you can pay an outrageous price to own it and hope to earn above-market returns.'

To improve his investing process and reduce the number of mistakes that he makes, Sanjoy suggests focusing on concepts such as *mindfulness*. He adds that while the awareness of the benefits exists and he has tremendous respect for those who practice it, he is still far from having embraced it fully. The optimism of a learner then springs out, 'I hope I do. But, in my case it is primarily analytical. When I reflect on my mistakes, I look at the facts and see where I have got them wrong.'

There may be judgements that one thinks as mistakes but which end up with favourable results. Then, one must deliberate if they were indeed mistakes and one got lucky by a change in circumstance that converted the mistake into a bonanza. He speaks about his tryst with SSI. SSI, a Chennai-based company which provided training to aspiring coders in JAVA, was hot property in 1997. He bought it a day after turning thirty-seven on 8 June 1997, essentially because a friend mentioned that the cycles were toppling in the cycle stand behind their office. Having vividly grasped the huge demand for their classes, Sanjoy lost no time in buying the stock. The need to do any homework or carry out any background checks was redundant, given the compelling narrative! And just to make sure the investment would have an impact on portfolio returns, he put a fair amount of money to work.

To cut a long story short, the stock multiplied more than 500 times by February 2000 because it found 'honourable mention' on the K-10 shortlist! Strangely, Sanjoy was scared silly by its vertical ascent and felt things were too good to be true. He felt incredibly relieved by selling the stock and paying a significant amount of tax, thanks to the capital gains. A live example of a lucky fluke where every action leading to the outcome was incorrect, but the result defied all odds!

Given Sanjoy's fascination with heuristics and intuition, it is par for the course that he frequently adopts rules of thumb to resolve dilemmas.

Rule 1: 'If you spend a disproportionate amount of time thinking about the price action of a stock and it prevents you from sleeping well at night, sell it.'

He is also an ardent fan of his colleague Ayaz Motiwala's homespun wisdom, '*jitna kharab, utna accha*' (the worse, the better). The corollary is also an immensely powerful truth.

Rule 2: Whenever a stock becomes excessively popular, the alarm bells start ringing.

Rule 3: Understand that risk is meaningfully different from uncertainty. Accept that the future is fundamentally unknowable and always act in a way that allows you to cope with the most damaging consequences of your behaviour.

His take on making the same mistake more than once is quirky and candid. 'It's not that I haven't repeated mistakes, but I think the crux of it is this: when you make a mistake, you shouldn't personalize it and beat oneself up because all that does is destroy your self-belief.'

'The key to getting better when you make a mistake is to try and understand what led to it and to see if you can figure out what is it that you could have done differently at that time. It is certainly true in my case that there are certain mistakes that I committed earlier which were repeated at a subsequent date. So, it's not that easy! If you have to hunt for palookas, this would be a great litmus test. Thankfully, the one thing I can honestly say is that this tendency of mine has declined somewhat with age!'

On analysing the nature of the mistake—is it omission or commission—and if one did not do what one should have or did something one should not have, his view is: 'When you fail to do something, the opportunity cost of not having done it is that you suffer, but there is actually no direct loss. Whereas, in an error of commission, there is a direct and immediate impact. You are responsible for the damage caused by errors of commission. Denial is wasted, whereas in an error of omission, all you can say is that I was asleep at the wheel and should have done better. But you haven't actually made yourself liable or responsible for anything that may have taken place in the future. So, errors of omission psychologically tend to hurt you somewhat less.'

He believes that type-one error can be truly destructive. Once you have acted, people may not be willing to let you off the hook, even though your intent may have been perfectly good. To my mind, avoiding errors of commission is far more important than errors of omission and for all of us in life, there will always be errors of omission simply because none of us can see the future perfectly. But errors of commission, based on what you have experienced and your circumstances, you can certainly avoid. Errors of commission do involve the future too! To that extent, one should be less harsh towards themselves for errors of omission but not everyone sees it that way. Most people see it in the context of how much they missed out and, I think, that is usually greed speaking. What is more important, and a basic principle of successful investing, is to avoid making or to make as few errors of commission as possible. In order to survive you have to make sure that you avoid making foolish decisions. To do that, the best method is to observe other people do so. As Buffett put it, to finish first, you must first finish.[2] Errors of commission do not sometimes allow you to finish. So, no matter how brilliant you are or what great ideas you have, if you make errors of commission that are fatal or end up badly, you're not going to reach the finish line.

How does one learn from mistakes in a way that it has a positive impact on future behaviour?

His take on this is pretty straightforward. One of the most cardinal mistakes in investing is to have an ego. No matter how smart you are, and how impressive your past record, the minute you begin to believe that you are superior to everyone else, you are setting yourself up for disaster. So, in my case, fortunately and for a host of other reasons related to investing, I had figured this out when I was pretty young; it is best to get ego out of the way at an early stage in life.

What does have relevance in my context, and this is truly important—staying rational. When you make a mistake, it shouldn't make you veer off course. Any attempt at rationalization or seeking excuses is wholly unproductive.

In large organizations, people are always seeking scapegoats. So, there is a strong tendency for people to deny reality. The best that you can do, when this happens to you, is go back in time and say, let's make this decision all over again and try to do it as sensibly and rationally as possible. Very often, some of these mistakes take place because of misplaced emphasis on certain factors. This is typically evident in hindsight, and the learning from that is, looking ahead, you have sorted out one aspect of your thinking that can trip you up. The tragedy is that you need to make new mistakes to become better and better.

Bizarrely, sometimes you can make a mistake, but what you think is a mistake turns out really well. This is called dumb luck, and most of us have been major beneficiaries of this phenomenon! Once again, denial is entirely useless. The best one can do is remain objective, examine each step critically and then see what you can learn, and apply it to the decision-making process. I think this is the only way to have a positive takeaway from such outcomes.

The key to making better decisions is to try and separate skill from luck. Avoid focusing too much on the outcome. Rather, ask yourself what went wrong and why? If it is a team decision and one guy got it right or wrong, you should not seek to pin the blame or success on one single member. No single individual has all the answers. Very often, it's not about experience, age, background or professional training; it's about how you think and how creative you are. That's really what leads to good outcomes. The ability to remain rational, to think in a way that is holistic and to be creative in defining both the problem and the answer is fundamental to a good process. Many of us are good at some but not all of these things. So, no single individual can get all the credit when you're working in a team, whether it is a small team or a large one.

Secondly, this is unlikely to be either the first time or the last time that you'll be working in a team. So, the most important thing in the team decision is to introspect, to learn why things turned out the way they did. The crux of teamwork is to ensure that future decisions benefit from past outcomes. The second is to not assign blame. Finally, the most important thing is to keep learning and improving in the hope that you will cut your mistakes going forward and, as a group, you will function better.

He adds that one of the strengths of the investment team at HDFC AMC was that after a slightly rocky start, they got this aspect sorted out! The way to really figure this out is to ask yourself that in the environment that you belonged to, were there a lot of prima donnas? If most people were treated well and the team went on to do great things in future, regardless of any single individual, you have the best possible result!

Elements of a good decision-making vs outcome: Different elements of decision-making

Sanjoy believes it's not about focusing on an outcome, it's about constantly trying to improve different elements of a decision-making process, which include framing the problem, looking at it holistically and understanding the possible range of outcomes. You rarely think in absolutes, particularly while investing in a mutual fund. Since performance is measured relative to a benchmark, it is much more about trying to understand a range of outcomes, a range of possibilities, and seeing which one on a probabilistic basis is something that you can live with. You don't have to be right about every single decision, the best possible outcome. You will get many chances in your life, and the important thing is to avoid making serious errors. You have got to hang around to be there when the fat pitch comes, and you will get fat pitches—the pandemic in 2020 was the ultimate fat pitch.

The role of exuberance and hubris in eliminating bad decisions

Sanjoy believes this is largely shaped by your upbringing, experiences and history. Excessive exuberance and hubris are probably the two most important factors that lead to serious mistakes. Once again, it is not about how smart you are, where you work, or the context. Ben Bernanke, former chairman of the US Federal Reserve, identified exuberance but did nothing about it. In fact, he was early in figuring it out, and he may have felt silly that he said that. But the excessive exuberance went on for one-and-a-half years and the economy continued to do well.

Time has a huge role to play because there are no immediate cause-and-effect relationships or outcomes that validate either exuberance or hubris, but the most important thing is that no amount of mental jugglery or fooling around in terms of trying to be smart and rationalizing the fact that you have done really badly can be an excuse for exuberance and hubris. If you attempt to do that, you are setting yourself up for even greater disaster. What leads to exuberance and hubris is usually massive overconfidence. If you don't tackle that, then you are certainly going to repeat it!

Can you alienate your mind between personal life and business life to arrive at a good decision?

Sanjoy shares from his experience, that per him, you can't in practice. You can't alienate your mind. The only thing to do when you are going through a difficult period in your personal life and you are an investment manager is to not try and do dramatic things—just avoid, just keep it really simple and stay with the herd for a short while; don't do anything fancy. Curb your natural instincts to, sort of, make new bets. It's just not possible to say that I have such outstanding abilities to compartmentalize that I can put away what affects me in my personal life and, at work, it just doesn't affect me.

He adds, but equally, 'I must say that I am blessed that as a consequence of my personal life, I have certainly made some good decisions and I've been happy and joyful, but I haven't gone off the rails. There haven't been many incidents where my personal life made me feel really upset. There are only a few incidents that I can think of when this happened. For instance, my dad's passing was one incident. I don't think I allowed myself to get affected to the extent that it came through in the way that I was making decisions at work. That didn't happen. But I was acutely aware of the fact that I was slightly disturbed and so I cut back.'

Mistakes and motivation

Mistakes can be a motivation when you learn from them, when you get smarter. That's the simple answer. Sanjoy says, 'I think, mistakes must never be seen in a unidimensional context. In the context of what happened. Mistakes will be seen as an opportunity, so you make a mistake, it's fine, it's not the end of the world. All of us make mistakes, no one can go through a happy and successful life without making a large number of mistakes. So, there is no reason to try and cover them up, to be unhappy about them, to beat yourself up—none of that. It is important to understand the nature of the mistake, its context and the reason for its occurrence, and get smarter by learning from it.

'There is a famous book by Carol Tavris and Elliot Aronson titled *Mistakes Were Made (But Not by Me)*. That's the really fatal part. When you say that I am so smart that I did not make any mistake, but I have witnessed a lot of others making mistakes. So, the first thing is to acknowledge that you made the mistake, to own up, and then starts the fun of having made the mistake. If it leads to serious learning, it can be fun. To ask yourself then: okay, what am I going to do differently now, going forward? That's it. That's when it can be a great motivation.'

Is India heading in the right direction? Do cracks in roads, potholes or frequent changes in policy and tax impact his decision to invest in India?

Sanjoy reflects, 'I think a lot of people believe that we are so far down the curve that things can only improve.' Being slightly more optimistic, living in India makes you believe that you can enjoy yourself working and living in this society. I think this country has a great future. That there are so many people across all age groups who are so versatile and so capable and so smart. And I am not saying this as a cliché. I think, as a nation, Indians are really good at problem-solving and getting ahead. If you look at Wall Street, Silicon Valley and the places where there has been the maximum value creation, wherever in the world it maybe—and these are people who have left India and gone outside. If you look at large American corporations, there are a disproportionate number of Indians who are CEOs. You look at whatever area you want to look, you get a sense of versatility and capability of Indians when you compare them across geographies.

'It's not about the potholes or the poor infrastructure—all the day-to-day negatives that you have. Hopefully, they will get better if they haven't got better for a long time. I have been living in Mumbai for a long time—for about forty years now—and forty years ago, the infrastructure was better, I feel, than it is now, which is really sad. But that's life. Someone keeps doing constantly well—it is an illustration of the hard work, the skill that person has—and there are many Indians, in athletics, in sports, in so many different areas; the one area, interestingly, that you don't see many Indians at the top is investing. India hasn't produced, in my mind, a truly legendary investor. We don't have one as yet. And, I think, that is disappointing. I cannot put my finger on why this is so, but it is certainly so.'

Converting a mistake into a winner

With his wisdom and experience, Sanjoy says, 'I don't think you can convert an unfavorable outcome into a favorable result. That often doesn't happen. But the first part of the question is something that I have experienced over time and it's something that will keep on happening to all of us. It's like a sport: when you play team games, very rarely can one individual determine the good or bad. One is, you got to mentally reconcile to the fact that when you work as part of a group, the group is larger than you.

'The second thing is, you shouldn't be obsessed about a single event. So if you are going to be part of the group for a long period of time—let's say five years, there will be multiple times when all of you will be together and when you will have a chance to do well. Occasionally, you won't do well, you will do badly. But, in your mind, you have to think in the long term and instill this belief that one outcome, by itself, does not matter as long as it doesn't set you back permanently. It is what you do over a period of time—over ten-fifteen years, or even fifty years—that matters. That is the key to the plot. So, if you have that mindset, it won't hurt you that much, or at least that's how I have treated it over time.

Reflecting on the past to reduce mistakes

The first thing Sanjoy highlights is mistakes in allocation.

He says, the allocation bit is the easy part. Mistakes in areas such as education can be tougher. Here, he believes, the mistake does have a meaningful impact. To explain, he elaborates his example. 'I studied statistics, which is a great subject, and it has actually given me a lot of advantages in terms of how I think, how I get various opportunities of figuring out the meaning of risk, figuring out the meaning of uncertainty. Because investing is really all about decision-making and the uncertainty, if you think about it. So, I think that I have a good education and, in many ways, the fact that I have managed to get to where I have, not that it's very far but I am quite happy with it. It is all, perhaps, because of the way I started out. But, I think, one of the ways to really get a good education is to have a broad education. In other words, to be exposed to a number of academic influences—what is called in the US a liberal arts education, where you look at economics, political science, neuroscience and whatever else, and things come together. The most important factor—when you are young—in your education is to learn how to think from first principles. In an IIT, they teach you how to think very smartly in solving problems which have definite answers. Left-hand side is equal to right-hand side—solve the equation and you are a hero. But life doesn't have definite answers. Funnily, as you become older in life, you'll figure out that asking the right questions is more important than finding the right answers.

'So, I did not get to that. I don't regret it, but if I were to do it all over again, I would consciously look to go in another direction and I would also love to learn statistics all over again. I should emphasize that because I think it has been a huge positive for me and it has shaped the way I look at problems and the way I look at opportunities and I think, to a large extent, most of the time, I'm very rational. I wouldn't change that; I will change the mix of it. I got damn lucky that I was born into a family where I was the son of a professor who taught at a business school. So, not only was I exposed to a lot of very bright students and very bright young people who would come to meet my dad, but equally, you know what was discussed at the dinner table most of the time was related to business. So, from a very young age, I have been exposed to thinking about—or hearing about—business and how it works and how it feels, the people involved, the characters, et al.

'Thirdly, the thing that I wouldn't change—but which has been crucially important, and I always have been blessed in this regard—is having outstanding bosses. Apart from my dad—although he was never my boss—having outstanding role models. What values to enhance and what values to gradually get out of the system. I was blessed that I had three such role models, of whom two were my direct bosses, apart from my dad. So that was very positive, and a large part of the credit must go to all three individuals. Apart from which, I'd say, I have smart friends but that's, I think, a choice that you make. I think, in India, a lot of us want to associate with people who constantly say that you are smart—'it's not so much about the friendship. It's about their saying how good you are and that's why you are friends. Fortunately, I didn't have that sort of a situation, and so my friends are guys who are happy to criticize me knowing that I will like them all the more for it. That's worked really well for me.

'As far as the other mistakes go that I would like to change over time—in other words, if I went back in time by getting a time machine—there are two that I think really stand out. One is what we spoke about, which is allocation. Now, historically saying, I have put in a lot of efforts, I have been very diligent, I have been rational when having come to a problem. I haven't had the conviction or the ability, for whatever reason—I think it's a psychological thing, in my opinion, to make a really big bet. Because if I had made that really big bet by design then, when it turned out historically later that I had got it right, the impact would have been far more meaningful. I think that comes also in a funny sense from being a professor's son, because then you are never exposed to wealth, or it's always you have to be very careful with your money. Your lifestyle is always simple and nuanced. The fear of being wrong and losing a lot of money is, I think, what held me back when I was younger and it stays with me, funnily even today, when circumstances are meaningfully different, I think I still suffer from this way of thinking.

'I wish I got to investing much earlier—I spent over five years in consumers marketing and the six years I spent in credit rating were really beneficial. I learnt, probably, the largest amount from that period of my life, but the subsequent period of five years that I spent in broking on the self-side, I don't think that did much for me. I feel you win some you, you lose some, I don't think you should worry too much about it. I think the biggest one is the difference in my education, and the fear of failure or the fear of getting it wrong.'

I next ask, when he manages public money, mistakes can also be caused by the public itself, for example, they may pull out when it is time to pull in. The result may show against him publicly. How does he balance the public image with rational decision-making?

'You don't. You continue to remain rational and recognize that you are acting in a fiduciary capacity, and you must not look for personal glory. If they pull money when times are tough, never take that personally. It's not a reflection of you or how you make decisions. And this is a sad truth about a lot of Indian investors—they are, basically, constantly looking for personal glory. This is not a business for personal glory. The fact that other people have faith in you and give you their hard-earned after-tax money to manage, that itself is the tribute. Their trust is your biggest reward and building that trust is a reward. It's their money and they have the right to take it out and take it away; it's not your money. So, for me, this is a non-issue, and it doesn't matter. It is about constantly trying to behave in a manner that justifies their trust and that justifies you are capable of the fiduciary responsibility. Just cut out the desire to become rich and famous when managing money. It is inconsequential.'

Sanjoy shares, 'I am one of the few who is selected to be part of this group that is not a public figure, and I don't think I am too much on TV, or that I am in the category of some of the other candidates who are part of this book. So I am not often under scrutiny. In fact, I was more under scrutiny fifteen years ago when I was more active in handling money and even then, I tried to, sort of, to the maximum extent possible, stay away from the limelight. I don't think it helps investment managers to step into the limelight.

Therefore, I certainly do not meet the first part of the question. But let me try and answer the second part of the question. In investing, luck plays a huge role—the fact that you are doing well doesn't mean that you attribute your success to your skill. I think I am probably a good example of that—a bunch of dumb decisions at a young age worked out very well, but it was not skill. Now that I think back on those decisions, they were really foolish decisions which had an unbelievably positive result. Actually, if I hadn't done that, I would have been part of the footnotes of history; no one would have ever heard of me. I wouldn't have been invited to the Bombay Stock Exchange to speak, which is the first time I met you, and this whole interview would have been redundant.

'How you think about these things—when people say, this guy is a public figure and he screwed up, this is what he did wrong—I don't think you should get carried away by the criticism. You should try to actually be honest with yourself and say, there must be some part of this criticism that is valid, and what is it—to the extent this allows you to go into the next level of thinking, and that's what matters. The point is not to be thin skinned when you manage money. The point is to try and take on more, and all, criticism that you face. And that can only be possible when you're not shooting for personal glory.

Many guys want to be heroes, they want to be famous, they want to be well-known, they want the world to say how smart they are. People get agitated by this kind of criticism. That is not driven by the desire to be harsh, it is the desire to be get you to become smarter and better. That is always the mindset which you should have. Ask why people are being ridiculed or criticized. If you hold someone up as a hero, and you criticize him, the guy that is supposedly the hero should think why this guy is criticizing me? It is because he wants me to do better. This should be a motivation, if at all.

Luckily, I have never been in this position so I can say things like this, but I guess it is a lot tougher when you are a true hero.

New mistakes

On this, Sanjoy shares that I think we all make new mistakes. He elaborates, 'There is a wide range of mistakes. I don't think you can say that in a career spanning four decades in investing, you are not going to err. There are so many different kinds of mistakes. I'm not trying to justify that I am stupid, but I think you can continue to make mistakes for a long period of time and if you look at history and if you look at the people in different areas—as generals or as politicians or as whatever coaches—the fact that you are continuing to make mistakes, I think, that is not something to be nervous about. As long as you are making new mistakes.'

'In fact, I say that it's a side part that you are evolving from making dumb basic mistakes to making mistakes that are drawn into because of complexities, because you're encountering complex situations in your life. I don't think that I am worried about making mistakes. I think if I'm being honest with myself, I have repeated mistakes that I made in the past even today. For instance, my inability to make big bets. It's because I find it very difficult to change fundamentally and psychologically, it's still embedded in me. I may be financially better off than I was before, but my mind still works like that of a guy who comes from a very humble and modest background. Overcoming that mindset, is not easy. It takes I don't know what; but it takes a huge amount of a calibrated desire to really move ahead in life to do even better. I think many of us at some stage say we've got this far and it's far enough; we don't want to push ahead further. I think I fall into that category. It's probably also because I continue to make mistakes, because there are many things—today, in many ways, the environment in which we are in, the society that we are in, is a more complex and challenging society then it was forty years ago. Then, life was a lot simpler in many ways. Today, with social media, the internet, a huge amount of networking—all of this leads to mistakes. Forty years ago, no one knew who anyone was. I mean, in India, if you're sitting in Delhi, you didn't know who someone in Ahmedabad or who someone in Chennai was. I mean, today, social media has totally collapsed the world. That kind of changes in our environment, I think, at some level, lead you to make mistakes. So, I don't think you got to change, I think you got to move the other way. You will soon know what is happening at the back of Iceland or wherever much sooner. What is more important is to have the ability to not react to many things and to just dismiss these things. This will keep you from making mistakes. This obviously takes a lot of time to figure out and put into practice. I actually see this as a process of change in investing, I am not shaped by the fact that I'm still making mistakes.'

What is Sanjoy's take for the readers of this book to avoid mistakes and do well?

Sanjoy shares a combination.

1. Save more.
2. Control your needs.
3. Stay flexible.
4. Develop patience.
5. Read more on the benefits of compounding than simple returns.
6. Try to balance greed and fear.
7. Set goals and time horizons.
8. Understand the difference in bubbles and investing by trying to understand value vs euphoria.
9. Don't undermine luck, but try and develop a good process that combines effort, objectivity and a lack of ego.
10. An ounce of character is better than a pound of knowledge. Behaviour matters.
11. Understand the maths of rules, relationships vs the psychology of emotions, risk and uncertainty.
12. Avoid studying extreme examples, focus on commonplace and frequently repeated patterns of success and failure.
13. Remember, Bill Gates said, 'Success is a lousy teacher. It seduces smart people into thinking they can't lose.'[3]
14. Remember Warren Buffett said that there is no reason to risk what you have and need for what you don't have and need.[4]
15. Don't fall for social comparison of wealth vs envy.
16. It takes discipline and consistency to become rich.

17. To stay wealthy, don't make big mistakes that impact your survival. Recognize the value of frugality, self doubt, humility.
18. Have a sense of purpose.
19. Be comfortable with what you own. Sleep in peace.
20. Daniel Kahneman said, 'The correct lesson to learn from surprises is that the world is surprising.'[5]
21. Understand room for error, margin of safety.
22. Strive for balance and endurance. Accept reality but move on from setbacks quickly.
23. The market will never give you free lunches forever.
24. Accept what you don't know, avoid the myth of forecasting.

CHAPTER 3

VIKAS KHEMANI

The financial architect on a quest for hidden gems

VIKAS Khemani is someone I knew initially less off personally. Till I learnt about his exemplary performance in the markets through his Carnelian Fund, and the more I got to know him and read on him, the more interesting he became.

For Vikas, his description on X is a telltale:

Love family, markets & poker. Deep interest in psychology, spirituality, fitness, politics & policy. Practices Vipassana. An internal optimist and proud Indian.

Also, for him, 'emotional intelligence makes you not only a better individual but a better investor' as this is what he learnt from reading works of philosophers like J. Krishnamurti.

Vikas's description teaches us the mistake of not following a multidisciplinary approach to life and embracing a journey of optimism and dreaming big, and along the journey, overcoming shortcomings to reach life's highs.

In one of his posts on X, you get a glimpse of who Vikas truly is when he quotes a beautiful poem by thirteenth-century Sufi poet, Jalaluddin Rumi, 'Unfolding the Rose':

It is only a tiny rosebud,
A flower of God's design.
But I cannot unfold the petals with these clumsy hands of mine.
The secret of unfolding flowers is not known to such as I.
God opens this flower so sweetly, when in my hands they fade and die.

In the realm of investing, where numbers dance and fortunes rise and fall, Vikas stands out almost as a seeker on the path of wisdom.

Renowned for his discerning eye in recognizing growth and his mastery in navigating market currents, Vikas, the founder of Carnelian Asset Management, embodies a journey akin to a spiritual journey.

For him, investing is not merely a practice but a sacred quest, one where success is birthed from making choices that are both objective and unclouded by bias. His creed emphasizes considering the probabilities of outcomes and the delicate balance of risk and reward. It must have resonated with Vikas long enough for, to quote Peter Lynch over his personal profile on X, 'although it is easy to forget sometimes, shares are not a lottery ticket ... it's part ownership of a business'. This gives you a clean view of Vikas's investing world, his philosophy and his modus operandi. It easy to see that Vikas is a person who is driven by the word 'ownership'.

Mistakes and upbringing: The tapestry of experience

Vikas's journey began in a small village of Mandawa, in Jhunjhunu district of Rajasthan. His father ran a tourist bus service and was away for most of the time. In his youth, he assisted his grandfather in a modest clothes shop, witnessing the art of negotiation as customers haggled over prices. This early experience instilled in him a mindset of seeking bargains beneath the surface. Seeking better grounds for business was probably in his genes as the family moved to Surat, Gujarat, for better trading prospects. This is where he read and learnt of the greatest names in business, such as Aditya Birla and Dhirubhai Ambani, among others. Eventually, Vikas bet a lot on bargaining, whether it was his bet on learning English—coming from a vernacular-medium early education in Mandawa—or moving to Bombay, for value creation, both professionally and personally. For years, this philosophy guided him, leading him to favour undervalued stocks while overlooking the essence of quality. It was as if he were holding a piece of precious silk, only to clutch it too tightly, failing to appreciate its true worth. With time, he learned to embrace the balance between price and quality, understanding that even in the pursuit of bargains, one must not lose sight of value.

Vikas is a chartered accountant with more than twenty-two years of capital markets experience. He founded Carnelian Capital in 2018, before which he was the CEO of Edelweiss Securities Ltd, where he spent seventeen years incubating and building several businesses to leadership position, including institutional equities and equity research. With a strong business acumen and deep understanding of the capital markets, he enjoys strong relationships with corporate India and is associated with several industry bodies and committees, including the CII National Council on Corporate Governance, FICCI Capital Markets Committee and Executive Council of Bombay Management Association. He is also a member of Young Presidents Organization (YPO), a global forum for entrepreneurs and CEOs, and was awarded Young Professional Achievers Award for the service sector by the ICAI in 2014.

Despite his illustrious trajectory, you will find an unusual emphasis on the emotional aspects of business and leadership on his social media profile (LinkedIn) where he describes himself as: 'I am passionate leader with keen interest in building scale businesses, investing in capital markets and businesses, nurturing talent and building leaders. I believe high EQ is the key to leading a successful and happy life, both professionally and personally.'

Crisis and judgement: The play of circumstance

In his public interviews, Vikas often refers to the influence of the Bhagavad Gita on his life and on his philosophies for operating in the market: 'Do your best and do not worry about the outcome.' In moments of calm and turbulence alike, Vikas acknowledges that mistakes are part of the divine play, a reflection of the cosmic dance of fate. During serene times, errors often stem from misjudgements or flawed analysis, akin to missteps in a quiet meadow. But during crises, when the storm rages and emotions cloud judgement, errors arise from the tempests of greed and fear. Vikas's habit of self-reflection and critical inquiry is his way of seeking the inner truth, a practice reminiscent of Rumi's quest for the Beloved. And it is Jalaluddin Rumi who Vikas reads for guidance. By questioning his own actions and remaining grounded, he avoids the trap of allowing minor setbacks to obscure his vision of the greater journey. He prefers to see the glass as half full, understanding that even in moments of darkness, there is always a glimmer of light. In fact, he even quotes Adi Slok's *Atm Chintan* series to say that 'the usefulness of a cup is in its emptiness'. He employs similar philosophy in the world of investing as well. It's only when a cup is empty can you decide to fill in.

Fixing errors: The path of acceptance and renewal

Given Vikas's intuitive and deeply conscious nature, his approach to correcting mistakes appears akin to a seeker's path of repentance and renewal. He advocates for the immediate acknowledgment of errors and the pursuit of solutions rather than dwelling on consequences, once again reposing complete faith in Krishna's utterances for Arjuna, 'karmanye vadhikaarastey maa phaleshu kadacha na'. You have the right to perform your actions, but you are not entitled to the fruits of the actions. Nothing exemplifies the stock market better; keep doing your karma but do not expect the outcome of what you do. This presupposes room for everyday mistakes with scope for everyday correction. Like an evolved human who finds solace in admitting faults and seeking forgiveness, Vikas believes that half of a problem is resolved once one accepts their missteps. Therefore, when an investment falters, his counsel for investors is to act decisively, sell the loss, and then reflect on recovery strategies, and eventually, move on. His method of managing risk mirrors the age-old practice of moderation and mindfulness, starting small and gradually increasing his position, thus ensuring that even in error, he may find the grace to rectify and move forward.

In the grand tapestry of business, Vikas Khemani approaches management with a reverence akin to recognizing the divine presence guiding a vessel through stormy seas. To Vikas, the quality of management is not merely a factor but the very essence that channels the currents of value creation. Just as a skilled captain navigates turbulent waters with wisdom and grace, exceptional management steers a business towards success with a blend of vision, integrity and resilience.

For Vikas, management is the heartbeat of an entity, infusing vitality and direction into the enterprise. We have heard Vikas highlight this over time that while business models and valuations hold their place in the hierarchy, for Vikas, they are secondary to the human element that drives them. In this light, investing becomes an art of seeking alignment—a harmonious blend where a robust business framework meets the guiding force of exceptional management characterized by competence, integrity and drive, all secured at a fair price and without employing devious means.

Vikas has also been known to draw immensely from the wisdom of Charles Thomas Munger. For those not yet fully initiated into the stock market, Charles was an American businessman, investor and philanthropist. He was also the vice chairman of Berkshire Hathaway, the conglomerate controlled by Warren Buffett. Buffett described Munger as his closest partner and righthand man, and credited him with being the 'architect' of modern Berkshire Hathaway's business philosophy. Vikas waxes eloquent about the book called *Poor Charlie's Almanack: The Wit and Wisdom of Charles T. Munger*. It is a collection of speeches, lectures and writings by Charlie Munger which, admittedly, has influenced Vikas like no other. The book, says Vikas, compiled by Peter D. Kaufman, offers insights into Munger's philosophy on investing, decision-making and life. It delves into Munger's unique approach to problem-solving, emphasizing the importance of mental models and multidisciplinary thinking. Rich with humour and wisdom, the book provides a blend of practical advice and Munger's reflections on success, learning and rational thinking. This, once again, makes us vouch for Vikas's emotional intelligence, his intuitiveness and his sense of proportion in business purposes, where he still puts the human on top of the stack! Quite predictably, Vikas maintains a vigilant stance against the shadows of ego and overconfidence. Just as saints and Sufis—whose teachings seem to have had a role to play in the life and philosophy of Vikas—spoke of the need to transcend vanity and embrace humility, Vikas acknowledges that true insight and success come from recognizing one's limitations and the inherent uncertainties of the market. This awareness is not a passive resignation but an active engagement with the dance of success and failure. By observing the ebb and flow of market trends, learning from the patterns of triumphs and setbacks, Vikas crafts a strategy that is both grounded and adaptable.

Much akin to the journey of any self-discovery, which involves navigating the inner and outer realms with balance and awareness, Vikas's approach to investing is a symphony of observation and reflection. He appreciates that errors and successes are but part of a larger, interconnected tapestry. This balance—between humility and vigilance, between learning from past experiences and adapting to new challenges—is where true wisdom resides. In embracing this ethos, Vikas remains attuned to the broader rhythm of business, understanding that each step in this journey is a reflection of both his inner growth and his engagement with the external world.

Turning mistakes into money: The dance of Fortuna

Speaking to Vikas is a discovery of sorts; his deeply conscious side is evident when you speak to him in person or watch him speaking at fora. To Vikas, the art of transforming mistakes into gains resembles a delicate dance with Fortuna, the goddess of fortune, who wields both chance and challenge with equal flair. In his view, this endeavor is a double-edged sword, where the thrill of initial victories can often lead to a dangerous overconfidence, ultimately resulting in unforeseen losses. Such a precarious game is not without its perils, as complacency and arrogance can subtly steer one off course.

Vikas reflects on his investment journey with a poignant awareness of these dynamics. He recalls, 'Mistakes, while often painful, are also profound teachers. They remind us that success is not merely about capitalizing on opportunities but also about remaining vigilant and humble in the face of both triumphs and trials.'

His experience with KEI serves as a striking example of this principle. Initially, he purchased KEI at a seemingly unfavourable price, only to witness it drop further. 'The initial drop was disheartening,' he admits, 'but it was through continuous evaluation and perseverance that I discovered the true value of patience.'

This investment story is emblematic of Vikas's perspective that through trials and tribulations, one discovers the essence of true success. Vikas's patience and steadfastness in holding onto KEI, despite its early underperformance, eventually yielded substantial rewards. He underscores, 'It's not the initial mistake that defines the journey, but how one navigates through it with resilience and clarity. True gains are often born from the soil of persistence.'

Rumi's teachings appear to resonate deeply with Vikas's experiences. Rumi's poetry often reflects the idea that trials and setbacks are integral to the path of growth. Vikas seems to embrace this wisdom, noting, 'Much like Rumi's belief that "the wound is the place where the light enters you", I have learned that it is through the cracks of failure that the light of understanding and eventual success shines through.'

Turning mistakes into money requires more than just recognizing the lessons learned; it demands an inner fortitude to persist despite setbacks. Vikas continues, 'Many times, favourable outcomes can make us complacent about our mistakes. I've found that the real test is not just in acknowledging errors but in remaining steadfast and committed to the journey, irrespective of the immediate results.'

This dance with Fortuna, where one must balance between seizing opportunities and navigating the aftermath of mistakes, is a continuous journey. Vikas's approach reflects an understanding that success is not a linear path but a winding road filled with both highs and lows.

He emphasizes, 'Turning mistakes into gains is less about playing a game of chance and more about mastering the art of resilience and learning. The dance is ongoing, and it is through this rhythm that one finds lasting success.'

Thus, Vikas Khemani's journey through the landscape of investment is a testament to the transformative power of patience, perseverance and the wisdom drawn from both successes and failures.

Avoiding repeat errors: The path of humility and awareness

In the intricate journey of investing, Vikas recognizes that the subtleties of human behaviour often eclipse raw financial acumen. For him, the fears of missing out (FOMO) and the dread of loss are like veils that obscure the clarity of the heart and then, mind. These fears, much like the illusions described by the mystics, can lead one astray from the true path of insightful investing.

Vikas's approach to avoiding repeat errors is deeply rooted in the practice of humility and self-awareness. He believes that true enlightenment in investing comes not from merely understanding market mechanics but from engaging in profound self-reflection and keen observation of the broader sway of success and failure. 'The market,' Vikas says, 'is a reflection of human nature. To navigate it effectively, one must first understand oneself.'

This introspective journey involves more than analysing past investments; it demands an honest examination of one's own behaviours and biases. By continuously observing and learning from the successes and failures of others, Vikas cultivates a mindset of humility. He understands that every error, whether born from overconfidence or complacency, offers a lesson in the grand tapestry of investing. 'The path to wisdom in investing,' he reflects, 'is paved with the stones of past mistakes and the insights gleaned from them. It is essential to remain humble and vigilant, for arrogance can blind even the keenest observer.'

'In investing, as in life,' he notes, 'one must tread the path of balance—neither overestimating one's prowess nor underestimating the complexities of the market.'

Vikas tends to achieve this balance through a constant process of learning and adapting. His emphasis is on avoiding repeat errors and not avoiding mistakes altogether. Recognizing patterns and adjusting one's approach accordingly is the path Vikas has been choosing to comfortable success. 'True growth comes from acknowledging our limitations and remaining open to the lessons each experience brings,' he advises. 'It's a continuous journey of refining our understanding and approach.'

In essence, Vikas Khemani's path in investing is a testament to the enduring value of humility, awareness and learning from others, all of it stemming from his humble upcountry beginnings. It is true that he left this approach not only helps him avoid repeat errors but also guides him towards a more enlightened and balanced practice of investing.

Error of commission vs error of omission: The balance of choices

Error of commission is a type-A or type-B risk, where you lose your capital. An error of omission is a type-C risk where you miss out on a significant opportunity. Both are equally dangerous. Very often, people don't realize the impact of error of omission in our lives. Not buying a big winner is poor capital allocation. This risk typically arises from two sources: a lack of knowledge and inherent human biases.

For example, he elucidates, 'my bias against buying expensive stocks prevented me from investing in companies like Asian Paints and Fidilite when I studied them in 2004. Despite understanding these companies well, I couldn't bring myself to invest. Even when I did buy small quantities, I quickly sold off after a modest gain. Continuous effort to address these issues can make a substantial difference.'

This was akin to navigating the dualities of existence. An error of commission, where one loses capital, is a direct and often painful lesson. An error of omission, where one misses a significant opportunity, can be more insidious, reflecting a lack of foresight and awareness. Today, his favourite stocks are PTC Industries, Capacite Infraprojects, Man Industries (India) Limited, and Chemtech Industrial Valves, the first three also happen to be his best performing stocks. This, for Vikas, underscores the importance of overcoming biases and embracing the full spectrum of potential.

The art and science of investing: The divine fusion

Vikas strongly believes that investing blends both art and science. The science part can be standardized, but not the art. For example, when in 2005, after attending a meeting with Ashok Leyland, Vinod Dasari joined, Vikas was highly impressed and confident in his potential, whereas his analyst had a negative perspective. This illustrates how two people can interpret the same situation differently. To balance differing views within a team, it's crucial to foster a shared culture and engage in thorough discussions about wins, mistakes and lessons learned.

Personal factors such as a troubled family life, poor health or strained relationships can impact one's ability to make objective and well-considered decisions.

Meditation can aid in balancing the mind. One can't avoid life challenges; they will come but one can learn to handle them through meditation. It took Vikas a decade to gain understanding of investing decently and illustrating that even a loss can become motivation if one remains focused.

He adds, 'I don't equate rational decision-making solely with success. Many well-considered decisions can lead to poor outcomes, and conversely, some poor decisions can result in success. It's crucial to stay focused on your core principles and remain somewhat detached from the outcome. While it's challenging, it's essential to keep striving for this balance.'

Are mistakes inevitable?

Vikas emphasizes that rational decision-making does not guarantee success. Greatest of decisions can lead to poor outcomes and many poor decisions can occasionally be winning trades. 'My advice is to stay focused on the core principles and remain somewhat detached from the outcomes'—sounds familiar, right? Same as Arjuna was advised by the divine! Challenging though, but continuous effort is necessary. Mistakes are an inherent part of life.

According to Vikas, experience is nothing but a collection of learnings from your mistakes. It is human nature to keep making mistakes. But the goal is to make newer and fewer mistakes by balancing between change and the status quo. Certain things evolve while a few things stay constant. When a mistake is critical and the chances of recovery are slim, it can result in quitting or leaving lasting scars.

Such experiences can also set a negative example for one's family and social circle, leading to a deep-seated aversion to the capital markets. Therefore, to manage mistakes effectively, one needs to learn from history and the people around. Vikas is known to possess a hugely observant mind and that helps him understand what is working and what is not. In a genuine sense, he seems to enjoy learning from others.

He says, 'over time, I've evolved by learning from both my own mistakes and those of others, through reading, self-introspection and observing the successes and failures of others'.

He warns that high ego, overconfidence, arrogance, FOMO and complacency are nearly certain paths to failure. While favourable outcomes are important, he shares that he prefers to work with individuals who bring a unique perspective rather than just conforming to the mainstream. And values those who can connect diverse dots and offer insightful, unconventional viewpoints.

If he would be fearful of making mistakes, Vikas would have never learnt English. As he admitted in different media conversations, when he was learning English, he would try, fail and try again. 'If people laugh at you, you laugh back at them.' Low expectations and low ego lead to a happy life both personally and professionally.

However, we would want to end this chapter on a brilliant professional, or on a less sombre note, especially for our young readers: remember, you cannot wait to take out your new car on the road on a day when all the traffic lights in the city will be green! As in life, with the red signals and speed breakers, also in the stock market, *'yehi umar hai, kar le galti se mistake'*!

CHAPTER 4

DEVINA MEHRA
The data-driven equity crusader

DEVINA Mehra, founder, chairperson and managing director at First Global, is an IIM Ahmedabad gold medallist. She comes from a banking background at Citi and someone who bid for a BSE ticket in 1993 when membership opened, only to face a committee that had doubts on how someone outside the 'exclusive club' would even qualify as a broker. Her knowledge of the market, however, stunned the committee, and there was no looking back. Starting as a research and broking house for large foreign institutions investing into India, by the end of the nineties First Global became the first Asian (excluding Japan) securities firm to become a member of London Stock Exchange in 1999, and then got an NASD membership in 2001.

Then came the move to asset management, first globally and then in India, via portfolio-management services (PMS). Here too she thought differently, using what she calls a human-plus-machine system where the core is an artificial intelligence and machine-learning system.

Devina has always thought big.

When I met her for this interview, and asked with great interest on her gold medal and topping status at IIMA, she quipped, 'I was always a good student. I always did well in studies and came first.' Though she cherishes the gold medal, what really stood out for her is the comments of the IIM director at her twenty-fifth alumni meet, where he shared that in his over thirty years' experience as a teacher, she was the best student he ever had, and that he particularly and fondly remembered her handwriting.

Counting her parents as her inspiration, Devina firmly believes that hard work, first principles thinking and data scouting, a positive attitude and the support of her parents and daughter are sources of her strength and her accomplishments. She also counts books as a mentor and is known to repeatedly share her liking of books on X.

Thinking, Fast and Slow by Daniel Kahneman, as well as his *Noise,* rank among her favourite books and every year she lists out books that she really enjoyed reading. The subject of her avid reading is so diverse that she exhibits a multidisciplinary approach to themes from history to science to travel to psychology, besides the focus on business, finance and economics given her profession.

She highlights, in her fav books apart from all *Daniel Kahneman* books, some really sharp names such as Amitav Ghosh, *Shoe Dog* by Phil Knight, Malcolm Gladwell books, *The Art of Thinking Clearly* by Rolf Dobelli, *The Halo Effect* by Phil Rosenzweig, *Lessons in History* by Will and Ariel Durant, *The Invisible Gorilla* by Christopher Chabris and Daniel Simons, *Misbehaving* by Richard Thaler, *A Man for All Markets by* Edward O. Thorp, *The Man Who Solved the Market* on quant revolution by Gregory Zuckerman and *Unflattening* by Nick Sousanis.

In her early years, Devina says, she was so committed to her work and research that she even explored the idea of not bringing up a family. She worked hard because the learning in this profession excited her so much, in addition to pursuing her passion for travel.

Little wonder, with her persistence and hard work came success, and she has often featured amongst India's top businesswomen and made it to many a magazine covers for her stupendous success in the field of finance and as a working woman. Her research also made it to the front pages of *The Wall Street Journal* (on oil) and the late Alan Abelson from Barron's called her research, by and large, quite credible and on other occasions, even more than that.

She, however, shares that 'things never turn out the way you plan, it could be better or worse'.

I ask her about her mistakes, amidst the success.

Devina shares that thinking about mistakes in her investment career, brings into limelight three aspects.

One involves the evolution of investment analysis and the process to come to better decisions.

Second is a better understanding of very hardwired human biases and thinking fallacies and, therefore, the methods to get rid of those.

And the third part—which actually dawns quite late in life—is to realize that some decisions will go wrong in investing—they are meant to. As they say in software, it is a feature, not a bug!

So she comments that the very definition of mistakes needs to change. She goes on to say, 'of course mistakes are related to levels of education, exposure, etc., and I don't just mean what degree you have but how much you have studied finance, investment methods and most important, your own thinking'.

As someone coming from a background where nobody had any interest or exposure to investing meant that she started from a clean slate compared to some people she knew.

Adding to this, she says, 'Till I went for my MBA I did not even know what a share was. It is difficult for me to say whether that was an advantage or a disadvantage, on balance. While I did not know even the basics, it also meant that I did not have any preconceived notions ... If I draw a parallel with how I hired at First Global, where I preferred to hire freshers as they did not have any unlearning to do, maybe the fact that I came in without a background in investing may have been an advantage at the end of it.'

Devina further adds that even when she went into equities research or securities research in the early nineties, that discipline did not exist in India at all. Nobody knew what equity research was, no company had an investor relations department. This was, of course, in her opinion, both good and bad, because you could then start actually from first principles rather than fit into an existing mode.

At that time, she actually thought of learning from foreign brokers from developed markets who had decades of institutional experiences but when she actually looked at the reports, she found that they had neither real substance (due to problems of both competence and integrity), nor great style, and she never looked at that route of learning thereafter.

The big difference between mistakes made in normal market conditions and in times of crisis, per Devina, is that in normal market conditions, often the mistakes are the result of missing out some component of the analysis, or not being able to foresee certain changes and so on—basically, they are errors of analysis of the business or the finances or, occasionally, the economy.

At times of crisis, it additionally becomes about discipline and control over your own mind. Do you panic or are you able to remain disciplined because then it is not about individual stock movements but the direction of the whole market.

She says, we humans are very much the product of our experiences. For example, Americans who grew up during the Great Depression avoided debt all their life, not only personally but even in companies that they led. For people in the markets having lived through market cycles, it gives you a very different kind of experience and understanding, which does not come from and cannot come from just looking at past charts, where it is very easy to see the bottoms and say that this is where I would have bought and this is where I would have sold. It is only when you live through multiple crises—from 1987 to the Asian crisis of 1998, the 2000 tech crash, 9/11, Covid in 2020 or the Russia–Ukraine war of 2022 and the many others—can you actually learn from those experiences, or closer home, some of the political changes-related falls that help you learn perspective, for instance, the possibility that the markets' immediate reaction after an election result may turn upside down in a matter of days.

That is why most great investors, or even traders, really come into their own in their fifties, after the great depression. Whether it is Warren Buffett, George Soros or Jim Simons, the pattern is pretty much the same. You need the hard miles of understanding financials and reading the investing books; you also need to live through the school of hard knocks.

In the beginning, in your mind, and also in the minds of your clients, a mistake means a decision with a wrong outcome. For example, when you are a research and broking house, you recommended a buy on a stock and it did not go up, or you recommended a sell and it not go down.

She says, 'For me, the problem was particularly acute as many institutional clients expected a 100 per cent hit rate from First Global. It often happened that a foreign institutional client would say that xyz stock you recommended did not do well. You would say, but that was one of ten stocks you had recommended in the last period and that was the only that where that happened. And for most other securities firms, the ratio was almost the other way around, but they would cryptically answer: We expect better from you.'

Further, she adds, 'what I did not understand, at least, articulate at that time was that this was actually a mistake of framework. Even though I see this theoretical concept in reports I wrote as far back as '96 and '97, at the time somehow did not connect it to what the clients were saying.'

What is this framework of mistakes, I ask.

She replies, the concepts that there is uncertainty in the market; investing is a game of probability; and the quality of the outcome is not the same as the quality of the decision are things that one has been able to incorporate in one's thinking only much later in investing and in life. That, per her, totally changes the framework of what constitutes a mistake in the first place.

Earlier a mistake meant a wrong outcome but now the benchmark is different; where you are evaluating now is *whether* the framework for and the process of decision-making was right or wrong, rather than whether the outcome turned out to be favourable or not. The two can be very different.

Devina then elaborates that a wrong decision can have a right outcome and vice versa: 'One of the largest amount of money that I made from my investments was in a stock (or actually a convertible) where I put in outsized investment. The stock went down about 60 per cent at a time when I was unable to sell due to a lock-in, and then from those beaten-down levels, went up hundred times! So I made forty times my original investment. But definitely that decision was a mistake! The reason why it went up was totally extraneous to the analysis done at the time of investment and could not have been foreseen in at the time.'

She adds, 'On the other hand, one may have passed up opportunities to buy stocks like Tesla which went up several times but the decision may not have been wrong as the company came close to bankruptcy several times between 2017 and 2019.'

In the nineties, Devina says, the effort was to keep refining the financial-analysis techniques and also add on other statistical techniques to refine factors such as demand forecasts. That is, every effort was to learn more so that fewer mistakes were made.

While in the very initial phase she started off with the regular analysis of the profit and loss account, margins, growth, valuation multiples and such, she says she realized very quickly that she was missing out on a great deal.

Then she came about understanding traditional cash flow and discounted cash-flow methods, along with drivers of return ratios.

And even in financial modelling to not resort to shortcut methods of forecasting but to forecast every line item separately with the understanding that not all of them vary as a percentage of revenues. Basically, let the forecasted numbers truly emerge rather than try to shoe-horn them into the hypothesis one had in mind.

Then on, it was a process of evolution and analysis. For a time, the discounted cash-flow method (the sort in books by Prof. Damodaram and Tom Copeland) seemed to make sense till one realized how sensitive it was to assumptions, especially terminal value assumptions. By tweaking the growth rate or the cost of capital even a bit, one could dramatically change the value and basically come up with whatever value one wanted.

That led her to devise measures to capture near-term cash flows. Even then there were gaps in what you could foresee. The whole rise of IT services in the nineties is something that comes to her mind as a mistake or a misreading of the situation.

At a time when even a P/E of 25 or 30 was considered high, these companies were trading at multiples of sixty-seventy times and she thought they were far too expensive, and recommended a sell, but they kept soaring past every target you could have had in mind.

This was in spite of the fact that on another dimension, she did see the potential of these companies and sector. First Global had done a report in the late nineties talking about employee strength of companies.

At that time, she recalls, the largest private sector employer was Tata Steel with about 65,000 employees. The IT services companies had less than

10,000 employees each. And she projected that in the not-too-distant future, each of these companies would employ more people than Tata Steel, which at the time everyone thought was absurd, but it did turn out to be true. The forecast was simply based on the revenue model, that if they had to grow at a certain rate, they would need these many employees.

And yet, despite seeing that growth, she did not relate it well to what looked like off-the-charts P/E multiples.

There are also calls which, to Devina, appear like errors for a short time and turn out to be correct eventually. She cites Satyam as an example. Elaborating, she says 'I remember meeting the company and Ramalinga Raju in the very early days just a year or two after the IPO. I came away and told institutional clients that I was not impressed with the management at all. I could understand that an entrepreneur may not be a technology expert and may not be able to talk tech, but not to be even able to give a sense of different market segments and what they were targeting and what could be expected in each, I thought was a red flag. The stock was just about forty rupees and had a multi-year bull run from there ... till the whole house of cards eventually collapsed, and the promoter/management were right in the centre of it.'

She adds, 'I would not have counted it as a win in my account if the stock had eventually crashed because of a business problem that arose years later but, in this case, the issue was exactly in the area that I had identified.'

Here, we are talking of specific errors but there are also things which you have to live through in order to really understand them at a deep level.

While she believed in the ten thousand hours of study to master a subject, the fact is that for investing, just the reading and studying part is not enough, you also have to live through markets to have the experience to implement the knowledge.

For example, the fact that asset allocation determines 85 to 90 per cent of your returns is there on page 1 of every investment book, but like most others in this field, you start off still looking for the best security that you can get, chasing the golden trail of the multibagger.

On the above, she shares that it certainly took her a long time to really assimilate the importance of asset allocation, and implement it as a key part of her investment strategy. And also to realize that multibaggers are always going to be only a few out of all the stocks you identify through a process; you will not know in advance which specific stocks are going to be multibaggers.

Then there are errors and mistakes which help you evolve into a better investor because you realize what are the parts missing in the whole picture.

For example, she says, one saw in the nineties that you could recommend a buy on a stock, but it would fall some more before starting its move up, or that you thought something was overvalued but it kept running up before falling. Even though your basic premise was correct, you missed out on a part of the move. So, while in the nineties, one concentrated only on financials and fundamentals and did a lot of refinements on that, she realized that some part of the picture was missing.

Which is when she added some techniques on timing and momentum—fairly elaborate systems for that. But even as the systems were refined more and more over the decades, she also realized by making errors in the market that these technical or timing or momentum trading—whatever systems you call them—were too noisy on their own. Their real value was only to better time an investment or trade that had been identified based on fundamentals and what she says she has seen since has not changed her mind on this.

She clarifies, 'Mind you, Safir, 'the systems I am talking about are much more rigorous and complex compared to the technical analyses of the sort that are featured every day on television. Even so, they will not give additional returns without the core being fundamental analysis.'

I take notes nodding and wondering on the depth of her points.

Realizing my somewhat trying to catch up with this learning state, she looks at me and shares, 'where they do help is cases like this: at one point, we had identified that it was a good fundamental switch to move from Dell to Motorola. Thereafter, we put it in our system to better time our call. And the Motorola share price actually fell from 22 US dollars when we had identified the trade to 18 dollars, and that's when the timing system signalled that it was a buy, so that is the additional part that such systems add.'

As for not allowing mistakes to become fatal, that again is something she says you get to after making crippling losses in the market. 'So now we have a very rigid stop-loss system, and while human fund managers can override on the buy side, they cannot override our stop loss because human beings are not good at acknowledging mistakes and taking losses. Therefore, it is very important to be disciplined and systematic on that side.' She now deploys her proprietary algos to try and reduce human error of emotions and ego.

On the whole, the big change to prevent mistakes has been to codify the expertise into a system which then can be applied on a bias-free, noise-free basis on the entire universe of stocks, which is really the only way to get rid of noise in a system—it is simply not possible to do it humanly. Realization and implementation of this has been the biggest step in eliminating mistakes.

Ultimately, she emphasizes that she is only really bothered about errors of commission. She says, 'you should never get very caught up in the errors of omission because there are always going to be some of those and the last thing you want is to make transactions driven by FOMO.'

Very many mistakes in the market are made because of FOMO, when people jump too late on to a trend. Fund managers like to launch funds on a theme that is running—whether it is an industry or small cap or NASDAQ, but usually almost all thematic funds underperform the market from the time of their launch, which is usually close to the peak for that theme.

One of her favourite quotes on this is by Richard Branson: 'Opportunities are like buses, there is always another one coming along.'

And since investing is a loser's game, the emphasis should be on avoiding errors of commission. Her advice is to not bother about the one that got away. Over time, you realize that investing is a game of luck and skill.

Hence, you are going to lose some, no matter how skilled you are. If you accept that and are actually geared towards it, it makes your life simple and your portfolio better.

Devina often says that the simplest way to improve your portfolio returns is to say every time you are buying a security that you may be making a mistake. If you can acknowledge mistakes and get out immediately, that is a superpower.

And if you are aware of this fact, you avoid falling into the trap whereby you attribute the good run to your skill and the falls in your portfolio to bad luck and unforeseeable risks—the classic attribution bias.

Getting swayed by your mood—like if you have a fight in the traffic, if you are hungry, and so on—is a human attribute, what is called noise. Over time, she says, she has overcome this simply by coding the investment expertise into an artificial intelligence and machine-learning system so that this noise element is eliminated and the entire universe of stocks can be ranked based on the objective criteria.

'There is no other way to eliminate noise no matter how experienced and expert you are. This phenomenon is dealt with in detail in Daniel Kahneman's book, *Noise*: "The real superpower of a machine system is that unlike human beings, it has no mental barriers to acknowledging a mistake and, therefore, can learn from both positive and negative outcomes."'

As far as public money is concerned, in principle, she does not charge any entry or exit load because she thinks that an investor must have ready access to their own money on demand, as they may need it. However, at times, she feels that an exit load would help when you see investors withdrawing at absolutely the wrong time. Even mutual-fund flows peak near the peak of the market, and less than half the investors are invested for more than even two years.

Reflecting on a mistake of wrong timing, she says that a breakup of mutual fund flows shows that investors tend to go towards themes which have performed well in the recent past, whether they are industry themes or small cap vs large cap kind of divisions. In all these cases, investor will make suboptimal returns on the average. You can say it is a mistake on part of the investor but one that is encouraged by the fund-management industry, which also brings in these thematic funds towards the peak of the cycle, because they are easy to sell at that point and time and get them AUM.

In order to learn from mistakes, she relies both on the experience above and on books as the best teachers. 'But before I blink,' she adds, 'you can make a mistake even in this area.' A category of books that people read often are those that describe the journeys and processes of successful investors and traders. While these might have insights, it is important to keep in mind that asking 'why someone succeeded' is not really the right question as, in order to evaluate a strategy, you have to see everyone who used that strategy and what was the probability distribution of the outcome.

Of course, it makes sense to learn from people's mistakes like the Long-Term Capital Management (LTCM) collapse, where Nobel laureates could not see the limitations of their process, which was essentially what assumptions were behind their models. Another was the junk bond boom of the eighties and the subsequent collapse when the action of the market participants in issuing large quantities of junk bonds itself changed the quality of the pool.

But even more important than understanding mistakes of famous investors or people in other fields is also to understand the drivers or causes for their success.

For example, someone investing in the US markets at the beginning of 1960 would have only seen their money go to 2.3 times in twenty years, whereas anyone investing in 1980 would have seen their portfolio go up ten times in the same time period just investing in the broad index.

That is why so many success stories of the most well-documented market, which is the US, relate to the 1980s and 1990s.

To her mind, the real smartness of Peter Lynch was not just in creating Alpha over fourteen years but the decision to quit at the end of those fourteen years when he was still a relatively young man. While he has never spoken about it explicitly, it is clear that he realized that these were extraordinary returns and related to a particular period—he could not hope to replicate those out into the future.

In addition, the books on finance or investing which tell you about the fallacies of your own thinking and the hard-coded biases in the human brain are very valuable. Also valuable is the understanding that these biases are hard-coded and only a few of them can be eliminated by understanding them—most cannot be eliminated without a system, even if you intellectually understand them.

Devina concludes by sharing, 'The process of refining your decision-making and eliminating mistakes is endless. Which is the fun part of the market. Even the smartest and most diligent investor or fund manager cannot have a perfect track record.'

She leaves the reader with her motto in life: 'Look forward, anything that doesn't kill you, makes you stronger' and her message 'don't let other people's opinion about you impact your performance'.

CHAPTER 5

MANISH BHANDARI

The strategic visionary and value hunter

AN easy way to start understanding someone's personality is to explore their social media handles to see their philosophy, likes and dislikes. You can learn about the books they read, the quotes they share and their focus on topics such as technology and world affairs, which can also give an insight into their investment philosophy.

When you check Manish Bhandari's X handle, you find the following description: 'Investment Manager | Falafel Lover | Novice Pianist | Failed Photographer | Thought-provoking views on Investing Landscape'.

What impression does this give of the striking fund manager who handles Vallum Investments? To me, it paints a picture of someone disarming and funny, who doesn't take himself too seriously and isn't afraid to take new paths, fail and share those failures with the world.

When these are your inherent tendencies, the market is a mirror of the same.

Your decisions throw back at you the results of what and how you choose. It shows a rather humble approach to life and investing as most people come on social media to get likes and glorify their accomplishments, while it takes a few to write on their mistakes. In fact, in my discussions across this book, I deliberately chose a few who were open to discussing mistakes, particularly, where they admitted mistakes as a great source of learning.

Manish begins by emphasizing that the complexity of the mind can lead to success, but also failure. With over two decades in the business of investing, he maintains a quiet composure about the ups and downs of trading.

He says, 'Risk lies in the eyes of the beholder, and usually, investors associate risk with unfamiliarity with the subject.'

As one of the more successful names known for outstanding performance in the last two decades of investing, Vallum Capital, managed by Manish Bhandari, delivered a return of 45.7 per cent in FY24 compared to 30 per cent for the benchmark index.

So, what does Manish bet on when other investors find a deal and its contours unfamiliar? For Manish, it's about playing on the 'acceleration phenomenon', which simply means that the return is increasing over time, and thus the price increases at an increasing rate.

He shares a lesson here—your mind has to be flexible and rigid at the same time to identify the pattern and to take a corrective step. We must, therefore, surround ourselves with smart people who will always keep a check on any possible exuberance on our part.

During my conversation with Manish, I am often struck by his unique perspectives. He tracks developments in China very closely and uses his observations to analyse opportunities in India, looking at both potential successes and impeding failures.

Manish also applies the 'acceleration phenomenon' to his investee companies. For example, in the case of a pharmaceutical company, he evaluates whether a new discovery could significantly accelerate the company's growth. Another example is, he talks of capex cycles in large companies, highlighting almost that 2 plus 2 may be 22 (capability meets expansion meets good allocation of capital).

So how does Manish arrive at these conclusions, what drives his learning and what mistakes does he make or avoid and learn from? Let's delve deeper.

From coins to shares

As a child, Manish had a keen interest in collecting coins, a hobby that taught him some of the most important lessons in trade and in life.

Collecting coins requires several skills: knowing what to collect, understanding where to find valuable coins, the ability to trade them for others, determining their worth, and having the patience to persist in the pursuit. These skills can also be applied to the world of investing.

Manish feels that a mistake many make is not understanding their own strengths. Is it trading, investing or playing cyclical stocks well? When passion and knowledge meet temperament and confidence, the learning process can be truly enriching and rewarding. This reminds one of the legendary Dhirubhai Ambani.

In the late 1940s, at the young age of seventeen, Dhirubhai went to Aden, Yemen, and began working as a dispatch clerk for A. Besse & Co., which later became a distributor for Shell. While managing the filling station at the port of Aden, Dhirubhai noticed that Yemeni rial coins, which had a high content of pure silver, were disappearing from circulation at an alarming rate. He anticipated the demand for the rial in the London Stock Exchange, purchased them in bulk, melted them and sold the silver to bullion traders in London.

Both Dhirubhai's and Manish's stories show us that success is not just about intelligence or talent but also about hard work, perseverance and a willingness to take risks and think outside the box. It isn't merely about making money; it's about the ability to look beneath the surface and find hidden opportunities.

Manish elaborates that mistakes can happen anytime, but can turn into a positive outcome, even though initially they may seem to go against. He teaches us that a mistake we make in judging an outcome too fast might actually be seeding itself, like a bamboo plant. The question to ask is not what the outcome is but what is the rationale for the outcome—a spread between market's short-term judgement and a company's long-term advantage, and whether that advantage is increasing over time.

Mistakes, says Manish, can surface anytime. It can happen due to inherent patterns or data errors. However, the mind must be flexible so that it can easily identify patterns to take corrective steps—not that every decision taken must always be right—and, therefore, to study the data error becomes important and a regular feature of a choice.

This is why it is important to surround ourselves with smart people who can keep the exuberance in check. His favourite quote of all time is 'hara wohi jo lada nahi'—those who have not fought are the ones who have lost.

While he would love to give it a fight, Manish's alertness to the possibility of mistakes in investing is beautifully articulated in a recent article he posted on his LinkedIn page. It's called '4 June Yaad Hai Na'. Says Manish, 'In the crime thriller movie *Drishyam*, the protagonist, Ajay Devgn, cleverly reminds the audience of 2 October, embedding it as a pivotal alibi in a meticulously crafted narrative to protect his family. By skilfully manipulating perceptions and creating a believable story, he outsmarts the police and the audience alike, showcasing the power of psychological influence. This mastery of narrative control parallels how politicians craft their own stories, shaping public perception and maintaining control amidst scrutiny. Just as Devgn's character creates a convincing illusion to achieve his goals, politicians often employ similar tactics to influence the masses and steer public opinion.'

He goes further to add, 'As India approaches 4 June, a date with potentially significant political and economic implications, investors should be particularly cautious. Any political or economic disappointment could trigger a substantial decline in the markets, amplifying the risks for retail investors. Therefore, it is crucial for investors to remain vigilant and not get swayed solely by the optimistic narratives being promoted.'

At the same time, if there is no meaningful political or economic disappointment, Manish leaves room to revisit 5 June as a new data point and take a view, a reason why on the fifth he remained substantially invested in his fund.[1]

For Manish, a mistake becomes a source of motivation when he learns the right lesson from it and applies it in other successful investments. This entails using the mind rather than letting emotions or background noise influence decisions. For example, as a shareholder in Rallis India during

2008–10, Manish achieved only marginal return, but the lesson learned was successfully applied in PI Industries, which performed exceptionally well in the subsequent years.

After encountering several new failures during the initial years, Manish and his team significantly enhanced their framework by integrating macroeconomic analysis with their bottom-up approach to stock selection, which greatly helped them in that investing phase.

Manish, the funny guy that he is, who thinks he is a failed photographer and a novice pianist, talks exuberantly about a mistake turning into a bonanza. 'Yes, it indeed has happened on a few occasions in the last two decades. We invested in a steel-pipe company with certain earning expectations, but a family feud broke out causing chaos with our investment. We were concerned about various potential outcomes and our position became more precarious than anticipated. However, after a few months, the situation stabilized and the investment yielded significant returns, and we had a sigh of relief.' Manish has called this a mistake as he believed that he did not build such a scenario during the investment phase and was totally unprepared for such circumstances.

He leaves us with a great process: the power of drawing inherent patterns, identifying data errors, scenario building and running sensitivity analysis.

Everyone is eccentric

While sanity is often considered the most desirable state of mind when making investment decisions, Manish argues that every individual carries some form of eccentricity that, consciously or unconsciously, influences their investment choices.

'We are ultimately a sum of our upbringing, beliefs, biases, education, circumstances, conditioning and more. Everything we experience throughout life contributes to shaping who we are,' he explains. These deep-seated influences, he believes, play a significant role in shaping our investing patterns. From the companies we choose to invest in, to the timing and strategies we employ, every decision is a reflection of our personal makeup. If you have a predisposition towards growth, momentum or value investing, it isn't just a random preference—it's a signature that mirrors your personality and experiences.

In essence, our investment choices are a canvas where our inner selves are painted, revealing the complex interplay of who we are and what we value.

Simple tastes

Despite his professional success, Manish leads a life grounded in simplicity and values. His favourite dish still is dimsum and a good plate of falafel, and he prefers the refreshing simplicity of a glass of lemon water over more complex beverages.

Beyond his culinary preferences, Manish's true joy lies in spending time with his two daughters, watching them grow and thrive. It's also quite evident that he tries to keep the child in him active through his piano lessons or the occasional photography escapades! I have read many books on why a child is the best state of mind to be, in terms of curiosity and open mindedness—a mistake we make is to diminish that by the overload of what is pushed towards us.

Spotting investment errors: The role of intuition in investment

Spotting investment errors is not easy, says Manish. He believes that the hero of the bull market is the villain of the bear market. Experts use various tools to weed out errors—and even then, some mistakes still slip in.

As we grow and evolve, we make different kinds of mistakes, one of which is allowing our frameworks to remain anchored in past events, preventing us from embracing new technology, adapting to changing investing landscape.

For example, investing in public sector companies and public sector banks has become a pariah in the last decade. However, in the current bull market, these very companies have been among the biggest value creators. Manish was quick to adopt to some of these and play either on their turning capex cycles or move towards efficiency and opportunity at a very reasonable enterprise value.

Manish also acknowledges the role of a sixth sense in business and investing. He references a quote by Sashidhar Jagdishan, managing director of HDFC Bank, in an interview with Rahul Jain of Goldman Sachs on 19 February 2024: 'Our bank's architecture has a sixth sense, which sort of knows when to grow, when not to grow or when to slow down. You may not see it now, but when the cycle changes, it will be far more visible.' Manish shared this quote in an article he published on LinkedIn.

For Manish, the sixth sense is a fascinating and somewhat elusive concept, blending elements of intuition, instinct and perception. He cites Warren Buffett's interview in 1999, where Buffett said that investors must fend for themselves and rely on their knowledge and intuition when searching for promising businesses to invest in.

As Naval Ravikant, tech veteran, says: 'It takes time to develop your gut, but once it's developed, don't listen to anything else.'[2]

All investment managers with experience have benefited during their careers from the use of the sixth sense.

Even the US Navy has invested millions of dollars in helping sailors and marines refine their sixth sense because intuition can supersede intellect in high-stake situations, such as the battlefield, shares Manish.

He admits to having benefited from his sixth sense by staying away from a merger news of a media giant with another global media company, based on his experience of dealing with the media sector as well as from a digital company which had a run with the regulator in 2024.

For Manish and his world of fund management, sixth sense serves as a compass, guiding through the complexities of life, offering insights beyond the realm of logic and reason. In today's world driven by analytics, data and AI, intuition is not merely a luxury but a necessity for success.

In Manish's firms, senior members share their vast repository of experiences with other team members, to hone up instincts of the team. 'So, the next time you find yourself at a crossroads, trust in the whispers of your sixth sense. For in those fleeting moments of intuition lie the seeds of greatness, waiting to be sown.'

Readers are leaders

An avid reader, Manish admits that books have broadened his understanding of life. From macroeconomics to the events that shape history, everything he has read has expanded his knowledge and given him different perspectives.

Investing is equally about observing trends—wisdom and follies of the crowd. Manish shares the art of fund management. He says that the crowd is mostly wrong at the start and end of any trend or direction, but is usually right in the middle of a trend.

Therefore, it is essential to understand this phenomenon and not completely ignore the crowd.

Manish Bhandari's investment philosophy

This is deeply rooted in the belief that one must not become a hostage to past experiences or mistakes, understanding that both life and investing are journeys filled with learning, growth, and the inevitable errors that come with the territory.

To grow as an investor, Manish emphasizes the importance of acknowledging these mistakes, learning from them, and then moving forward without allowing them to constrain future decisions.

In the context of his own investment journey, Manish has continually demonstrated the ability to adapt and evolve with changing market conditions. This flexibility is crucial, especially in the dynamic world of finance, where clinging to outdated strategies can quickly lead to obsolescence. He believes that staying nimble, continuously learning, and being open to new ideas while remaining intuitive are essential qualities for any successful investor. This approach has enabled him to navigate various market cycles and technological shifts, ensuring that he remains relevant and successful in an ever-changing landscape.

Manish's refusal to dwell on the past has also influenced his approach to embracing new technologies and exploring emerging investment landscapes. By staying current and open to change, he has positioned Vallum Capital to take advantage of opportunities that others might miss due to their attachment to outdated methods or strategies.

This forward-thinking mindset not only prevents stagnation but also fosters an environment where innovation and growth can thrive. In essence, Manish's investment success can be attributed to his belief in the importance of adaptability and continuous learning. By not allowing past mistakes or successes to define his future, he has cultivated a resilient and forward-looking investment philosophy that serves both him and his clients well.

Regrets of an investor

If he were to reverse the clock, what would Manish regret? Well, he says he would invest in exceptional business managers who would be capable of transforming simple stock into a multibagger. Although he often reflects on past errors and wonders about the potential missed opportunities, he ensures these regrets do not influence his current investment decisions. And what would he do if he had a time machine? Manish says he would like to revisit and learn from past mistakes, but in the absence of one, he remains focused on enhancing his understanding of how other successful professionals manage businesses as custodians of capital. Moving forward, he says, 'I will study how to identify outstanding business managers, what makes them unique and how they translate a mundane business into multibagger stock and reward shareholders.'

Personal life and investing

Maintaining equanimity and controlling emotions can be challenging, says Manish, especially when people tend to make more mistakes during favourable times. However, despite errors, one should not be disheartened, rather serve as motivation to learn from the mistake. Staying calm has a huge role to play in recovering from a mistake to move further on. It is here that one must see from where all Manish draws his lessons.

In a recent post, Manish quotes, 'Remarkably calm rescue ops from a burning aircraft speaks highly of Japanese discipline, work ethic and the dividends of giving blue-collar jobs status.'[3] Even when the Japanese go wrong, they still do something so right that they come out winners. Here lies a crucial clear give-away of Manish's value systems for investments. Manish must have wondered how did they rescue 379 passengers from a burning plane in less than twenty minutes? Zero deaths! Fact is, Japanese are very, very stoic and very calm people. They are very good at following orders for their own benefit.

These qualities come to everyone's rescue while it's a physical or an economic emergency.

Learning from mistakes is an integral part of the curriculum but criticism on a public platform can have a negative impact. It is common for investors to publicly criticize managers to showcase their own superiority, which can discourage managers from openly discussing their mistakes. It is very common for the investors to pull down managers in public to showcase their upmanship. Such acts result in managers shying away from discussing their mistake openly. To avoid this, Manish has made a habit of discussing his decision in public by writing them in annual shareholder letters.

The public admission of mistakes encourages deeper introspection and growth, which is also how he handles things with his family and young daughters—being open, discussing and seeking views, rather than putting others down, which can demoralize them.

I admit, I have a lot of learn from this mistake of mine!!

Amidst personal challenges, making sound business decisions has always been challenging, says Manish.

In the market, professional investors have two key advantages: duration edge, which involves the length of capital commitment and strategic reviews, where private equity often excels over public market investments; and temperamental edge—do you buy when others are sellers in the market or in the stock. Successful investing requires duration and temporal edge by capital allocated.

As a manager, it is crucial to be more careful with money and relationships, especially during good times rather difficult times. It is a human tendency to commit mistakes during prosperous times. Manish's strive has always been practising equanimity in his investing journey.

Vallum's way of investing

To establish a standard operating procedure for minimizing errors, Manish has introduced Vallum's Earning Cycle Analysis (VECA). This checklist assists in refining the selection of shares before purchasing them. There is also a way to do basic earning analysis before taking risky bets.

Manish says, 'It's important to balance differences of opinion amongst the teams. Therefore, to align everyone, we use investment checklists and test our frameworks under various market conditions to reach a final outcome.' He adds, however, 'The value of intuition and wisdom gained from diverse experiences cannot be replaced by education or committee structures. A well-rounded approach helps navigate differences within the team.'

Reflecting on his career, Manish admits to having made many mistakes, but he has also developed defining frameworks to improve success rates. One important strategy has been to invest in a company for one business cycle (three to five years). With a portfolio turnover of around 22 per cent, one of the lowest in the industry, Vallum focuses on the statistical likelihood of a company performing well within a single business cycle. This approach has helped the firm maintain the fine balance between rigidity and adaptability in its collective mindset.

Errors during hard times

While errors can be made at any time, the pandemic has provided a unique opportunity to observe and learn from them. Despite witnessing market losses, staying true to the vision has ultimately been rewarding. The checklist that Manish talked about, and the frameworks, guide them in these situations, helping them stay on track and balance things over time. Manish says, 'At Vallum, we are fortunate to have investors who are truly long-term and patient. During investor meetings, the review showed our client attrition remained as low as 1 per cent even at the peak of Covid-19.' There can be no better testament to Manish and his team than integrity and focussed attention to the genuine needs of his clients.

Errors of omission vs errors of commission

Errors of omission occur when you fail to act on an opportunity you had identified through analysis and due diligence. You thought there may be an opportunity for investment, and then, for whatever reason, you decided not to act. The error becomes apparent later when the company performs contrary to how we expected.

Errors of commission, however, are mistakes where you failed to act when you should have. Errors of commission are those where you chose to do something—you acted and were proved wrong. These are instances where you conducted analysis and performed due diligence on a company, involve taking action that leads to loss or impairment of capital, making them harder to accept.

Manish says that in public money management, both types of errors cost dearly. Errors of omission can lead to severe underperformance of the fund relative to the benchmark, while errors of commission can lead to loss of capital. Identifying these mistakes is straightforward but employing a strong investment framework can help minimize errors of omission, and using checklists can aid in avoiding errors of commission.

Discussing about correcting the errors, Manish says that investing is inherently filled with mistakes. Let's recap the famous investing mistake of investors of IT sector of 2000, retail stocks in 2008, pharmaceutical stocks in 2014, NBFC in the year 2019 and the chemical sector in 2022. There is lot to learn from micro bubbles in sectors and various asset classes and once we learn, it will improve our reflexes; remember Manish's bet on intuition?

Corrective measures for mistakes

Manish acknowledges that corrective measures are essential for monitoring mistakes. After extensive deliberation, the Vallum team developed a checklist to guide their investors through the investment process. Central to this is VECA, as mentioned earlier, which aims to avoid investing in companies during elevated earnings cycles, as this often leads to inflated price-to-earnings (P/E) ratios.

Manish shares an example: 'Some in the investing community went on a buying spree in diagnostic and FMCG shares during and after the Covid period. The tailwind of earnings from Covid and network expansion created a surge in earnings for diagnostic companies in the short run. Investors mistook acceleration of earnings and expanded valuation multiples. As the dust settled, the normalization of earnings revealed the real picture, resulting in significant drawdowns in the valuations of such companies. At Vallum, we conduct a detailed ECA before investing in a company to avoid such pitfalls.'

In conclusion, Manish's journey as an investor is a testament to the value of intuition, looking for hidden opportunities, spotting roadblocks, adaptability and continuous learning, as well as the importance of not being a prisoner to one's past. His success is not merely a product of his financial acumen but also of a philosophy that values resilience and forward-thinking. By embracing change and remaining nimble in the face of evolving market dynamics, Manish has managed to stay ahead of the curve, ensuring that Vallum Capital continues to thrive. His belief that growth comes from moving beyond past errors and staying open to new possibilities serves as a guiding principle for aspiring investors. In an industry often characterized by rigidity and tradition, Manish stands out as a beacon of innovation and enduring relevance.

CHAPTER 6

RAAMDEO AGRAWAL

The luminary with an eye for long-term success

I first heard of Raamdeo Agrawal—one of the prominent names in the stock market—not because of his success or media presence, but because of the 'feel good' reputation he carried. Many people I met early on in my market journey praised him as a 'sound investor'. At the time, I did not fully understand what that meant. Influenced by stories about Harshad Mehta and Ketan Parekh, I assumed that being a sound investor meant being someone who made a lot of money, often by questionable means.

However, the more I learned about Raamdeo, the more I realized that making money through investing wasn't about schemes; it was about following a sound investment process. Some called him the 'Buffett of India', and naturally, I was keen to learn more about him. As I studied his methods, I came to understand that investing is based on financial analysis rather than on speculation.

Today, Raamdeo Agrawal stands tall as one of the market's most respected investors and a highly successful entrepreneur, co-founding Motilal Oswal Financial Services Limited.

My first learning from Raamdeo was an introduction to 'value investing' followed by a more pertinent concept that was new to me—'value migration', a term inspired by Adrian Slywotzky's 1995 book by that title.

If there were an Olympics for value investing and value migration investing in India, Raamdeo would be standing proudly on the podium, gold medal in one hand and a balance sheet in the other. He has seen it all—from the dizzying heights of the bull market to the gut-wrenching lows of the bear phases. Yet what sets him apart isn't just his knack for picking the right stocks; it's his ability to laugh at his own mistakes.

Born in a small town in Rajasthan, Raamdeo's journey to becoming one of the most respected names in the Indian financial market is the stuff of legends. Imagine a young boy with stars in his eyes and numbers on his mind, wandering through the dusty streets, dreaming not of becoming a cricketer, but of analysing balance sheets. While other kids were trading marbles, Raamdeo was more interested in trading stories about market dynamics.

Determined to pursue a career in finance, Raamdeo went on to study chartered accountancy in the early 1980s—a time when calculators were huge and Excel was something you did in your school exams. This qualification didn't just open doors for him; it handed him the keys to the financial kingdom. It was during this time that Raamdeo learned the holy trinity of investing: patience, discipline and the ability to spot a dud stock from a mile away.

Raamdeo dove head first into the stock market. He quickly realized that the market doesn't care if you topped your class. It's a place where even the best of the best can, and will, make mistakes. But instead of being daunted by his early missteps, Raamdeo embraced them. Each mistake was a lesson in what not to do. And with each lesson learned, he sharpened his skills and honed his instincts.

Today, Raamdeo Agrawal is celebrated not just for his victories but for his willingness to acknowledge and learn from his mistakes. His journey is proof that even the best investors get it wrong sometimes—it's how you respond to those mistakes that defines your success. So, if you find yourself disheartened by a bad investment decision, remember Raamdeo's golden rule: 'The market might be unforgiving, but that doesn't mean you can't forgive yourself.' After all, every misstep is just another step towards greatness.

Raamdeo's professional journey began in 1987 when he teamed up with Motilal Oswal to co-found what would become a powerhouse in India's financial sector—Motilal Oswal Financial Services Limited. Picture this: two ambitious young men with a modest brokerage business and a dream bigger than their combined bank balances. They started with little more than sheer grit and a few calculators that were probably older than they were.

Raamdeo's strategic vision—combined with a healthy dose of stubbornness—pushed Motilal Oswal to incredible heights. Under his leadership, the company diversified into investment banking, wealth management, asset management and retail broking, among other things. It was as if they'd grown from selling lemonade on the corner to running a beverage empire.

In the stock market, Raamdeo is like a Jedi master, wielding the power of value investing like a light sabre. A disciple of the legendary Benjamin Graham and Warren Buffett, he has made it his mission to navigate the market's ups and downs with the precision of a seasoned trader. His investment decisions are meticulously researched, rooted in fundamentals and always focused on the long game.

Consider his early investments in Hero Honda and Infosys. While others chased the latest market fads, Raamdeo placed his bets on these under-the-radar gems, turning them into multibagger success stories. It was the kind of move that leaves other investors wondering, 'Why didn't I see that?'

I once asked him why he chose these investments, and his answer was simple: 'value migration'. In one case, he saw human effort migrating to technology while in the other, he noticed a shift in demand from scooters to motorcycles, which offered glamour and power and were much in demand as gifts at weddings as status symbols.

Raamdeo didn't stop there. He shared his stock-picking strategy with the investment community through his 'QGLP' framework—quality, growth, longevity and price—which is his mantra for picking winners: find a high-quality business with strong growth potential, the ability to endure and a price that doesn't make you wince.

Through his books, interviews and speeches, Raamdeo has generously shared his playbook, turning everyday investors into savvy market players. His insights are like those rare stock tips that actually pay off, guiding investors towards sound principles and away from the pitfalls of chasing the next hot stock.

In the wild world of the stock market, Raamdeo Agrawal stands out not only as someone who knows how to pick a winner but also as someone who is willing to teach others to do the same.

Early life lessons aiding investment philosophy

Reflecting on his early life, upbringing and education, Raamdeo points out that even the best of investors can trip up when the market throws a curveball. He often jokes that investment mistakes are as inevitable as a bad haircut—you're bound to get one eventually, no matter how good your barber is.

He believes that common errors like skipping research, rushing decisions or letting greed drive your trades are often rooted in upbringing, education and exposure. If you're taught that money grows on trees, you might find yourself chasing get-rich-quick schemes rather than taking a slower, more measured approach to investing.

Raamdeo was lucky—his chartered accountancy background gave him a solid foundation. But even with that edge, he emphasizes that the stock market isn't a set-it-and-forget-it game. You have to keep learning, adapting and staying sharp. In his words, 'Education might teach you how to read a balance sheet, but life teaches you not to bet your entire portfolio on one.'

Mistakes come in all shapes and sizes, and Raamdeo has experienced them all. Here, he gets philosophical: he believes that mistakes made in calm times are like spilling coffee on your shirt—annoying, but manageable. On the other hand, mistakes made during a crisis are more like accidentally setting your kitchen on fire. Yet sometimes, the market gods smile upon you, and from that burning kitchen comes a Michelin-starred meal.

Raamdeo finds that context is crucial in investing. During events like Covid-19 or 9/11, if you were a net buyer, you might have ended up profiting from investments that initially looked hopeless. Sometimes, a disaster can turn a dud into a diamond. Reading and grasping the context is the key.

Throughout his career, Raamdeo has stuck to a portfolio approach, treating his investments like a well-curated menu rather than a one-dish wonder. And he's diligent—some might say obsessively so—when it comes to tracking his investments. He's like that friend who checks the stock market app every five minutes, except in his case, it actually pays off. The first hint that he's made a mistake usually comes when a stock starts dropping faster than a hot potato. That's when his spidey sense starts tingling, and he knows it's time to reassess and adjust.

In Raamdeo's world, mistakes aren't just slip-ups—they're part of the process. And thanks to his knack for catching them early, he's managed to turn potential epic failures into valuable lessons, and sometimes, even profits.

Raamdeo is the first to acknowledge his mistakes, but unlike most of us who might hit the panic button, he focuses on swiftly making the necessary corrections. He knows that in the investment world, letting a mistake linger only leads to worsening losses.

Raamdeo avoids getting stuck with underperforming stocks by tapping into his vast arsenal of investment ideas. He reallocates his capital efficiently, ensuring every rupee is working as hard as it can.

To keep mistakes from snowballing, he follows a few tried-and-true practices. For one, he takes a disciplined approach to investing, making only a handful of decisions each year. It's like choosing your moves in a chess game—fewer moves mean fewer chances to mess up. He also swears by quantitative analysis and a disciplined process, treating his investment strategy like a well-oiled machine that doesn't go off track easily.

However, Raamdeo isn't all about numbers and spreadsheets. He's also a big fan of old-school tools like meditation to keep his mind sharp and clear. He firmly believes that a focused mind leads to better decisions—or at least fewer panic-induced sell-offs.

But even Raamdeo knows that every now and then, a mistake ends up turning out well not because of skill, but because of luck. He's wise enough to know that counting on luck is like trying to time the market—it's a gamble, not a strategy.

In Raamdeo's world, there's a clear distinction between skill and luck, and he places his faith in skill. While he occasionally benefits from a lucky break, he doesn't rely on it—he's learned that in the long run, discipline beats luck every time.

Raamdeo emphasizes the importance of avoiding fatal mistakes. He has mastered the art of walking the fine line between taking smart, calculated risks and steering clear of anything that could blow up his portfolio. It's like navigating a minefield, where the mines are bad stocks, market crashes and the occasional too-good-to-be-true opportunity.

He has the humility to admit that the market is a vast, ever-changing puzzle with plenty of pitfalls. No matter how much he learns, there's always another mistake waiting in the wings. But that's what keeps him sharp. Instead of getting complacent, Raamdeo is always on the lookout, striving not to make the same mistakes. It's this blend of caution, curiosity and continuous learning that has shaped him into the savvy investor he is today and keeps him ahead of the curve.

Raamdeo's mantra is simple: Make mistakes, but never the kind that send you packing. If you can learn from someone else's mistake instead of making your own, that's smart investing with a dose of schadenfreude.

Raamdeo believes in the value of introspection to learn from mistakes. He carefully analyses what went wrong so he can improve continually. When it comes to throwing good money after bad, Raamdeo knows better than to let his ego get in the way. He's learned that doubling down on a losing position rarely leads to success and often results in deeper losses.

In team settings, Raamdeo appreciates a good debate and values diverse viewpoints. But when it's time to make the final call, he leaves it to the manager responsible for that stock. This approach allows for a thorough evaluation while making sure that accountability and decision-making are clear.

Raamdeo firmly believes in the value of a successful team. By fostering trust and continuity, he allows his team to build on their successes and learn from their missteps. However, he knows that a large, successful team can sometimes mask mistakes. To avoid falling into this trap, he champions process codification and transparency. This helps keep everyone on track and minimizes the chance of taking a wrong turn because of overconfidence.

When it comes to the impact of personal life on decision-making, Raamdeo acknowledges that personal circumstances can influence his choices. He is committed to keeping his personal and professional lives separate, ensuring that personal challenges don't cloud his investment judgement. He balances the ups and downs of life with the temperament of a seasoned investor, using personal experiences as lessons rather than excuses.

He views mistakes as his chance to refine strategies and improve performance, giving him the resilience to stay focused on long-term success. When mistakes feel overwhelming, he reminds himself that setbacks are part of the investment journey—like speed bumps on the road to success. This balanced perspective helps him stay optimistic, even when the market feels like it's testing his patience.

Reflecting on his journey, Raamdeo knows that understanding companies deeply before investing is crucial. Thorough research and careful allocation are essential to avoid unnecessary slip-ups, especially when managing public money. Even though public perception can be swayed by various factors, he stays committed to his sound investment principles, treating external pressures as mere background noise.

When it comes to media and social media scrutiny, Raamdeo maintains a healthy balance—he owns up to errors while celebrating successes, creating a transparent and accountable approach to investing.

To conclude, Raamdeo Agrawal's legacy isn't just about the success of Motilal Oswal Financial Services Limited but also his contributions to value investing in India. Through his writings, seminars and mentorship, he's inspired a new generation of investors to adopt a disciplined and research-driven approach. His journey is a testament to how vision, perseverance and adhering to fundamental principles can lead to extraordinary success. As he continues to guide and inspire, Raamdeo's impact on the Indian financial landscape will be felt for years to come.

CHAPTER 7

ATUL SURI

The insight strategist and market alchemist

It is often said in light humour that one must take Atul Suri seriously for he lives in Pali Hill!

Atul has decades of experience, a passion for scuba diving and a unique ability to blend technical and quant with fundamental analysis in his journey of wealth creation. Despite his expertise, he does lesser churns than any trader per se and is fixated on long-term trends than daily charts and candlesticks.

Atul began his career as a fundamental analyst at Parag Parikh Financial Advisory Services in 1991, gaining expertise in identifying high-quality stocks. Starting his journey alongside the legendary Parag Parekh laid a solid foundation for his success.

He then decided to pursue a Masters in banking and finance from the University of Technology Sydney, Australia, delving into quant and technical analysis.

Returning to India in the late nineties, Atul joined Birla Sun Life Securities, leading the private client group business. In 2003, he founded

Marathon Capital, focusing on trading index derivatives, which further deepened his understanding of financial markets. In 2008, he took another leap by joining RARE Enterprises as an analyst, gaining invaluable experience under India's big bull, the late Padmashri Rakesh Jhunjhunwala. Indeed, Atul credits Jhunjhunwala as being instrumental in shaping his professional journey. He then went on to launch his own portfolio-management services (PMS) fund.

Having worked alongside mentors like Parag Parekh and Rajesh Jhunjhunwala, Atul has learned a great deal and is always willing to share his learnings, be they in finance, travel or the finer things in life. He sometimes reminds me of the scene in the Bollywood film *Zindagi Na Milegi Dobara*, where after a scuba dive, Hritik Roshan's character experiences a moment of revelation about balancing unrealistic expectations with reality. Perhaps Atul draws similar inspiration from scuba diving, seeing the vast opportunities that lie in the depths of the ocean as a reminder to keep discovering and learning.

Leveraging his diverse experience, Atul successfully moved on to managing trend-following strategies at Marathon Trends Advisory. His trend-following investment approach is inspired by the legendary trader Ed Seykota. Combining fundamental and technical analysis with a deep understanding of market trends, his strategy helps his team navigate financial complexities and deliver superior investment outcomes.

Atul's success stems not only from his financial expertise but also from his holistic approach to life. So, who is Atul beyond the world of finance.?

The CEO of Marathon Trends PMS once said, Atul had a sharp eye for talent assessment. This trait, which his friends and associates vouch for, is often referred to as intuition—a gut feeling that helps one pick up on subtle signals. His personal passions—marathon running and scuba diving—reflect his perseverance, patience, stamina and focus, qualities that shape his portfolio-management skills. Indeed, at Marathon Trends Advisory, everyone recognizes that Atul's interests contribute to his holistic perspective as a portfolio manager. His passion for marathon running highlights the importance of physical fitness, long-term goal setting and commitment. Likewise, scuba diving emphasizes exploration and uncovering hidden opportunities, which is reflected in his investment strategies.

Atul's example highlights the need for cultivating a multidisciplinary approach to life that can aid adaptability in investing. Some cultivate this through poker, some through bridge, yet others by developing analytical skills, seeking great mentors or learning from life and its lessons. The learning process is truly endless.

Mistakes: An integral part of the learning curve

With disarming straightforwardness, Atul recognizes that mistakes are an inescapable part of life but valuable learning experiences.

He says, 'Investing is intrinsically tied to life. The decisions we make, whether they lead to success or failure, often stem from deep-seated psychological biases developed over the years. The correlation between life and investing is undeniable. My extensive work in this area, particularly in collaboration with Ed Seykota, a pioneer in trading, and the Trading Tribe, has made it evident that the subconscious imprints from our childhood play a significant role in shaping our personalities. These personality biases then spill over into the realm of investing.'

While many perceive investing primarily as an intellectual activity, Atul has always believed that it is largely driven by psychology. In his estimation, only about 10 per cent of investing is intellectual; the remaining 90 per cent is deeply rooted in psychology, often tracing back to our earliest life experiences. This connection underscores the profound link between one's upbringing and their approach to investing. I tend to agree when I tie this back to a young seventeen-year-old Dhirubhai Ambani's silver-coin arbitrage shared in another chapter.

We often read about biases, and while it all sounds apt, in reality, we do little work to eliminate the biases. Hence, the psychology of investing needs us to visit, re-visit and repeatedly visit these biases and the traps they lay. Easier said than done but the journey towards doing is the real learning of an investor. By being fixated on biases, we make mistakes, and sometimes even repeat them.

Atul notes, 'Mistakes are an integral part of the learning curve and offer pivotal growth opportunities.'

Let us now look at Atul's journey as a financial advisor, illustrating how he transformed challenges into valuable lessons.

Errors in times of uncertainty

How does Atul differentiate between mistakes made in calm times versus those made during crises such as Covid-19 or 9/11? For him, errors during times of extreme stress hold significant weight. Having navigated the market for over thirty years, he has encountered such high-stress moments periodically. Every time, upon reflection, Atul recognized that while the specifics of each situation varied, making it impossible to be fully prepared, the solution tended to remain consistent: adherence to one's process.

Take, for instance, the market plunge during the Covid-19 pandemic. No one had faced anything like it, nor could they rely on historical accounts. The challenges transcended market fluctuations—humanity's very survival seemed at stake. Images of overcrowded hospitals and alarming contagion theories rocked our foundational beliefs, making investment decisions even more challenging. It's during such times that the propensity for mistakes is magnified.

Yet, when Atul harks back to events like the 2008 financial crisis, he is always reminded that while the severity and duration of the downturn were unprecedented, the solution was familiar or inevitable. Relying on simulations and back tests from those periods, it becomes evident that the best strategy in such adversity is unwavering commitment to one's process.

Like many other fund managers and lead investors, Atul emphasizes, while the nature of mistakes made in calm times differs from those made during crises, the remedy for both is the same: trust and adherence to the process that you have established and has stood the test of time.

As someone who learns every day, Atul advises documenting your process: note what led to successful outcomes and what resulted in failures. Identify a pattern that works for you, and stick to it, through good times and bad.

Two steps back, three steps ahead.

Throughout his career, Atul has recognized mistakes when outcomes deviated significantly from the expected results. These deviations have served as cues for him to reassess his process. In nearly every instance, Atul found that the root cause was a deviation from his established procedures. Such moments serve as a wake-up call, emphasizing the importance of returning to the foundational investing process.

The first step in dealing with a mistake is admitting to them. Many shy away from this, blaming other factors rather than examining their own processes and judgement. This often leads to buying high, selling low and blaming market irrationality rather than reflecting on their own actions.

Atul starts by acknowledging a mistake. While this recognition induceses a poignant sense of discomfort, they prompt him to review his process, analysing how things might have unfolded had he remained faithful to it. More often than not, the root of these missteps lies in our inherent human biases—particularly fear and greed—which skew decision-making. When he realizes that he is the primary architect of the predicament, Atul recalibrates quickly, recommitting to his established process.

He admits that while short-term recalibration can be challenging, experience has shown him that it yields favourable outcomes in the long run.

Atul elaborates further on tools and practices that can ensure a more balanced and disciplined approach to investing. Meditation provides clarity and equanimity, helping him stay centred during market volatility. Quantitative analysis provides data-driven insights, acting as a counterweight to emotional biases. Finally, an advisory group serves as an external check, offering diverse perspectives and challenging potential oversights.

For Atul, each perceived misstep is an opportunity to revisit and refine his processes. This continuous improvement not only elevates the quality of his work but also increases profitability. Thus, what may seem like an error in the immediate aftermath can, over time, pave the way for more favourable outcomes.

Throughout his journey, Atul has gained immense insights by observing and interacting with others. Engaging with accomplished investors and learning from their successes and failures has been enlightening. He has had the privilege of collaborating with some of India's top investors, gleaning invaluable lessons. Seminal works like *Market Wizards* by Jack Schwager have also profoundly influenced him, providing insight into the psychology of successful investors and equipping him with the wisdom to navigate challenges more effectively.

Despite all this knowledge, Atul acknowledges that the human psyche is susceptible to greed and fear. Awareness is crucial but applying that knowledge consistently can be difficult. Over time, he believes his ability to apply risk-control measures has matured, enabling him to better manage the emotional tumult of investing.

In decision-making, errors of omission and errors of commission carry distinct connotations for Atul. Errors of omission arise from ignorance—a lack of understanding or insight. Each mistake often reveals a knowledge gap, illustrating this type of error. For Atul, the process of addressing these gaps and continually expanding his understanding is a lifelong endeavour.

Conversely, errors of commission are missteps made despite being aware. Such errors are linked to the psychological aspect of decision-making, where emotions like greed, fear and other inherent human sentiments play a role. Atul acknowledges that no one can claim complete mastery over their emotions, which makes these types of errors an ongoing challenge.

In essence, for Atul, the investment journey entails a dual challenge: constantly learning to rectify errors of omission and striving for emotional discipline to minimize errors of commission.

Balancing ego and commitment bias in the stock market

As an investor who relies on stop-loss mechanism for risk management—not as a foolproof method but as a threshold beyond which the system can no longer tolerate further losses. He views the triggering of a stop loss as a clear indicator of a mistake, often prompting him to exit the investment. However, he admits that he dreads overlooking his own stop-loss criteria. In the volatile market environment, Atul believes the gravest risk is financial ruin, and ignoring a stop loss brings one perilously close to this threat.

There are times when a stock rebounds after a stop loss is triggered, which can lead to moments of reflection and even regret. One might wish they had stayed with the investment.

Despite this, Atul has witnessed numerous instances where investors, swayed by conviction or narratives, held on to stocks beyond their stop losses, leading to significant financial loss or even total ruin. For Atul, effective risk management takes precedence over conviction—it's the safety net that ensures the sustainability of one's investment journey.

Decision-making process

In the world of professional investing, unlike individual investing, decisions are often made by multiple people in a team, some of which may be right and the others wrong. Atul firmly believes that the essence of successful investing lies in the individual's mindset and emotional discipline. Some of the world's most acclaimed investors, like Warren Buffett and Rakesh Jhunjhunwala, have primarily been solitary decision-makers rather than relying on committees. Learning from them, Atul is sceptical of committee-based decision-making in investing. Multiple decision-makers can introduce challenges like ego clashes and internal politics, clouding the investment process.

Atul believes that investing should be driven by clarity and sincerity of thought. When these attributes are overshadowed by personal biases and competing interests, decision-making suffers. He therefore favours individualistic investment decisions over those made by teams or committees, as this approach maintains the sanctity and artistry of investing.

Atul also emphasizes the need for caution when on a winning streak, as the market, with its inherent levelling nature, has a way of humbling even the most seasoned investors. He often advocates investing with a reputable fund manager, especially during their drawdown phases. Given the cyclical nature of markets, periods of success and setbacks are inevitable. Ultimately, he believes, adherence to a solid investment process is what prevails in the long run.

Exuberance, hubris and the stock market

As we have seen, Atul is an ardent believer in the power of a well-defined investment process. A sound, meticulously crafted process serves as a bulwark against the inherent biases of the human psyche. During prosperous times, it's all too common for investors to succumb to overconfidence, even arrogance, mistakenly believing they are invincible. Such overestimation often results in pitfalls like over-investing and over-trading, which are typical snares during an unchecked bull market.

Conversely, during market downturns or periods of significant drawdowns, fear can cloud judgement, resulting in missed opportunities.

The goal of establishing, and even coding, a robust investment process is to counteract these extreme emotional states—whether it be euphoria or paralysing fear—that can distort decision-making.

For Atul, adhering to a rigorous investment process is among the most vital components of enduring success in the investing realm.

Role of personal life and circumstances

Atul aspires to ensure that his personal life does not influence his investment decisions. However, experience has brought him the humbling realization that the emotional baggage from one's personal life often permeates into investing biases. The realm of investment serves as a vivid stage, laying bare a human being's internal conflicts and unresolved issues.

To mitigate the impact of personal drama on his investment choices, Atul has cultivated a simple, transparent and disciplined personal life. A particular emphasis for Atul lies in both physical and mental fitness. They not only provide an outlet for emotional turmoil but also instil a rigorous discipline that translates directly into his investment decision-making.

Risk reward and where to play

Just as in investing, substantial returns aren't necessarily guaranteed by backing the most prominent, established or popular entities, Atul emphasizes that the most significant gains often come from stocks with a favourable risk–reward profile.

Drawing a parallel, Atul views India not as a 'large-cap index' country, but rather as a 'mid-cap play' with an exceptional risk–reward proposition, which is where he intends to channel his investments for fruitful returns.

Earlier, India's infrastructure deficits might have cast doubt on its potential. However, Atul now sees this very gap as an opportunity, offering vast room for growth for those willing to invest. In contrast, several Western nations, with their established infrastructures, offer limited opportunities. In such mature markets, while opportunities are well-known and pursued by many, the risk–reward dynamic isn't as enticing.

This is why Atul sees India as a mid-cap stock transitioning into the large-cap arena. This transition, coupled with the potential transformation that the nation is undergoing, is why, despite infrastructural challenges, he remains bullish on India's prospects.

Taking remedial action

When I asked how he approaches turning what might seem like a mistake into a favourable result, Atul explains:

'In the complex web of investments and markets, not all outcomes are a direct result of our own actions. At times, people find themselves on the receiving end of others' mistakes, just as occasionally, we reap the benefits of another's strategic move, even without our active involvement. It's a game of balances, akin to the undulating scales of fate: you win some, and you lose some.'

Amidst all the narratives, rationalizations and the propensity to assign blame or claim credit, the market possesses a pristine clarity. The stock price remains the ultimate arbiter of value and sentiment. Returns, encapsulated in numerical precision, cut through the noise, providing a clear and objective measure of performance. In the intricate dance of numbers, narratives and nuances, there's an inherent beauty: everything eventually reflects in the stock's valuation. And, as with many facets of life, the highs and lows, the gains and setbacks often find a way to balance out in the grand scheme of things.

The public image with rational decision-making

Atul sounds almost philosophical when he says he truly believes managing public funds is a high-wire act that demands not only financial acumen but also a deep understanding of human psychology.

In the world of investing, an investor isn't merely an architect of wealth but also a steward of trust. It's a dance, a delicate balance between the cold logic of numbers and the warmth of human emotions. As the curator of this trust, Atul has often felt the tremors when clients, driven by the winds of market fluctuations, decide to disembark. He likens it to the pain a craftsman feels when his art isn't appreciated.

But with time comes wisdom. One learns that the journey isn't about those who leave but about staying true to the destination. Each station brings its own set of challenges and opportunities, and it is in navigating these nuances that the essence of the journey lies.

One should strive to evolve to a position where transparency reigns supreme and objectivity is the cornerstone. By refraining from sugar-coating and speaking candidly, one not only builds trust but also reinforces the authenticity of the process.

This journey, with its ebbs and flows, will continually test one's mettle. But staying steadfast, keeping one's eyes on the goal and understanding that the journey itself is the reward can make all the difference. For Atul, the voyage of managing public funds is not just about the destination; it's about the stories, the learnings and the resilience one gathers along the way.

Managing the media

Atul has learnt, by observing Rakesh Jhunjhunwala up close, that there are times when one's portfolio may be doing well overall, but if one is a public figure, then the media and investors often focus on the mistakes to highlight negative results.

That is why in today's age of ubiquitous communication, Atul prefers to tread carefully in the digital realm. Navigating social media and the media at large can be a double-edged sword—it offers a platform to amplify one's voice but also serves as a battleground where opinions clash, often drowning out reason and measured discourse.

Therefore, Atul chooses to engage on platforms that foster a conducive environment for sharing one's thoughts without being mired in trolling and negativity.

Atul picks his battles wisely as he considers maintaining mental equilibrium paramount. Platforms like television and YouTube provide a semblance of control, allowing for a structured and focused discourse. However, platforms like X, while powerful in reach, can sometimes devolve into a whirlwind of confrontations.

Atul believes not everyone is equipped to endure this storm of often unwarranted critiques. Thus, prioritizing mental well-being by selectively choosing the media channels that align with one's comfort and intent is not just a choice for him—it's a necessary strategy in today's hyper-connected world. Atul likes to craft a communication strategy that serves the purpose without compromising peace of mind.

Life lessons and mistakes

Atul believes that making mistakes is an inherent part of the human experience. His words here are almost sage-like yet easily relatable: 'Within each of us, there's a tug-of-war between our rational selves and our impulsive, sometimes emotional "monkey mind". This internal conflict can propel us to the zenith of achievement but can just as easily send us spiralling into errors. Our journey through life isn't merely about the destinations we reach or the successes we amass; it's as much about navigating these internal battles and learning from our shortcomings.'

Atul continues, 'In this labyrinth of experiences, there's an undercurrent of spirituality, a quest to understand the deeper nuances of our existence and purpose. In many ways, our evolution is a dance between learning and unlearning. Even as we amass knowledge, gain experiences and read countless times, we remain vulnerable to error.'

But therein lies the beauty of the human experience: we are fallible, yet we are capable of growth, introspection and transformation.

Atul's life lesson seems to be that no amount of education or experience can shield us entirely from making mistakes. But each misstep is an opportunity for growth, a chance to better understand our inner workings, and a lesson in humility and resilience. After all, it's not the absence of mistakes that defines us, but our response to them and our relentless pursuit of betterment that does.

Observing and learning

Atul finds great value in observing and learning from others' mistakes. It provides a vantage point, a window into the possible repercussions of actions without having to bear the consequences ourselves. Observing human behaviour, studying the decisions of others and understanding the broader ecosystem is an enriching exercise for Atul. It offers insights and cautionary tales.

However, there's a difference between knowing the path and walking the path. When Atul personally navigates challenges, makes choices and experiences the outcomes, the lessons take root in a deeper, more impactful manner. For him, life, in all its unpredictability and complexity, is a continuous journey of growth and discovery. Each twist and turn, every stumble and rise contributes to his evolving understanding of himself and the world around him.

Atul believes that while it's wise to observe and learn from the world around us, it's our personal journey—with all its trials, tribulations and triumphs—that truly shapes and defines us.

CHAPTER 8

SANKARAN NAREN

The anatomy of an investment mistake—lessons from the school of hard knocks

IN the peculiar world of investing, mistakes are like that awkward cousin at family gatherings— you don't want them around, but they're always there, lurking with a life lesson you never asked for.

Our protagonist, Sankaran Naren, let's call him 'Naren', has spent decades wrangling with the stock market, and he's got the scars to prove it. Despite the scars, his fund, ICICI, has stood out shining like a silver armour.

He shares that while many think investing is all about precision and sharp calculations, it's far from that. During our conversation about the importance of mistakes in his career, Naren compared investing to trying to herd cats in a thunderstorm while wearing a blindfold.

But let's not get ahead of ourselves—let's start with the basics as Naren shared during our conversation.

The engineer's curse: Determinism vs the market

Naren's journey into the world of finance began with a solid education. Unfortunately for him, that education was in engineering. Engineers are a curious breed, trained to believe that the world operates in a neat, orderly fashion. If A happens, then B must follow, like night follows day. It's a world of cause and effect, where precision is king. A well-designed bridge will bear weight, a properly constructed circuit will light up, and a correctly calculated trajectory will send a satellite into orbit. Errors are met with rigorous analysis, followed by systematic corrections. But what happens when you throw an engineer into the chaotic, unpredictable world of the stock market?

Precision vs chaos

Naren put it best in his own words: 'The result is often a mix of bewilderment, frustration, and misplaced confidence. The market doesn't care about your deterministic equations or your precisely calculated projections. The stock market is a wild, untamed beast, more in tune with chaos theory than Newtonian mechanics.' With a chuckle, he adds, 'the market often laughs in the face of your carefully plotted graphs and mocks your neatly laid-out plans.'

Looking back at where it all began, armed with his engineering degree and a head full of equations, Naren entered the stock market with a level of confidence that only a novice could muster; almost like that kid who jumps into a swimming pool for the first time without being aware of either it's depth or the pressure of water around him.

He was certain that with enough analysis, he could predict market movements with the same precision he had used to design circuits. He pored over financial statements, constructed elaborate models, and created spreadsheets that would make any accountant proud. Yet, his early forays into investing were met, as he says, with a series of humbling defeats.

His first big mistake was an overreliance on historical data. Like many engineers, he made the mistake of believing that empirical data from the past could accurately predict the future.

He would analyse years of stock performance, identify patterns, and then invest heavily based on these patterns.

He elaborates that he failed to consider that the market is driven by human behaviour, which is anything but predictable. Just because a stock had performed well in the past didn't mean it would continue to do so in the future. We often make the mistake of looking at past performance as a certain guidance for future returns, although the variables of earning, valuations, competitiveness, policies or even relative valuations may have changed. When the market took an unexpected turn, his meticulously planned investments crumbled, leaving him with significant losses.

Naren admits that it wasn't just the data that misled him. He also fell into the trap of believing that his engineering skills gave him an edge in the market. 'I failed to see that investing was neither a problem to be solved, nor a puzzle to be completed', says Naren.

But the stock market is far from a problem—it's a complex, dynamic system influenced by countless variables, many of which are beyond the control of any one person or even a group of intelligent ones.

So, what could have been his greatest folly at this stage? Naren was disarming in admitting that he learned this the hard way—by making aggressive bets in a bid to turn small capital into big returns, only to find himself face-first in a puddle of regret.

The lesson? His answer was an unambiguous and resounding admission: 'Look, your upbringing and education can lead you straight into a brick wall when it comes to investing, but don't despair—that wall is just the beginning of your real education. Turn your regrets into ongoing education.'

Calm waters, turbulent times and the big mistakes

Naren makes an important distinction between the types of mistakes made in calm markets and those made during crises.

'In calm markets, mistakes are like paper cuts—irritating but rarely life-threatening,' he explains. 'You might lose some money, but the overall market stability cushions the blow.'

However, crises are a different beast. Mistakes made during turbulent times can have far-reaching consequences. Reflecting on events like the 2008 financial meltdown and the Covid-19 pandemic, Naren emphasizes the importance of quick thinking and decisive action during crises.

'In a crisis, the greatest opportunities often arise from the ashes of panic,' he says.

During the 2008 crisis, as financial institutions collapsed and markets plummeted, many investors succumbed to fear and sold their assets at record lows. Naren, however, saw this as an opportunity to buy undervalued assets. His conviction paid off during the subsequent recovery.

Similarly, during the Covid-19 pandemic, Naren relied on ICICI Prudential AMC's Balanced Advantage Fund model to guide his decisions. Despite widespread fear and uncertainty, the model indicated a clear buying opportunity in equities due to attractive valuations. 'Many questioned whether the old model still applied in a post-COVID world. But we trusted the process, and it worked. In retrospect, that was a great decision along with the decision to go overweight on equities in 2020,' he says.

During crisis, asset/sector allocation decisions become important whereas during calm times it's more bottom-up stock picking.

The challenge of acknowledging mistakes

For Naren, the first step in learning from mistakes is admitting them—a step that many investors struggle to take. 'In my stockbroking days, I noticed that those who refused to admit their mistakes rarely improved. Recognizing and analysing your errors is the only way to grow as an investor,' he says.

He recalls a humbling moment for investors during the dot-com bubble of the late 1990s. The trailing P/E ratios were absurdly high in 1999. Naren had observed that the sky-high market caps of those IT companies could not be justified. Convinced that tech boom would burst at some time, he remained patient for reversion to mean theory to play out and stood behind this conviction call. He avoided the IT sector and invested in underperforming sectors like cement and steel which handsomely rewarded investors by 2002. He graduated as an investor by avoiding the fall, post 2000, which saw IT stock prices plummet.

Tools for avoiding repetition of mistakes

Over the years, Naren has developed tools and practices to minimize the recurrence of mistakes.

Meditation

Meditation plays a crucial role in Naren's decision-making process. By reflecting on the day's events and decisions, he gains clarity and reduces emotional biases. 'Meditation helps me absorb what I've learned and approach decisions with a calmer, clearer mind,' he explains.

Checklists

Naren relies on checklists to ensure that past mistakes are not repeated. These checklists are not static—they evolve with time and market conditions. 'The world is constantly changing. Our processes must adapt to ensure we're learning from past errors and avoiding new pitfalls,' he says.

Collaboration

Recognizing the limitations of individual decision-making, Naren places great value on teamwork. At ICICI Prudential AMC, he fosters a culture of open dialogue, encouraging diverse perspectives. 'Different people bring different strengths to the table. By collaborating, we reduce blind spots and make better decisions,' he explains.

Turbulence and its impact on your portfolio

One such mistake occurred in 1994–95. Naren, while enjoying the fruits of a long bull market, says he became fixated on maintaining his portfolio's price-to-earnings (P/E) ratio at a consistent level.

He was convinced that by selling high P/E stocks and buying low P/E ones, he could maximize his returns while minimizing risk.

On paper, it appeared to be a sound strategy, grounded in decades of financial theory. In practice, however, he says it turned out to be a disaster.

By 1997–98, he realized that he had created a junk portfolio in this process. My learning from this was, as the bull market expands, you need to improve the portfolio quality and increase the P/E or price-to-book (P/B) value of the portfolio, rather than reduce the P/E or P/B of the portfolio.

The lesson here was painfully clear to Naren and this is how he cautioned: 'When the market is in a bull run, you can't afford to sit on your laurels. You need to upgrade your portfolio quality, not cling to rigid strategies.'

His insistence on maintaining a consistent P/E ratio had blinded him to the reality of the market, leading to significant losses.

It was a stark reminder that the stock market doesn't care about your theories or your carefully constructed models—it moves to its own rhythm, and if you don't keep up, you'll be left behind.

Sitting on past laurels tends to make you a one-Olympic wonder! But as damaging as mistakes during calm periods can be, Naren says they pale in comparison to those made during times of crisis. 'When the storm hits, it's all about quick thinking and decisive action.' Naren shares his crucial learning that asset allocation during a crisis can make or break you. In times of severe turbulence, the rules change. 'The strategies that worked during calm periods suddenly become obsolete, and survival depends on your ability to adapt and rhythm yourself differently.' Just like taking physical control of an airplane from the autopilot mode when facing severe storms in the skies.

Take the 2008 financial crisis and what it taught Naren, for example. As the housing market collapsed and banks began to fail, he found himself in uncharted territory. His carefully balanced portfolio, designed to weather normal market fluctuations, was suddenly exposed to extreme volatility. Stocks that had been deemed safe investments plummeted, and the global economy teetered on the brink of collapse. In the face of such uncertainty, many investors panicked, selling off assets at rock-bottom prices in a desperate bid to cut their losses. But Naren already had the learning of his past mistakes and he took a different approach. He realized that 'in a crisis, the greatest opportunities often arise from the ashes of panic'. Instead of selling, he began to buy—carefully, selectively, but with a clear understanding that the market would eventually recover.

The lesson here? Learn from your past mistakes, put the learnings to practical use and do all of these with objective optimism. It was a gamble, to be sure. There was no guarantee that the stocks he bought would rebound, or that the crisis wouldn't deepen further. But, as Naren says, 'I had learned that in times of crisis, fortune favours the bold.' His strategy paid off. When the market began to recover in 2009, his portfolio was well-positioned to take advantage of the rebound, leading to substantial gains.

Test of the theory of risk and reward

This experience reinforced another key mistake and its lesson: in times of crisis, the greatest risk is often not taking one, because no one solution is ever either the most correct or the best. While it's natural to want to protect your assets during turbulent times, those who have the courage to seize opportunities when others are fleeing can come out ahead. Naren's ability to navigate the 2008 financial crisis was a testament to his growth as an investor—a growth that was fuelled by the mistakes he had made during calmer times.

The epiphany—usually too late

So, I ask Naren, when does an investor realize they've made a mistake? Is it like a lightbulb moment, a sudden flash of insight? Not quite, chuckles Naren. 'More often than not, it's the slow, painful realization that comes when your portfolio starts looking like a scene from a financial horror movie.' For Naren, these moments are less about sudden epiphanies and more about the gradual, creeping dread that settles in when the numbers just don't add up.

Balancing ego and rationality

Investing often tests one's ability to manage biases like the ego and the commitment bias. Naren acknowledges that even seasoned investors are not immune to these pitfalls.

He shares an example of a long-term bet on a differential voting-rights instrument. While the investment ultimately paid off, Naren reflects on the fine line between conviction and ego. 'It's important to question yourself constantly. Decisions must be driven by rationality, not emotion,' he says.

Motivation from mistakes

For Naren, mistakes are a source of both motivation and introspection. He finds demotivation in missed opportunities—errors of omission that could have been avoided with better preparation or awareness. At the same time, mistakes resulting from irrational market behaviour motivate him to refine his framework and improve.

'Every mistake, whether small or significant, adds to your learning. The key is to ensure that each mistake leads to new insights,' he says.

A lifelong journey of learning and adaptation

Despite his decades of experience, Naren acknowledges that mistakes remain an inevitable part of his investing journey. 'Investing is not a perfect science. It's a dynamic process influenced by constantly changing variables like geopolitics, technology and human behaviour,' he says.

His resilience comes from embracing the idea that investing is a continuous learning process. By staying open to new ideas, reading extensively and learning from others, Naren has built a philosophy centered on humility and adaptability.

The role of exuberance and hubris in investment decisions

In our discussion, Naren touched upon the role of exuberance and hubris in eliminating bad investment decisions. He believes that the investment world often rewards humility and punishes arrogance. 'Exuberance and hubris can sometimes cloud judgement, leading investors to overlook emerging risks or to stick too rigidly to failing strategies,' Naren explained. He reflects on how, in his experience, staying humble and open to new information has been crucial in navigating the highs and lows of the market.

Naren shared anecdotes about times when the market's exuberance, especially during bull runs, tempted many to make overly aggressive bets. He contrasts this with his approach during such times, emphasizing the importance of maintaining a balanced perspective and not getting carried away by market euphoria. 'The key is to remember that the market will always be a mix of predictable cycles and unpredictable events. Staying grounded allows you to see both,' he stated.

Impact of personal life and circumstances

Discussing the impact of personal life and circumstances on investment decisions, Naren opened up about his own experiences. He recounted a particularly challenging period during which his son's genetic disorder diagnosis coincided with a turbulent time in the markets. 'It was a tough year, both personally and professionally. But these personal challenges forced me to focus and refine my approach to risk,' he shared.

Naren believes that personal hardships can sometimes lead to a deeper focus and a better understanding of one's priorities and risk tolerance. 'Separating personal emotions from investment decisions is crucial, yet our personal experiences inevitably shape our risk perceptions and decision-making processes,' he added. This introspection helped him not only manage his professional responsibilities with a clearer mind but also taught him valuable lessons about resilience and adaptation.

Understanding external influences on mistakes

Naren also discussed the role of external factors in influencing investment mistakes. He emphasized that not all mistakes are a direct result of an investor's own actions; often, they are caused by broader market movements or unforeseen geopolitical events. 'Investing is an interconnected activity. Sometimes, external factors can cause the best-laid plans to go awry, and these are not necessarily a reflection of one's investment acumen,' he observed.

He highlighted instances where external economic crises or sudden market shifts led to losses, despite sound investment strategies. 'In such situations, it's important not to be too hard on oneself. Learning to distinguish between self-caused mistakes and those driven by external factors is key to maintaining confidence and objectivity in investment decisions,' Naren advised. This understanding helps in developing resilience and ensures that investors do not lose heart but instead learn to navigate the complexities of global markets with enhanced insight and strategy.

Navigating investor psychology and market missteps

When discussing the intricacies of investor psychology and the impact of collective market behaviour, Naren highlighted the importance of understanding both. 'Investing is not just about analysing numbers and predicting market movements; it's also about understanding human behaviour and collective psychology,' he stated. This perspective stems from his experiences during market fluctuations, where he observed that investor reactions often amplify market volatilities.

Naren recounted instances where he had to differentiate between his own investment decisions and the broader market's irrational behaviour. 'There are times when the market is overwhelmingly pessimistic or optimistic, which can lead to significant mispricing of assets,' he explained. This understanding allows him to capitalize on market overreactions, turning what might seem like a mistake into a strategic advantage. He emphasized the need for a balanced mindset that can distinguish between genuine investment errors and opportunities created by market sentiment.

The challenge of managing public perception

In a further reflection on the complexities of managing public investments, Naren discussed the challenges of public perception, particularly when managing large funds. He noted that sometimes, despite a fund manager's best efforts, external factors can lead to underperformance, which may be perceived negatively by the public and investors. 'It's essential to balance public perception with rational decision-making. Sometimes, the right decision might not immediately yield positive outcomes, but it's crucial for long-term success,' Naren observed.

He also touched on the importance of communication and transparency in managing investor expectations. 'At times, educating investors about the nature of the markets and the rationale behind certain decisions can help mitigate negative perceptions and maintain trust,' he added. This approach not only helps in managing expectations during turbulent times but also reinforces the foundation of trust and credibility essential for long-term investor relations.

Adapting investment strategies to changing global dynamics

Lastly, Naren spoke about the necessity of adapting investment strategies to global economic changes and market dynamics. He described how shifts in geopolitics, economic policies and technological advancements necessitate continuous learning and adaptation. 'The only constant in the investment world is change. As fund managers, our strategies must evolve with the changing global landscape to mitigate risks and capitalize on new opportunities,' he asserted.

This adaptability has been crucial in navigating past financial crises and market downturns, allowing Naren to adjust his investment approaches in response to new information and changing conditions. He emphasized the importance of staying informed and proactive, which helps in anticipating market shifts rather than reacting to them. 'Being adaptive in our investment strategies is akin to steering a ship through changing seas—sometimes you need to adjust your sails to continue on the right course,' he concluded.

Mistakes, the path to mastery

Naren highlights the power of hindsight as the rear-view mirror in your vehicle. So, how and what do you conclude out of these experiences, I ask Naren. He says 'I say I like to firm up on the almost cliched lines used in investing in stocks, the realization that mistakes are the path to mastery, of course, when every mistake is a new one and not a rehash of a past one.

As Naren's story, along with those of all the others in this book that the reader would have gone through so far, reiterates that investing isn't just about making money—it's about learning, growing and becoming wiser with every decision, good or bad. In a field where the only certainty is uncertainty, mistakes are an inevitable part of the journey. But as Naren has demonstrated, 'your mistakes do not define you; what truly does is how you handle them'. 'So, the next time you make a mistake, remember—you're in good company,' says Naren with his characteristic nonchalant sarcasm. 'Embrace it, learn from it, and let it be the fuel that drives you to become a better, more resilient investor. After all, in the unpredictable world of investing, every mistake is just another opportunity in masquerade. And if all else fails, just remember there's always humour in hindsight. Because at the end of the day, if you can't laugh at your mistakes, you're probably taking the stock market and yourself a little too seriously.'

While saying bye to Naren, I recalled the words of the delightful Maya Angelou who once said, 'don't trust people who don't laugh'. As an investor/fund manager, you would always want to be trusted, right? So your ability to acknowledge and laugh at your mistakes takes you a long way in building investor trust in you; remember, you are a human first.

CHAPTER 9

VIJAY KEDIA

The melodic rationalist with a legacy of success

BORN in Kolkata (then Calcutta), Vijay Kisharlal Kedia began investing at the age of nineteen—or fourteen, if you include his early trading on family accounts. Having lost his father while still in school, he felt compelled to enter the investing world to provide for his family.

His initial foray into the market was challenging, and he suffered repeated losses. Shuttling between Calcutta, where he lived with his Marwari family, and Bombay, he suffered setback after setback. Burdened with financial responsibilities and an early marriage, he recalls a time when he could not even afford milk for his child. Losses mounted, and he spent many a sleepless night in the small room he shared with six family members. The situation became so dire that his mother had to sell her jewels to make ends meet. With nothing left, Vijay faced a choice: give up or fight. He chose to fight, analysing the mistakes he had made in investing in worthless companies, spurred by his dreams of getting rich quick.

Vijay's first lesson is clear: 'When you are wrong, evaluate the mistake. Don't just give up. If you are made for it, don't distance yourself from it.'

In 1990, armed with the lessons he had learned, Vijay started investing based on fundamental analysis. Starting with a modest sum of Rs 35,000, he invested in Punjab Tractors, a company he says he got lucky with in 1992 during the Harshad Mehta boom when the market soared and all boats rose with the tide. His investment tripled in three years and grew sixfold over time. He sold the stock, and based on a market analysis, focused on another Harshad Mehta favourite, Associated Cement Company (ACC), purchasing shares at Rs 300. While the stock remained stagnant for a year, it soared tenfold the following year, enabling him to sell it at Rs 3,000 and buy his first house in Mumbai.

Despite the success, he was lured towards what he now calls and recognizes as 'satta' (gamble trades) and over time, started recognizing how his profits lay in investing, not gambling. He says 'trial and error' teaches you a lot. Losing money in trading made him realize, 'Trading is injurious to your wealth. If you are smoking, you may die in twenty-thirty years, whereas by trading, this may happen the next day.'

Here Vijay teaches us not to be deterred by the past as long as you learn to not make the mistakes of the past. One of his favourite quotes is: 'Your investment belongs to the market and your profits belong to you.' Another is: *Jab khone ke liye kuch nahin hota, to paane ke liye duniya hoti hai* (When you have nothing to lose, you have everything to win).

To succeed, one must embrace failure and its lessons and have the hunger to move, where your passion, knowledge, temperament and skill sets can cause a shift. He quotes, 'regret is a lifestyle disease of investing' and 'like cricket, you must change your game plan per format' to win.

Today, as the founder of Kedia Securities, Vijay has gained renown for his long-term investment strategies. A regular guest on Indian business channels and a motivational case study at several leading institutions, he has become a role model for investors.

He proudly claims that he is now meticulous with his approach and likes to listen to no one when making decisions on investments. He lives independently of others' judgements and does not dwell on past errors. Believing in karma, he maintains that learning from one's own mistakes as well as others is essential.

Vijay's infectious smile and affable personality draw people from all walks of life. He has a creative side, reflected in his flair for crafting quirky songs on current affairs, reminiscent of the commentary of the iconic Amul girl. His songs also reflect his investment philosophy and are popular amongst his friends and admirers. Vijay has also coined memorable terms like 'bhangar cap' to describe microcap or penny stocks with no fundamentals, which he likens to 'barsaati maindak' (frogs that sing when it rains but disappear when it doesn't).

In this exploration, I delve into Vijay's investment criteria, guiding principles and the invaluable lessons he has learned from his own, as well as others', mistakes.

The childhood factor

Vijay asserts that the decisions one makes are influenced by one's birth, place of birth and DNA, which collectively shape one's personality. Upbringing—influenced by parents, relatives, friends and education—plays a significant role in moulding one's character. The choices, and even the mistakes, one makes are deeply rooted in these foundational aspects.

He draws a parallel to Mary Kom, who once remarked that her poor financial circumstances in childhood prevented her from playing sports like tennis or badminton, which required expensive equipment and facilities.[1] Instead, she took up boxing—a sport that needed little financial resources. Indeed, necessity is the mother of invention and highlights how one's upbringing can foster the hunger to succeed. For Vijay, this hunger stemmed from his inability to provide milk for his child during his early struggles. Later in life, he even purchased a milk company as a symbolic gesture and to apologize to his wife for his early missteps.

Fondly remembering his school days, Vijay recalls[2] a couplet by the renowned poet Abdul Rahim Khan-i-Khanan:

रहिमन चुप हो बैठिये, देखि दिनन के फेर।
जब नीके दिन आइहैं, बनत न लगिहैं देर॥

The verse roughly translates to: 'Remain silent during bad times, for when good times come, they will come in abundance.'

These lines convey the wisdom of weathering the bad times and not quitting. Vijay reflects on how inactivity can also be a form of activity and indecision can also be a decision. It is, therefore, essential to remain patient during trying times, as positive results are often closer than they seem.

Fundamentals of Vijay's journey

As it is rightly said, success lies in the continuous pursuit of knowledge, and for Vijay, this rings especially true. His success in the market is due in large part to his reliance on data and information, which are an integral part of Vijay's decision-making process and serve as tools for preventing mistakes.

A calm mind, achievable through practices like meditation, is another tool for achieving better results. A clear and composed mind fosters unprejudiced decision-making, leading to better outcomes. On the other hand, decisions made with a restless mind often result in errors.

While a referral board can sometimes help in processing mistakes, Vijay feels this approach can only help to a certain extent. Different people will have different opinions on a problem, and these opinions may be biased. Thus, it is essential to trust one's own experience and intuition when making decisions.

Intuition plays a significant role in Vijay's career, but he cautions that intuition must be supported by data and information. Decisions based solely on intuition and not backed by facts amount to what he calls 'satta' (gambling). He compares this to playing card games like teen patti, where one tends to rely on intuition rather than data to win the game.

An important part of making intuition-based decisions is remaining neutral and unbiased. Vijay avoids seeking advice from others and focuses on gathering data and conducting his own quantitative analysis. He notes that 90 per cent of the time, the data is accurate, guiding him to make better decisions. And if the outcome of such a decision is not as expected, then it serves as a lesson to identify and correct mistakes.

Revalidation, according to Vijay, is essential for understanding and correcting mistakes. Here, again, he relies on data, rather than on others' opinions, to analyse his mistakes. He summarizes the three key elements of decision-making as intuition, results and validation, which together help recognize and address mistakes.

Vijay also values learning from others' mistakes, asserting that life is too short to rely solely on learning from personal experiences. He advises observing not only others but also oneself as growth comes from reflecting on personal mistakes and drawing insights from the experiences of those around us. He acknowledges the role played by mentors, parents, teachers, gurus and friends in providing guidance that minimizes errors caused by inexperience or naivety.

He notes that just as repeatedly falling when learning to walk teaches a child the concept of gravity and the importance of support, failures in childhood impart valuable life lessons. He asserts that committing a mistake is not inherently wrong and that 'every mistake has its take'. It is missing the opportunity to learn from mistakes that is the greater error.

Vijay reflects on how the market, like life, is constantly evolving. As the famous song from the Shah Rukh Khan starrer *Kal Ho Na Ho* goes, 'Life changes from moment to moment, sometimes there is shade, sometimes there is sun'. Similarly, the market is always changing and fluctuating, offering numerous opportunities to learn and grow. Each rise or fall becomes a learning curve for investors.

He acknowledges that with mistakes come regrets, but he strives to live a life free from them. Vijay avoids dwelling on past missteps, choosing instead to carry forward the lessons learnt from them.

He maintains a checklist to prevent mistakes and revisits it when errors occur to identify what he missed or points of deviation. This analysis helps him learn and commit not to repeat the same mistake. For Vijay, demotivation is short-lived and serves as a catalyst for motivation.

However, not all mistakes lead to failure. At times, there are decisions that one may think were mistakes, but they eventually result in favourable outcomes. Vijay recalls an incident involving an NRI friend who insisted on partnering in one of his high-stakes projects. Although Vijay was initially reluctant as he did not want the deal to impact their friendship, he eventually agreed to offer his friend a 25 per cent share. However, on presenting this offer to his friend, Vijay was dismayed to receive an e-mail from him that delegated the negotiation to his CFO. The CFO then attempted to bargain further, and Vijay, who was already sceptical of the deal as he had agreed to the partnership out of friendship rather than based on professional ability, retracted the offer. He realized the importance of preserving mental peace over financial gain. He believes that 'mental capacity is more important than financial capacity' as mental exhaustion can be harder to recover from than financial losses.

The project was eventually completed under Vijay's sole direction after being on hold for a few months and surprisingly, gave him 100 times the profit he had initially expected.

Taking calculated risks while avoiding critical errors

Vijay advises his children to make mistakes as frequently as possible as they can serve as valuable learning opportunities, but to avoid those that carry severe or irreversible consequences.

He elaborates on this through a personal anecdote: when his young child once jumped off the second floor of a building, Vijay explained the importance of recognizing and avoiding mistakes that could have disastrous outcomes, such as severe injury or death. He applies the same principle to his own decision-making process, ensuring he only makes mistakes he can recover from, both financially and mentally.

In essence, Vijay advocates the approach of 'being ready to hit a sixer on a no-ball', or taking calculated risks while avoiding critical errors. Following this approach, he takes very few decisions in life and prefers to be a long-term investor. He believes that every decision carries the potential for mistakes, so reducing the number of decisions can help minimize errors at the ground level.

He further emphasizes that the ego is a significant obstacle to a good decision-making process. It is crucial to eliminate one's sense of superiority and the belief that 'I' cannot make mistakes. He shares a personal experience where he was invested in a company that was doing well and ignored the advice of an industry expert and well-wisher to exit the company due to concerns about its irregular internal workings. His ego stepped in, and he did not heed his friend's warning, resulting in huge losses as the company eventually went bankrupt. There is a fine line between one's ego and self-belief, akin to the 'Laxman Rekha', which when crossed can result in disaster. Therefore, setting aside one's ego is integral to moving ahead in life.

Despite treading the path of learning from one's mistakes, Vijay acknowledges that destiny is something that one does not have control over. What lies within our control is hard work, passion and resilience—a philosophy beautifully captured in the popular verse from the Bhagwat Gita: 'Do your duty, but do not concern yourself with the results'.

Vijay also warns against the pursuit of instant gratification, which he sees as a bane rather than a boon. One of the lessons Vijay has learnt from his mistakes is that what is written in one's destiny shall happen. He believes in the power of the universe, which, he says, understands one's ultimate destination.

In summary, Vijay has gained insights through others' mistakes, his own experiences, and his keen observation of human behaviour, all of which serve as a guide to success.

Eliminating mistakes: The role of unconventional thinking

To minimize mistakes, Vijay emphasizes the need for unconventional thinking. When investing, he often chooses companies unfamiliar to most, which requires one to think out of the box. While well-wishers and friends often warn him about investing in relatively new companies, Vijay remains confident. He believes that innovative thinkers embrace the seemingly impossible but only take risks they can afford, maintaining a margin of safety. Vijay believes that if he does something extremely unconventional, failure will not result in catastrophic consequences.

Therefore, thinking out of the box can accelerate success but carries risks. However, risks are a part of life. One can get hit by car or meet with an accident no matter how careful one is, but that doesn't deter people from stepping out of their houses. Similarly, one shouldn't fear risk in the market. He cites the saying, 'A ship is safe in a harbour, but that is not where a ship is meant to be'.

Vijay recognizes that life lacks fixed formulas, and what works for one person might not work for another. Similarly, making one or two correct decisions does not guarantee future success.

For him, mistakes are a part and parcel of life. The real lesson is to learn from them. He doesn't rely on other people's opinions or advice, preferring to make his own decisions. He believes decisions should add challenge, thrill and adventure, rather than playing it safe and blindly following what is preached. He compares life to a cricket match, where every decision starts from zero and the outcomes are unpredictable.

A happy personal life: Key to career success

Vijay believes that personal life significantly influences professional conduct. For instance, starting the day with a fight with one's spouse or children can directly impact work-related decisions and conversations throughout that day. Thus, it is important to have a happy life at home to lead a successful career. Thus, training the mind to distinguish between personal and professional life is essential, no matter how hard you wish to strike a balance between both worlds, one's personal life can still impact professional success despite efforts to maintain balance. He emphasizes that a happy home life is essential for achieving success in one's career.

The India story

One cannot change their place of birth or upbringing, as these are destined aspects of life. Vijay finds it gratifying to see India flourishing, appreciating the country's efforts to provide for its people despite challenges such as a low number of taxpayers and inherent corruption, and he feels comforted by the way India operates and progresses. India has miles to go before it sleeps, and it is in fact great to witness India flourishing. Vijay embraces this growing India with all its flaws.

As we conclude, Vijay shares some quotes that resonate with his ideology of investing:

'A bull market is very much like being in love. You don't realize its value till it's gone.'

'Don't always trust what you see. In a bull market, even a duck looks like a swan.'

Finally, he leaves readers with this multibagger mantra: 'Find companies that are small in size, medium in experience, large in aspiration and extra large in market potential.'

CHAPTER 10

AYUSH MITTAL
The young fin-tech trailblazer

AYUSH is someone I really trust for being an amazing combination of knowledge with simplicity at the core.

He hails from Lucknow, and while I admire the progress the city has made, I was struck by how he and his brother Pratyush, in spite of being based away from the usual market hustle of Mumbai or other financial centres, developed one of India's most advanced financial tools—Screener. This platform aids in investment research and offers a vast repository of data along with customizable screens and alerts, enabling investors to make informed decisions like never before.

When I asked Ayush why Screener is available at a nominal cost, he shared that it is the passion for the market that drives him and not the desire to earn. He believes that for a small investor, access to fundamental data is critical for understanding some sense about the underlying company, to reduce mistakes and make better investing decisions, and it should be freely available up to a certain point, so that lack of data is not a bottleneck in an investor's journey. Ayush and Pratyush find joy in seeing investors learn and grow through analytical tools. Earlier, the brothers were also active on platforms like

ValuePickr, sharing company and sector insights. However, they have now scaled back on such activities since the launch of their portfolio-management services (PMS) due to regulatory concerns.

Today, while Ayush manages a registered PMS, Screener continues to serve as a trusted resource for investors navigating turbulent markets. It remains a powerhouse of data, offering insights from credit ratings and annual reports to management meeting notes.

Ayush has an exceptional ability to identify opportunities in small-and mid-cap companies, often steering clear of large caps. To me, this approach symbolizes the spirit of Lucknow, where small and medium businesses have grown into big names, and the city itself has evolved from a place that was not traditionally regarded as a cosmopolitan metro into a name to reckon with.

Ayush believes, much like his father, who is also a skilled investor, that when you invest in the right small- or mid-sized company, the returns can be exponential. Just as a small plant quickly grows into a bamboo tree, the right small-cap investment can flourish at a remarkable pace.

It is not surprising that Ayush is known for the sharp picks he has made throughout his career, including Avanti Feeds, Astral Poly, Ajanta Pharma, Sandur Manganese, Mayur Uniquoters and Shivalik Bimetal. He identified these companies when they were still small and moreover, when no one was looking at sectors such as aquaculture or pipes and fittings as their past performance was not encouraging. What sets Ayush apart is his ability to understand the differences among companies in a sector. He doesn't shy away from rigorous follow-ups to strengthen his convictions, ultimately smiling at the mammoth returns.

Ayush's success with small- and mid-cap companies can largely be attributed to his upbringing and his father's influence. His father began investing in the early 1980s, and Ayush's childhood was shaped by observing his father's investing journey and habits. Despite lacking a formal education in finance, his father demonstrated the impact of a thoughtful approach to financial decisions, one that led to few regrets. This approach was marked by an emphasis on simplicity over complexity, a focus on value over price and a willingness to explore the unknown and yet to be discovered.

For Ayush, his father's faith in small caps played a pivotal role in shaping his investment philosophy and style. He acknowledges that, like most beginners, he initially focused on large-cap or well-known names when he started. However, his father's strong emphasis on investing in the small- and micro-cap space was a life-changing influence. The family's consistent focus on this space for over thirty to forty years, while avoiding large names, has largely contributed to their success.

Apart from upbringing, Ayush believes that one's environment plays a significant role in shaping how one thinks and behaves. During extreme times—whether good or bad—emotions often take over, and instead of relying on rational and analytical thinking, fear or greed tends to drive decision-making. Surrounding oneself with like-minded believers can provide both the reassurance and the motivation to continue in the long-term wealth-creation journey.

Overconfidence obscures judgement

Ayush recalls his experiences in 2017 when he was riding high on confidence as he had done exceptionally well in the small-cap space during the bull market of 2012–17. With this success, Ayush believed that these small, undervalued companies would continue do well. He started investing in companies like Prakash Industries (despite corporate governance issues, the company was posting strong numbers and there was China + 1 theory), Suzlon (which had started showing strong numbers) and Reliance Capital (the company was growing at over 30 per cent yet trading cheaply). However, when the market fell, these stocks plummeted by 25 to 30 per cent in a short span. Confident, thanks to his recent success, Ayush started averaging these companies equally to try to bring down their costs. It was only when these stocks fell further by 50 per cent did he realize that he had made a mistake. His judgement froze, and he decided not to sell in the hope of a recovery. It wasn't until these stocks had dropped by nearly 70 per cent that he finally sold, accepting his mistake.

Ayush acknowledges that this misstep was due to his overconfidence, FOMO and adopting shortcuts during the bull market. He reflects that during bear or stable markets, we usually do lot of work and scuttlebutt which we missed. Also in hanging on to price of buying as an anchor rather than reality check on their worth.

Similarly, during the Covid-19 pandemic, when there was panic in market, Ayush made the mistake of selling shares of Pokarna Limited. He had initially invested in the company due to its large expansion in quartz and granite. Shortly after he sold, the stock bottomed out and subsequently rallied, rising tenfold over the next two years.

From these experiences, Ayush believes that the most significant mistakes often occur during market extremes. In bull markets, FOMO often pushes one to make hasty decisions based on limited research. On the contrary, when the markets are quiet, one can make more rational and calculated moves and take advantage of the opportunities in the stock market.

Corrective measures: Turning mistakes into opportunities

Ayush acknowledges that recognizing one's mistakes is challenging, especially when overconfidence leads to poor decisions or when a company has previously delivered strong results. Self-realization often comes when a company reports unexpectedly poor results or experiences extreme price movements, prompting him to question his initial hypothesis and reassess the company's trajectory based on its current situation.

Ayush cautions against fixating solely on stock prices as he believes price is not always the right indicator. He shares that many of his successful investments, such as Poly Medicure Ltd, Avanti Feeds and Shivalik Bimetal, experienced sharp drops of 50 to 70 per cent in a short span of time due to market downturns or temporary issues faced by the companies. Selling these stocks during steep price drops would have been a mistake, which he avoided by remaining calm.

This also explains why Ayush doesn't follow the stop-loss theory, as he believes that a fall in price alone does not define a mistake. Stocks will recover and even cross previous highs as long as their core strengths remain intact.

Amongst the measures Ayush employs to take corrective action following a misstep is open discussion. He begins by sharing his thoughts about the concerned companies with various groups of people, seeking to understand their point of view and the reasons for their concerns. This enables him to form a more balanced view, allowing him to develop a clearer and more informed opinion about the company. Ayush also returns to the basics—re-reading annual reports, talking to people and examining the company's track record—rather than being fixated on short-term issues.

Another corrective measure, which he learnt from his father, is taking small steps in times of negativity or a falling market. Ayush explains that when faced with losses, a typical reaction is to hold on and sell when the prices recover. However, the key is to start small, selling only 100 or maybe 500 shares out of a larger holding. This helps the mind adjust to the situation. The same shall help you sell more if a particular theme is playing on the negative. So, that way one can get out of the mistake.

Further, something which has really helped Ayush as a corrective measure of a mistake is switching from one stock idea to another rather than just thinking of buying and selling.

These strategies have helped Ayush manage and correct mistakes more effectively.

A strong network and continuous learning: Keys to smarter investing

Ayush emphasizes that successful investing largely depends on one's mindset. He advocates maintaining a strong network of friends, family and mentors for support in making informed decisions in life. He believes that being open to sharing concerns and seeking diverse opinions is crucial as even a small piece of good advice can significantly influence one's investment process and foster a balanced perspective.

For example, Dr Onkar Singh, one of Ayush's mentors, has remarkable wisdom and is an avid reader of books and magazines. Around 2005, Dr Singh sent Ayush an article predicting that stock brokering was among the top five businesses that were likely to decline. This prompted Ayush to shift focus from his side family business to investing full-time. Dr Singh also recommended books like *The World Is Flat*, which encouraged Ayush to focus on export-oriented companies, a move that has proven highly beneficial.

Similarly, through my interactions with Ayush, I have had the opportunity to provide him with critical feedback—both positive and negative—on companies he was researching. We have also talked about the power of brands and their impact on investing.

Ayush is passionate about learning and constantly reads about various companies. Platforms like ValuePickr.com allow him to keep abreast of companies that interest him. He likes to explore diverse perspectives, including negative discussions, so that he is aware of public sentiment regarding his investments. He credits ValuePickr and Donald Francis for changing his approach to investing. Before 2010, Ayush relied solely on desk research. However, after working with Donald and others at ValuePickr, he began doing ground-level research, meeting company representatives and asking in-depth questions.

Ayush's website Screener also helps him track developments across more than 2000 companies on his watchlist. This tool allows him to conduct comparative evaluations and make sound investment choices.

Finally, Ayush believes that maintaining a calm mindset plays a key role in ensuring a balanced and rational approach to investing.

Judgements and mistakes: Navigating the highs and the lows of investing

Ayush observes that in the stock market, high volatility often excites investors, while prolonged stagnation or a decline in stock value can be perceived as a 'mistake'. However, he emphasizes that some stocks, after testing an investor's patience for years, can eventually outperform expectations, turning a perceived 'mistake' into a bonanza.

Ayush recounts an interesting example from the period between 2006 and 2010 when his father had identified Poly Medicure very early at a market cap of between Rs 60 crore and Rs 100 crore, with sales of between Rs 50 crore to Rs 60 crore. They did more research on the company and were very excited about it. However, the stock only doubled over two to three years, despite a raging bull market for micro caps. Then, in 2009, the global meltdown caused many Indian companies to suffer significant forex losses, including Poly Medicure. The company's 2009 annual report revealed losses of over Rs 30 crore, while its annual profit was less than Rs 10 crore. By the time these details emerged, the stock price had dropped by over 70 per cent.

Ayush was shocked and worried about whether the company could even survive. However, he attended the company's annual general meeting and spoke with the management. Their honesty in acknowledging their mistake and transparently sharing their plan to resolve the issue instilled enough confidence to remain invested. The company not only recovered but also grew significantly.

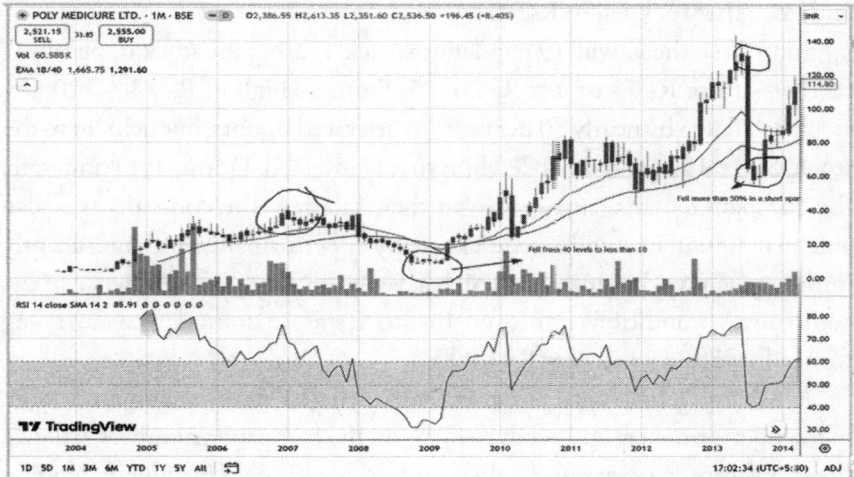

However, in 2013, Poly Medicure found itself in the midst of a political controversy, which caused a 50 per cent drop in the stock. While such events prompted Ayush to sell Poly Medicure stock from time to time, fortunately, he retained some exposure. Today, the company has a market cap of Rs 25,000 crore—all testament to his patience and conviction.

Ayush believes that for most good long-term stocks, there are often short phases—lasting a year of two—when the companies face severe challenges, resulting in significant drawdowns of 50 to 70 per cent from their peak. During such times, it is difficult to determine whether the fall is temporary or permanent, making it challenging to decide whether to stay invested or exit.

Ayush recalls his investment journey with one of his multibaggers, Shivalik Bimetal, to illustrate this point. He invested in the company in 2017 when its share price was around Rs 60–70 and it had a market cap between Rs 250 crore and Rs 300 crore. He selected the company as it was developing a new product with immense potential in the evolving electric vehicle (EV) industry. Ayush had learned about the sector's huge growth prospects during his classes with Professor Bakshi and was keen to invest in it. At the time, Shivalik had already secured a billion-dollar customer. Initially, the stock went up to around Rs 130-140, but then the company slowed down, and its profit margins took a hit. The company reported poor results for over two quarters and several fellow investors were quick to pass negative judgements and exit. The stock fell to Rs 75.

Soon after, the Covid-19 pandemic struck, causing the stock to plummet further—from Rs 75 to just Rs 20–25. From its high of Rs 130–140, the stock had fallen by nearly 80 per cent. Ayush faced doubts, but held on to the stock. Several factors convinced him to stay invested. During the pandemic, the company's management waived their salaries. The company was also able to maintain its numbers, quickly recover performance and significantly improve their working capital, which gave Ayush renewed confidence in the company. As conditions improved, the stock started doing well again, rising from a low of Rs 25 to over Rs 1,000.

Ayush firmly believes that rather than relying solely on a company's stock market performance, one needs to focus on the company's numbers, balance sheet, promoter moves and subtle communications. During challenging times, insights into these parameters help build confidence and elevate the quality of one's research, leading to better investment outcomes.

For Ayush, errors of commission are particularly troublesome as they consume significant time and effort, impact one's confidence and weigh heavily on the mind. He emphasizes the importance of avoiding such errors. Ayush believes that these mistakes tend to occur more often in the early stages of an investor's journey, largely due to poor data availability and limited analytical capability. However, he has been able to reduce such errors with the help of better data access through his Screener website.

He has learned the hard way that even after conducting in-depth research and developing a strong belief in a stock, it is crucial not to ignore red flags or negative opinions about the company. He admits that, in the past, he would dismiss these signals instead of considering alternative perspectives while making decisions.

Ayush recalls his experience with Kitex Garments, one of the largest manufacturers of infant apparel. Based on his research, he believed (and still believes) that the company had a unique business model, robust infrastructure and excellent clients such as Gerber and Mothercare. However, there were several aspects of the company that were red flags. Despite this,

Ayush continued to justify his decision to stay invested, even seeing the stock go up tenfold. Eventually, however, a prolonged period of underperformance and corporate governance issues began to impact his returns significantly. The situation caused immense mental strain as he continued to hold on to the stock even as it plummeted and erased all his gains. Ayush realizes it would have been wiser to acknowledge the red flags earlier and take corrective action.

In contrast, Ayush is less concerned about errors of omission. He believes that if little effort has been put into a decision, then one doesn't deserve any resulting wins either. Besides, the Indian market offers a sea of opportunities and there are always some ideas that will do well. It is better to learn from these success stories rather than dwelling on missed opportunities.

Ayush believes that, as humans, mistakes are inevitable. However, what can be truly demotivating is not the mistake itself but the failure to take action to correct it. Until a mistake is addressed, one tends to remain in a negative frame of mind, often panicking or worrying. On the other hand, once corrective action is taken, the focus shifts to the next stage—exploring new investment opportunities. Ayush shares that he starts looking forward to new prospects, and that is what keeps him going. The motivation to address mistakes also comes from freeing up capital that can be redeployed into better opportunities.

Mistakes can also become demotivating when they are compounded by external factors such as prolonged bear markets, or abnormal events like wars or the Covid-19 pandemic, which can crash the market for extended periods. In such scenarios, despite all your efforts, heavy losses may still occur. To mitigate the impact of such situations, Ayush stresses the importance of diversification. By maintaining a diversified portfolio, even a significant mistake in a single stock will not severely impact the overall portfolio.

This strategy thus helps minimize critical errors. He advises against allocating more than 3 to 5 per cent of one's portfolio to any single stock on a cost basis. Additionally, he is cautious of companies with high debt, excessive working capital requirements, frequent fundraisings, or those operating in highly competitive industries. Recognizing such red flags helps him avoid potential pitfalls.

Ayush also advises a mix of cautiousness and spontaneity for outperforming the market.

Reflecting on his journey, Ayush believes that his company is evolving rapidly, constantly adopting new techniques to ensure their work is far more detailed than it was five years ago. He observes significant improvements in his company every three to five years but acknowledges that the stock market is like an ocean, offering endless opportunities to learn and grow. One key improvement in his investing style has been tweaking his research process to hold on to winners for much longer than he managed in the past. He often continues to hold on to stocks even when there is little happening in near term—sometimes over one to two years—bearing the opportunity cost.

The core idea, according to Ayush, is to keep evolving through continuous learning. He places great value on learning from peers and friends, recognizing that shared insights offer opportunities for growth and improvement.

Reflecting on mistakes and navigating the highs and lows of investing, he encourages investors to embrace risk. He believes that mistakes often stem from a lack of willingness to explore new ideas and opportunities. Taking risks disrupts monotony, keeps investors engaged, and offers valuable lessons and rewards through both successes and setbacks.

However, Ayush clarifies that when he talks about risk, he refers to 'perceived risk' rather than actual risk. Once he narrows down on a company, he works to reduce the unknown or perceived risks by using tools such as those provided by his website, analysing cash flows in annual reports, studying management and competitors, and conducting case studies.

Team player

Ayush strongly believes in giving space and freedom to every member of his team. When someone puts in hard work on researching a company and their analysis has merit, Ayush incorporates it into his strategy, often buying shares in the relevant company and tracking the investment. He values having a broad range of ideas—twenty to thirty core ones and a long tail of over a hundred ideas—rather than limiting himself to just ten to fifteen names. Ayush believes that no one can predict which idea might turn out to be the next big success. As a result, he continuously experiments with multiple opportunities. As he gains insights and confidence in certain ideas, he scales up his investments in those opportunities. He considers it essential to give team members the freedom to pursue their own experimentation and learning.

Talking about his clientele, Ayush focuses on onboarding clients who share a similar long-term horizon and understand his investing philosophy. This is important, as having a client who does not share your mindset can lead to challenges during downturns. In difficult times, a client's panic may make an investor feel guilty, potentially impacting their own judgement and performance. So, over the years, Ayush has become cautious about managing money for strangers or the general public. Instead, he invests for a select group of individuals, offering them highly customized services.

Personal life impacting investing

Ayush believes that investing is influenced by one's frame of mind. A bullish outlook can justify a stock at any valuation, while a bearish mindset can lead to dumping the same stock at any low price. He acknowledges that it is not easy to prevent personal situations and problems from impacting one's investing journey. It is extremely important to have a positive personal life, and he feels blessed to have the unwavering support of his wife, Roopali. She has been a pillar of strength since his CA coaching days, enabling him to devote most of his time to investing. She recently also joined the family's investment business, contributing significantly to Screener.

To give you a practical example, during covid time, it was very scary to see that people around were falling ill or dying. Businesses were shut in lockdown and reported heavy losses. Who could have imagined about a big stock market opportunity back then. Ayush heard Rakesh Jhunjhunwala who said that 'You know one bad year in the life of a company is immaterial. One bad year doesn't matter. Just write it off. Just forget this Covid year.' Ayush felt this was so logical and after hearing this, he just ignored the bad numbers that came for next two-three quarters. At the same time, he ignored the people who were selling in panic and had he listened to the latter category, he may have made a disastrous mistake of his life.

India: A country of progress and potential

Ayush acknowledges that India's size and diversity present complex challenges, yet he firmly believes that a growing country like India offers boundless opportunities. Despite sometimes feeling disheartened by short-term issues, he sees India as an extraordinary story of progress.

Looking at his hometown, Lucknow, Ayush observes that the city undergoes dramatic changes every five years. The infrastructure development and transformation taking place in the city fill him with immense pride.

Another impactful area of India's growth that is gaining attention is the digitization and automation spreading across nearly every sector. He notes that India has surpassed many developed countries in areas like banking and transaction speeds.

Ayush also praises India's stock market, considering it one of the best in the world. He believes the entrepreneurial spirit in India is unmatched globally, and with such a young and hard-working population, one cannot but be bullish on India.

Small regrets

Looking back, Ayush says he could have improved his focus, patience and reading habits to enhance his knowledge and temperament. He regrets allocating too little to good stocks and exiting them too early without strong reasons. There are many instances where he invested in promising companies but sold the stock after making a good return in the short term. Later, these companies became multibaggers.

Ayush believes that having access to better information, conducting more detailed analyses and valuing the qualitative aspects of companies would have significantly enhanced his investment journey.

CHAPTER 11

GAUTAM TRIVEDI
The global strategist with an Indian twist

GAUTAM Trivedi is the co-founder and managing partner of Nepean Capital, overseeing a portfolio-management services (PMS) and a family office that manages a media-centric fund with substantial investments (and, in some cases, majority) in some of the leading media companies.

With over twenty-six years of experience in the Indian and the Asian financial industry, Gautam's illustrious career includes roles such as CEO of Religare Capital Markets and managing director and head of equity distribution at Goldman Sachs India. He also pioneered the Great India Roadtrips and has worked with Reliance Industries, DSP Merrill Lynch, CLSA Asia and Jardine Fleming (Hong Kong).

He serves on the boards of several organizations including Collective Artists Network, Extramarks Education, Landmark Cars, Maddock Films and UFO Moviez. He is also a member of the India Advisory Board of the USC Viterbi School of Engineering.

Apart from his professional pursuits, Gautam is an avid traveller and enjoys penning his experiences in travelogues. Given his varied interests and outgoing personality, conversations with Gautam often lead to interesting insights on everything from food and travel to investing.

I begin our discussion by asking Gautam about his early years and whether his upbringing, education and exposure have shaped the way he makes decisions.

Gautam reflects on how his generation grew up in an India of limited resources, restricted choices and curiously, limited wants. He attributes this to the fact that the country at the time was largely cut off from the world and most goods were in short supply—two-wheelers, cars, telephones, TV sets and more.

He adds that life was in a sense simple, yet constrained. He believes that the socialist policies followed by India's founding fathers were a failed economic model. As a result, many Indians grew up with a short-term mindset and believed that a better future awaited them overseas in Western countries. Gautam admits that his generation lacked the foresight to think long term. For example, few could have predicted that the NIFTY50 would rise twenty-seven times, from 890 on 1 January 1999 to 24,800 today. 'One of the few people I know who betted on India was my friend, the late Rakesh Jhunjhunwala,' he fondly recalls.

Gautam's father, a lawyer, had hoped that one of his two sons would join the legal profession. While both Gautam and his brother studied law, his father made the mistake of agreeing to send them to the US for an MBA in the early nineties. This decision, Gautam says, changed everything.

Studying in the US exposed him to an entirely new world of finance, one that he admits he had little knowledge of. He calls the US the 'poster child of capitalism' and credits his two years there with opening his eyes to what capitalism could do to a country's economic growth.

Gautam shares an interesting story from his time in the US. In August 1991, he moved into his off-campus apartment at the University of Southern California (USC) in Los Angeles. Coming from India, where citizens were subjected to the whims and fancies of a state monopoly, MTNL (Mahanagar Telephone Nigam Limited), he was accustomed to bad service and exorbitant costs—Rs 150 a minute to make a long-distance call to the US. 'Ironically, today long-distance calls are free via WhatsApp and MTNL is a basket case.'

The apartment, he recalls, had a telephone connection, but the line was inactive. His neighbour told him to call Pacific Bell, a local phone company that was one of the 'Baby Bells' carved out from the break-up of AT&T. Using his neighbour's landline, Gautam called Pacific Bell and was surprised by the polite and helpful operator who answered the call. She activated his landline within minutes and then asked a question he would never forget: 'What long-distance operator would you like?'

That question, he admits, left him confused as in India, there was only one long-distance phone company—another state-owned monopoly called Videsh Sanchar Nigam Limited (VSNL). Curious, he asked the operator how many operators were available, and her response—'over a hundred'—stunned him. 'It took me a full minute to understand her reply,' Gautam recalls. He eventually chose AT&T as it was the only name he recognized. This experience illustrated the impact of capitalism. It brought about competition and gave consumers choices.

He further shares, 'My second eye-opening experience was my first visit to Las Vegas, a city that epitomizes capitalism more than even New York City. I had not seen anything like it before.' The idea that American corporations were willing to bet billions of dollars on building hotels, restaurants and entertainment venues struck him as remarkable. 'The thinking was, "if you build it, they will come".'

The Las Vegas Strip, he explains, is lined with around thirty hotels and casinos, with enormous signage and neon lights that make them the brightest spot on the planet. 'NASA published an image taken by astronauts on the International Space Station (ISS) showing just how bright the Strip looks from space,' Gautam shared. Comparing it to India, he highlights that Las Vegas alone has over 1,56,000 hotel rooms whereas all of India has around 1,90,000. 'Casino operator Las Vegas Sands spent a whopping $1.5 billion to build the Venetian, which has over 7,000 rooms—that's twice the number of rooms that the Oberoi has in India—and fifty-two bars and restaurants.'

Alongside his learnings from the US on infrastructure and capitalism, Gautam shares another experience that influenced his investment process—his proprietary writings and visits on the Great India Roadtrips. He recalls that a month after joining Religare Capital Markets in late 2011, he met with the CEOs of their non-banking financial company (NBFC) and retail broking businesses and discovered they had a nationwide network of over 2,000 offices, including both owned and franchised outlets in more than 500 towns. He saw this a potential opportunity, but initially wasn't sure how to leverage it.

'After about a month, it hit me,' he says. 'Why don't we start road trips to tier 2 and 3 towns and villages? The objective would be to take investors to places they hadn't been before. Most institutional investors, whether Indian or foreign, have only been to around ten cities—barring holiday destinations. These include the four metros—Mumbai, Delhi, Kolkata and Chennai—plus Hyderabad, Bangalore, Pune, Ahmedabad, and maybe Coimbatore, Chandigarh or Indore. That's it.'

Paraphrasing the famous *Star Trek* line, Gautam envisioned these road trips would 'boldly go where no investor has gone before'.

Gautam explains that the goal of these road trips was not necessarily to find new companies but to conduct 'channel checks' to understand how large companies were performing through their dealers, distributors or even consumers. By creating a 'feedback loop', his team could conduct research on several listed companies. For example, during these trips, he and his group met local dealers and distributors in many sectors, including:

- Automobile companies like Maruti Suzuki, Hyundai India, Tata Motors, Ashok Leyland and Eicher Motors
- Two-wheeler brands including Bajaj Auto, Hero MotoCorp and TVS
- Cement manufacturers such as Ultratech Cement, Ambuja Cement, ACC, Shree Cement and various regional players
- Financial institutions including local branches of SBI, ICICI and NBFCs
- Consumer goods companies like Hindustan Unilever, ITC, Dabur and Emami
- Farmers, village sarpanches and traders

Encouraged by the findings of these trips, Gautam toyed with several names before settling on Great India Roadtrip. He figured that for the venture to be successful, the name had to be grand. 'If people asked investors where they were last weekend, the reply would be, "I was on the Great India Roadtrip".'

The purpose of these trips was to garner intelligence from the Real India, as opposed to sitting in an air-conditioned office in Mumbai, detached from ground realities. Gautam notes that unlike his model, most sell-side research analysts rely on annual or quarterly earnings reports, plant visits and discussions with investor-relations teams to forecast future revenues and earnings. These road trips, however, could provide a major differentiating factor for Religare and its analysts. They offered insights into how the rest of India looked, functioned and behaved.

Gautam shared some of his learnings and insights gained from the road trips.

He recalls being shocked at the number of knock-offs of branded fast-moving consumer goods (FMCG) products sold in smaller towns. In Patna, for instance, a distributor of a large multinational company revealed that knock-offs accounted for almost 50 per cent of the goods sold in Bihar. Similarly, a dealer of a popular cigarette brand shared that counterfeits, which looked identical to the original, sold for just a fifth of the price.

Gautam also highlights the dominance of India's cash economy. While GST has curbed this to some extent, cash remains king, especially in real estate deals. Tax evasion has been a long-standing issue in the country, and he says he met several traders who admitted to disclosing only a fraction of their sales to the tax man.

Another insight from these road trips was the aspirations of people in smaller towns. They too want to enjoy the kind of life people lead in the big cities—they want to wear the latest fashions, try different cuisines and travel abroad. He believes that as India's per capita income rises, the demand for these goods will explode. He cites a recent Thomas Cook presentation, which projected that the expenditure on tourism by Indians would jump by 173 per cent from $150 billion pre-Covid to $410 billion by 2030. Two-thirds of this will be spent on domestic tourism with the rest on outbound travel.

Gautam also emphasizes the importance of engaging directly with farmers to understand the issues they face. He recalls visiting Lasalgaon in Maharashtra, Asia's largest onion market, in 2015, when unseasonal rains had severely damaged the onion crop. He met the head of the Agricultural Produce Market Committee (APMC), who made an interesting point: while the media makes much of food inflation, property prices have risen five to ten times across India in the past ten years, and people willingly pay Rs 300 for a movie ticket in a multiplex.

He recalls meeting Ramanbhai, a farmer in Gujarat, who shared that the younger generation did not want to work in the fields, toiling under the sun for over twelve hours a day. They wanted to work in cities and towns. His two sons, for example, preferred trading in cumin seeds in Unjha to working in the fields. Ramanbhai also noted that it was easier to find a bride working in a town as opposed to on a farm, even if the latter earned more.

Over time, competitors began recognizing that Gautam's road trips were resonating with investors. In 2015, the initiative received a significant boost when CNBC India started covering them. Through various TV appearances, Gautam promoted the findings of these trips, fuelling even greater interest. 'No one was doing them; no one could do them at the speed, scale and depth that we could,' he proudly exclaims.

I next quiz Gautam on making mistakes, even when processes like the one he articulated earlier are followed. Gautam candidly admits, 'One mistake most of us make during a crisis—be it 9/11, the global financial crisis or Covid—is that we lack the courage to buy when the market or our well-researched stocks fall by 15 to 20 per cent. We think that this time it will be different, the fall will be even steeper, and so we wait for a lower price point. But the market always bounces back, and in hindsight, you wish you hadn't been so pessimistic.'

He draws a difference in believing it's the right time to buy in companies well researched when they fall vs convincing the mind to let go of fear in times of cracks.

When I ask him to elaborate on a specific mistake he has made, he is quick to share an example. 'The one stock that I missed buying was Indian Hotels. Pre-Covid, the stock was priced at Rs 150, but when Covid hit, it crashed to Rs 65. Hotels were empty, tourism had come to a grinding halt, and the world was apparently coming to an end. No one had dealt with a global pandemic the size of Covid before, so it was impossible to know when things would turn around. Even after Covid receded, I didn't have the conviction to buy Indian Hotels as historically, the stock had traded in a band of Rs 60–150. I didn't factor in the turnaround that the new CEO, Puneet Chhatwal, had initiated in the company, which has since driven the price up by 900 per cent in the past four and a half years.'

He adds that the irony was that in June 2021, he had hosted Puneet as a guest speaker in his Nepean Capital Leadership Series, an online fireside chat with CEOs, economists and foreign investors. During his session, Puneet had clearly outlined his plans to an audience of about two hundred guests, detailing initiatives such as adding more hotels through an asset-light model, and expanding Ama Stays, Qmin and the Ginger Hotels brand. He shares, 'I still didn't buy the stock as it had doubled from its Covid bottom, hitting a fifteen-year high of Rs 150. Little did I know that the stock would triple thereafter.'

Reflecting on this, Gautam highlights the mistake of not acting even when the research is sound, perhaps due to blind spots.

He says, 'Full marks to the Tata Group for finding a remarkable CEO like Puneet and empowering him to make changes in India's largest hotel company. He had spent the previous forty years in Europe and was new to India's hospitality sector. Yet, he has done an incredible job creating shareholder value and taking the market cap to over $10 billion. I am confident that Indian Hotels will soon be the eighth Tata company to cross the Rs1 lakh crore mark.'

Next, Gautam reflects on mistakes, realization and the ensuing action taken.

He explains that some mistakes become apparent when companies declare results, often within two to three quarters of purchasing the stock. He elaborates, 'I run a long-only fund and have more patience than the average investor. Being an entrepreneur or promoter in India has several challenges. While the ease of doing business in our country has improved, we still have miles to go. As a result, if a promoter estimates that a company's new plant will start on a certain date but misses that by one or two quarters, it's okay—it's not a big deal.'

He points out that investors often make the mistake of using a disappointing result as a reason to exit a stock. Analysts frequently share polls comparing 'expected results' versus 'delivered results', leading to a fixation on the short term. Stocks often fall when companies miss expectations, even if they remain on track to achieve their long-term vision. Gautam cautions against judging a 'speed breaker' as the end of a company's journey.

Gautam emphasizes that in investing, admitting a mistake is the first step towards making corrections. He shares an example to illustrate this: 'One theme that has worked very well in India over the past six to seven years is private equity (PE) funds conducting buyouts of listed mid-cap companies while keeping them listed. The market perceives this positively, and the expectation is that the PE fund will fix any existing problems and turn the company around. We have invested in several such special situations. For example, we invested in the pharma company J.B. Chemicals, where the founding family sold their stake to KKR.'

However, he acknowledges that he made a mistake in assuming that the strategy would have a 100 per cent success rate. 'We erred in our analysis of one specific company. We thought the foreign PE firm would use their global relationships and significantly increase the company's topline. It never happened—it's a mystery why— and the rectification was to sell the stock.'

From this, Gautam drew a key lesson: never take your analysis for granted. Continuously evaluate your investments, and when you sense a deviation that appears to be worsening, re-evaluate and exit if needed.

I ask Gautam how he tracks a promoter with a history of poor corporate governance, where investors have previously lost money. Can such a company truly change for the better?

Gautam reflects and acknowledges that human nature often succumbs to greed and excess, causing people to make the same mistakes. He elaborates, 'While you may first meet promoters or management at a conference or even casually in a hotel coffee shop, the following meetings are always held at the company's offices. Personally, visiting the office tells you a lot about the company—whether the décor and furniture are frugal, extravagant or practical. I also make it a point to check out the promoter's car. I observe the behaviour of the promoter and his team. Is there genuine reflection on past mistakes, or does the promoter sweep them under the rug, dismissing them out of ego?' Gautam believes that the culture of change, or lack thereof, becomes evident in such interactions.

Gautam explains that a significant challenge fund managers face is knowing when to sell. Gautam advises asking yourself whether India's growth will remain strong over the next ten to fifteen years, and whether the company in question will participate in that growth. If the answer is yes, he suggests buying good stocks and holding on to them for the next ten years or more. Good stock, he believes, must exhibit both strong performance and reasonable valuation.

He elaborates on this through an example: 'One of our best performing stocks is Varun Beverages, the bottler and distributor of PepsiCo's beverage portfolio in India and select overseas markets. When we started building a position in 2019, the company covered around 45 per cent of India's geography. Soon after, PepsiCo sold them an additional 45 per cent. So here you have one of the world's biggest consumer companies giving one company 90 per cent of the geographic reach in one of the world's largest consumer markets. Isn't that amazing? It speaks volumes about the management of Varun Beverages.'

He continues, 'Another reason we bought stock in the company was that it offered an opportunity to take advantage of the electrification of India. Over the past ten years, the Modi government has significantly expanded the country's power generation, transmission and distribution infrastructure. As a result, towns that used to get only five to ten hours of electricity a day now receive double that. This has enabled people in towns and villages to plug in mini refrigerators and Visi coolers (Varun has deployed over a million nationwide) and serve a cold drink. This has led to a huge spike in beverage consumption across India. The stock has gone up 23x over the past ten years!'

Gautam concludes by emphasizing that when you find a good company with strong potential and at a good valuation, and the economic climate in the country is favourable, the returns from holding such investments long-term can far exceed those from trading in and out.

Gautam believes that currently, India is the most expensive large equity market in the world.

He explains, 'Today, it is trading at 21x one-year forward P/E or at a 60 per cent premium to MSCI Asia (ex-Japan) and a 115 per cent premium to China. As a result, many Indian stocks are trading at huge premiums compared to their Asian and global peers.' To illustrate, he cites an example: 'One such stock is Dixon Technologies, the poster child of the EMS (electronics manufacturing services) industry in India. When we first looked at it some five years ago, at 28x one year forward P/E, we found it too expensive and passed on it. Little did we know that over time, the stock would appreciate 22x.'

The lesson to be learnt from this is that the market is prepared to pay a premium for stocks that demonstrate exponential growth, especially when only one or two companies in a sector are listed. Even today, despite having about ten EMS companies listed, Dixon continues to perform well.

Gautam acknowledges that deciding what to buy amongst many options is always a tough choice. He explains that his decision to buy a stock is made by comparing it to other attractive options at the time. The risk–reward ratio is measured based on the company's fundamentals and technical aspects.

Drawing an analogy, he adds, 'It's like needing to hire an analyst from a shortlist of seven or eight resumes. When one of our analysts recommends a stock, we often discuss and debate multiple factors before taking a final call. If the pros outweigh the cons, we go ahead.'

Gautam also shares a valuable lesson from his experience: 'If the outcome of one investment is favourable, there is no guarantee that you will be right the next time. Don't take success as a given based on one outcome. Each stock is different and its evaluation should be treated as such.'

He adds that fund managers who have been in the industry for a long time invariably develop an 'I know it all' syndrome. However, it is important to stay current and grounded. 'I believe no one is too junior to recommend a stock—ideas are not anyone's monopoly,' he stresses.

He shares that there are times when a fund manager bets on a founder or promoter, only to be let down by poor performance, lapses in corporate governance or even outright fraud. While such experiences can be demotivating, it's important to limit that demotivation to the specific company and not let it affect your overall investing approach. Similarly, one success shouldn't overshadow all past mistakes.

To minimize mistakes and improve success rates, Gautam suggests incorporating certain practices into one's due diligence, apart from financial analysis. These include visiting company plants, meeting promoters in their offices (rather than in the coffee shop of a five-star hotel), and assessing the capabilities of the next generation that will take over the company.

He also shares that there are times when public markets struggle with how to value a company or sector when it's new. He comments on the mistake of comparing valuations between private companies and those in the listed space.

A prime example is the new-age tech sector. Over the past two to three years, a clutch of companies such as Zomato, Nykaa and PayTM launched their IPOs. Despite having little or no profits, they commanded extraordinary valuations in the private equity world. However, when the public markets collided with the private markets, reality struck.

Public market investors rely on metrics such as EBITDA (earnings before interest, taxes, depreciation and amoritization), net profits and real cash flows, rather than metrics such as the monthly burn rate. Listed companies that had been in existence for decades and were PAT positive were left questioning why they weren't valued at 10 to 30x revenue. As a result, the new-age tech companies saw their stocks crash by 50 to 70 per cent within months of listing, resulting in huge losses for IPO investors.

Thankfully, Gautam says, his fund steered clear of these companies and didn't lose money. However, he highlights another mistake: believing that a company's fall means you should never participate in the market. He adds, in the context of these tech IPOs, 'We also missed the bottom. At some point, the public markets became comfortable with the valuations of the new-age tech companies, and the stocks saw a 180-degree turn. For example, Zomato listed at Rs 115 (against an IPO price of Rs 75), hit a high of Rs 154, then soon dropped all the way down to Rs 40—a fall of 70 per cent. That was rock-bottom, and since then, the stock has rallied 400 per cent as the company started reporting net profits, albeit tiny compared to its topline.'

Gautam concludes our discussion by summarizing that despite years of experience and education, fund managers will still make mistakes. One common error is believing that a previously rogue promoter has turned a new leaf, a mistake often made during bull markets. Another risk lies with newly listed companies—every year, forty to fifty new companies are listed with unknown promoters and insufficient background checks. Investors can thus be misled by false promises or even outright fraud. Lastly, one can make a mistake in betting on the next generation, particularly in India, where almost two-thirds of listed companies are family-owned. As a result, the next generation believes it is their birthright to inherit the throne, no matter their competence.

CHAPTER 12

RAVI DHARAMSHI

The guardian of marketing fundamentals

RAVI Dharamshi is the founder and CIO of ValueQuest Investment Advisors, a SEBI-registered firm providing discretionary portfolio-management services (PMS) to its clients. He holds an MBA in finance from McCallum Business School, USA. After completing his MBA, he undertook a brief internship at Salomon Smith Barney, returning to India.

I begin my conversation with Ravi by asking him how he handles mistakes.

Ravi views mistakes as an integral part of the learning process and embraces them as a part of his entrepreneurial journey. One of his favourite quotes is: 'Show me a man who has never failed, and I will show you a person who has never tried.' He does not believe mistakes are related to upbringing or education, interestingly in sharp contrast to many other fund managers featured in this book. They are more a result of one's behaviour than of education.

You can equip yourself with more knowledge and that can be a big factor in reducing chances of mistakes as the more you know, the better prepared and the less ignorant you are. So do more fact-scouting, and if you make mistakes, accept it as an inevitable learning. Your only goal should be to learn from your mistakes and not repeat them.

One cannot have an investing strategy that focuses on the extremes of the market all the time. In fact, focusing on the same can be counterproductive. He explains that every future market correction feels like a threat and every past correction appears as a missed opportunity in hindsight.

He differentiates between mistakes made during calm times and those made during crises, emphasizing that the latter can be more impactful and defining for investors. The former, he says, are not the ones where opportunities are lost. Mistakes in crisis carry greater weight because others are making them too, and that's when one has the chance to stand apart from the pack.

Ravi advises evaluating one's actions in calm times versus during crises and not fall for irrational exuberance in a fall basis commonality of action, highlighting that the behaviour of crowds can be misleading to long-term outperformance. He recalls the words of his mentor and ex-boss, Rakesh Jhunjhunwala: 'The worst of mistakes are made in the best of times.' This quote is prominently displayed in his office as a reminder to stay vigilant and humble.

He elaborates on how easy it is to become complacent when things are going well, often forgetting that markets are supreme. Crises, he argues, can be an investor's best friend. Reflecting on events like Covid-19, Ravi notes that such periods of widespread gloom and uncertainty can present once-in-a-lifetime opportunities. During the pandemic, his fund invested a significant amount of money, but he feels they could have done more, as such opportunities are rare in an investor's lifetime.

Ravi considers this as a personal lesson: the mistake of not taking a crisis as an opportunity and betting big.

He acknowledges that investing is a probabilistic game, akin to poker, but the best part is there is immediate market feedback on how right or wrong one is. Also as one progresses, he says he hopes to become less susceptible to the 'boiling frog syndrome'. This metaphor describes a frog that, if placed in boiling water, would jump out immediately but, when placed in tepid water that is gradually heated, fails to perceive the danger and stays until it is too late. This highlights the tendency to ignore or fail to react to gradually emerging threats. Similarly, many investors make the mistake of holding on to overvalued stocks, disregarding corrections like the frog, only to get burnt in the end.

Ravi quotes legendary investor Peter Lynch, who said, 'In this business if you are good, you will get six out of ten right' and for sure there will be some wrong turns in the journey. The key is not to repeatedly take the same wrong turns.

Ultimately, Ravi's key takeaway is to learn from mistakes and avoid repetition, fostering continuous growth and improvement by some cardinal rules that you learn from as you progress. Such as never invest at unreasonable valuations, never run for companies which are in limelight, never make same mistakes again.

It takes time to gain the maturity and realize a mistake. He recalls that early in his investing career, it took him longer to realize errors. Over time, you can crunch the learning time curve, recognize faster and correct faster.

Hence once should not be discouraged as an early investor who makes mistakes but keep the course and observe over time what such mistakes teach you about your behaviour that needs a course correction and then try to rectify them asap than repeatedly deferring the correction.

As an example, he adds, 'underestimating the size of an opportunity and the potential of a business' were some of his painful mistakes as misses. He was an early investor in Bajaj Finance, but sold too early. While he got good gains, he recalls missing out on bulk of its late rise. Here, he shares a mistake that many of us make, which is 'selling out too early'.

One must distinguish between a trend and a mega trend, or a major business turning around versus an inflection point where the turn could be way longer. Then one needs to sit tight and let the business ride. Thus a one-time earning may be different from a turn of earnings.

Luckily, over the years, he says, he is getting better at this.

To minimize mistakes, Ravi and his team utilize various strategies, including the 'tenth man rule' for contrarian thinking, a risk-revisiting investment committee and a mentor board for diverse insights. He also practices mindfulness through music and sports to maintain focus.

According to the tenth man rule, if ten people are involved in a decision-making process, then one person should be assigned the role of challenging the prevailing consensus, operating under the assumption that it could be wrong. The goal is to ensure that every angle of a problem has been considered and that policymakers don't fall into the pitfalls of group-think. It is similar to the principle of 'invert, always invert', which inspired Charlie Munger to say, 'All I want to know is where I'm going to die, so I'll never go there.' His thinking was influenced by the German mathematician Carl Gustav Jacob Jacobi, who often solved difficult problems using a simple strategy: 'man muss immer umkehren' (loosely translated as 'invert, always invert').

Ravi explains that his investment committee regularly revisits past mistakes. They evaluate whether risks are internal to a company or external, unique to the company, or common to the industry. For example, how much exposure towards exports a company has or what could be the implications of a longer drawn war, say in Israel, on a company. They revisit the process and rationale of investing and their systems when there are such flashpoints.

He also has a mentor board to bounce ideas off, emphasizing that the board's vast experience and diversity help uncover potential blind spots. Ravi says he is not much into meditation as a tool of mind balancing but music and sports help him in decluttering and thus in decision making.

He adds, 'What you see is important, but what you cannot see is even more important.'

Notably, he acknowledges the role of luck in investment outcomes, referencing Annie Duke's book, *Thinking in Bets*.[1] He highlights that there are two key factors that influence how our lives play out: the quality of our decision-making and luck. Learning to distinguish the difference between the two is the book's central message, which he highly recommends. He observes that sometimes one may get favourable results despite flawed processes, and warns, 'You must realize you got lucky and not overstay your welcome as you did not deserve this outcome in the first place due to a flawed process.'

Ravi stresses the importance of adaptability and humility, quoting John Keynes, 'When the facts change, I change my mind.' He also references an old stock-market adage, 'There are old investors and bold investors, but there are no old, bold investors', emphasizing the need for self-awareness and the ability to admit and learn from mistakes. Overcommitting can lead to fatal errors, and he advocates humility as a safeguard.

He draws inspiration from his brother and mentor, Kalpraj Dharamshi, who advised, 'Never buy on impulse, sell in panic and hold in hope.' Ravi has grown through experience, learning from his own mistakes and those of others, and acknowledges the impact of greed and fear on decision-making. However, he believes that experience and knowledge can mitigate these influences.

Ravi aspires to shorten his learning curve by not repeating the same mistakes but making new ones instead. Quoting Warren Buffett, he stresses, 'It is good to learn from your mistakes. It is even better to learn from other people's mistakes.' He emphasizes that reading widely and spending time in the market enables one to learn not just from one's own errors but also from those of others.

Ravi differentiates between errors of commission and errors of omission, acknowledging both as detrimental. As a public fund manager, errors of commission are more focused on reputation and the funds tied to it, but as a learning investor, errors in omissions are the ones you should try to reduce,

Both types of errors, he asserts, are harmful. Errors of omission occur when one fails to act and there the cause would probably be more of potential of opportunity loss and in some cases, not selling enough or not buying enough, so there is a case of 'potentiality'. Errors of commission, however, are much worse as they indicate a flawed hypothesis and the risk of capital loss. Ravi admits, 'I have experienced both and aim to avoid both.' To achieve this, he draws inspiration from the late Rakesh Jhunjhunwala's advice: 'Don't be afraid of making mistakes, but make sure you make those that you can afford.'

He also notes that errors of omission can have greater mathematical significance, with unlimited potential upside and limited downside risk.

Ravi reflects that as one grows older and gains more experience, one becomes more objective in assessments. The realization sets in that one doesn't have to make money from the same investment. You start dispassionately looking for the next opportunity instead of clinging to old ones. Here Ravi warns against the common mistake of becoming 'married to a stock' and believing it is the only way to make money.

He remarks that if mistakes never occurred, there would be no differentiation among people, and life would no longer be exciting. The game would become merely a matter of addition and subtraction, and we would become a race of bookkeepers with plodding minds. It's the guessing that sharpens the mind, as making an accurate guess demands intellectual effort. While all investors make mistakes, the successful ones are those who acknowledge them, learn from them, and work to understand what went wrong.

Ravi views investing as both an art and a science, as it is as much about psychology as it is about maths, and as much about faith as it is about data. There must therefore be a continuous improvement in your process and craft.

Ravi also emphasizes that investing—and having conviction in it—is a lonely exercise. While one may debate and discuss matters with one's team, the ultimate decision-making is a personal action.

He quotes M.S. Dhoni: Focus on the process and worry about the controllable. Don't worry about what you cannot control if your process is right.[2] When asked how to achieve this mindset, Ravi acknowledges that there is no universal blueprint. 'Each investment and each outcome is unique. You have to follow your gut and imagine which company or industry is at the cusp of an inflection point, which can scale the maximum and where the opportunity size is bigger.'

Quoting Howard Marks, Ravi says, 'There is no such thing as superior investing, there is only superior judgement.'[3] He believes that this judgement is the value he, as a fund manager, brings to the table.

Echoing the teachings of the Bhagavad Gita, Ravi advises, 'One should focus on the process not the outcome.' He adds, 'Irrespective of who you are, the process and the thought behind are important. Outcomes will follow. Our basic fiduciary duty to our investors is to create a framework that works and then follow it. People, processes and judgements are the inputs, while returns are the outcome.'

He highlights that taking advantage of market exuberance and hubris is the dharma of any balanced and mature investor. Quoting Howard Marks and his 2012 memo on mistakes, Ravi emphasizes, 'Superior investing is all about mistakes—and about being the person who profits from them, not the one who commits them.'

Ravi says risk control is the art of avoiding psychological and analytical errors. He advises against leaving too much to chance or emotion, urging investors to back their decisions with an established process, analysis and data. 'Treat all mistakes the same way, whether big or small,' he says. 'Learn from them and ensure you learn well.'

Ravi draws inspiration from many songs. 'I am a complete music buff,' he says, 'and my taste ranges from Kishore Kumar to Imagine Dragons. There isn't one specific song I can pinpoint, but 'Don't Stop Believin' by Journey is one of the most inspirational songs I have heard. As the lyrics go:

> Workin' hard to get my fill
> Everybody wants a thrill
> Payin' anything to roll the dice
> Just one more time
>
> Some'll win, some will lose
> Some are born to sing the blues
> Whoa, the movie never ends
> It goes on and on and on and on
>
> Strangers waitin'
> Up and down the boulevard
> Their shadows searchin' in the night
>
> Streetlights, people
> Livin' just to find emotion
> Hidin', somewhere in the night
>
> Don't stop believin'
> Hold on to that feelin'
> Streetlights, people

Ravi also finds inspiration in books, movies and TV series. Two that stand out for him are *The Swimmers* and *Rise*, both stories of migrants making it against all odds and succeeding under adverse circumstances. His all-time favourite book, however, is *Reminiscences of a Stock Operator: The Life and Times of Jesse Livermore*. He appreciates how Jesse balances ego and commitment bias to strive for a better tomorrow.

Ravi shares that he, too, recognizes the importance of balancing ego and commitment bias in investment decisions. He advocates for objectivity and dispassion, acknowledging that mistakes are inevitable but emphasizing the need to admit and learn from them.

Ravi believes that decision-making can be impacted by our circumstances and environment. For example, we are sometimes influenced by the people we meet. 'There is no secret sauce to eliminate this. As humans there is always something going on in our lives that can impact us. The key is recognizing when something in your life—say, A—will impact another—say, B—and then handing over control temporarily.' He advises creating a process to minimize the overlap of personal life and professional lives. 'Talk and dream and live the equity market, love what you do and if you do this, you don't have to worry about external factors.'

Mistakes as motivation

Reflecting on the mistake of selling too early, such as his experience with Bajaj Finance, Ravi shares that missteps can serve as motivators. 'We pat ourselves on the back on recognizing that our initial hypothesis to buy was right, and so was the investment. The fact that we did not see the investment through its natural journey was a mistake, but it motivates us to continue the journey, investing in other stocks and learning from this mistake.'

Ravi believes that striving for self-improvement and reducing mistakes should become a habitual practice. Motivation levels can ebb and flow, but habits and processes will help maintain stability and focus.

He acknowledges that mistakes result in both commercial and notional losses, which impacts one's mental space. Prolonged mistakes can therefore dominate the mind, affecting future decision-making and performance. To prevent this, Ravi advises moving out of the 'regret' mode as soon as possible and focusing on transforming mistakes into opportunities.

He gives an example of linking negativity to positivity towards a long-term investment approach. He says that for the many potholes we read about, new roads are being built. While there are construction lapses, metros are also being developed. There is traffic and chaos, but that reflects the growing aspirations of Indians as they are buying more cars.

Ravi believes that despite these challenges, India is on a growth trajectory. Being optimistic about opportunities in India, he prefers to see the glass as half full. While he acknowledges that there are infrastructure lapses, he feels they are reducing and significant progress is being made in the sector. Structural shifts like reducing corruption will take time, but the ecosystem is changing to ensure accountability and discourage corrupt practices. Over time, the culture will change.

Look at the big picture

As he reflects on his successful journey, Ravi shares that he wishes his education had been more diverse, extending beyond business, finance and markets. He emphasizes the value of a multidisciplinary approach to learning, saying, 'Maybe studying psychology or behavioural science could have added value.'

He says allocation is a common mistake, and mastering it comes only with experience. One needs to give oneself time to survive in the market—only then will one find endless opportunities to make money.

When managing public money, Ravi recognizes the impact of public expectations and actions on mistakes. He prioritizes avoiding the cycle of bad timing and unrealistic expectations, even if it means saying no to certain investors. He considers humility and the ability to publicly admit mistakes to be a superpower that cannot be taught. His focus remains on rational decision-making and controlling what he can, allowing the results speak for themselves rather than prioritizing public image.

With a growth mindset, Ravi advocates confronting mistakes head-on, conducting in-depth analyses to learn from them while avoiding analysis paralysis. He stresses that the lessons learnt from mistakes should drive future improvement and refine one's investment approach, prioritizing long-term success over short-term gains.

Ravi concludes by highlighting the critical role of mistakes as catalysts for growth and learning. He believes that embracing mistakes is essential for evolution and ensuring that successes outweigh failures. He acknowledges that mistakes are universal, affecting various aspects of life—sports, politics and human behaviour—and stresses the importance of remaining vigilant and curious. He notes that investing is an intellectual pursuit, and what constitutes a mistake for one person may be an opportunity for another. He believes one must understand contextual truth, pointing out that right and wrong are not always binary.

'It's a game of probabilities. Keep your losses small and wins big,' Ravi advises. He lives by the mantra 'stay hungry, stay foolish', continually learning from the world around him, whether it be politics, sports or business case studies. By doing so, he stays adaptable and open to new perspectives, ensuring that his investment approach remains refined and informed.

CHAPTER 13

E.A. Sundaram

The philosopher of wealth and wisdom

E.A. Sundaram, often hailed as the 'thinking investor,' has established himself as a prominent figure in contrarian investing in India. In the world of value investing, Sundaram stands out with his unique approach, which he describes as 'common-sense investing'. His philosophy is simple: investment success can be achieved not only by making the right decisions but also by avoiding the wrong ones.

Sundaram often recounts his early days with humorous anecdotes about the 'investment advice' he once gave that didn't quite pan out, humbling him in the process.

But like all great investors, Sundaram learned from his missteps, eventually becoming a trusted name in the investment community, known for his disciplined, thought-through approach.

With over twenty-nine years of experience in the investment industry, Sundaram has consistently demonstrated his knack for taking significant contrarian positions. Notable examples include being underweight on technology in 1999, on infrastructure, utilities and power in 2007, on midcaps in 2017, and excluding non-banking financial company (NBFC) exposure in 2018. These strategic decisions reflect his ability to learn from his mistakes and use them as a springboard for growth.

Armed with an MBA in finance from the prestigious IIM Ahmedabad, Sundaram's professional journey began with roles at various financial institutions, where his sharp acumen and composure during market turbulence quickly set him apart. Over the years, he has held key positions such as manager (research) at SBI Mutual Fund, head of research and fund manager at Zurich India Mutual Fund, senior portfolio manager at HDFC Mutual Fund, portfolio manager at M3 Investment Managers (a family office) and CIO and Portfolio Manager at PGIM India Mutual Fund.

Sundaram's extensive experience and strategic insights have made him a respected figure in the investment community, exemplifying the principles of common-sense investing. With nearly three decades of experience in Indian equity investing, he is primarily known for his expertise in mutual funds, portfolio-management services (PMS) and family-office investing. At the time of writing, he serves as the executive director at BugleRock Capital, formerly o3 Capital.

Delving deeper into his philosophy, it becomes evident that Sundaram has a natural curiosity for numbers and a talent for finding value in the most unexpected places through keen observation and common sense. Though he began life far from the chaotic world of stock markets, in a quiet, academically inclined household, his exposure to his father's meticulous budget planning planted the seeds of financial prudence early on.

However, it wasn't all smooth sailing.

Mistakes and childhood

I ask Sundaram if there is a correlation between upbringing and the mistakes we tend to commit today. His response is a nuanced perspective on the relationship between upbringing, education and the errors one makes in investing.

He suggests that drawing a direct link between upbringing and investment mistakes is a complex endeavour. While acknowledging that inadequate education can lead to analytical missteps, he emphasizes that investing transcends mere analysis.

The essence of investing, according to him, lies equally in one's temperament—a trait that education alone cannot shape. He points out that the emotional forces of greed and fear are at the root of most investment blunders. These sentiments, he argues, are deeply ingrained and cannot be easily eradicated by education or upbringing alone.

Sundaram explains that investing is as much about one's early experiences as it is about academic knowledge. Formative experiences significantly influence an investor's thought processes, shaping their approach to investment decisions. The mistakes that arise from these decisions often reflect the exposure—or lack thereof—individuals had in their early lives.

More crucially, Sundaram emphasizes the importance of learning from these exposures. Whether an investor learns from their experiences often determines the likelihood of repeating the same mistakes.

While acknowledging the importance of education and upbringing, Sundaram asserts that they are not the sole determinants of an investor's success or failure. Instead, it is the combination of temperament, experience and the ability to learn from past errors that truly guides one's investment journey.

Mistakes during bad times

Two distinct emotions come into play when making mistakes during periods of calm or crisis. Sundaram notes, 'As an investor, speaking from my experience, I can say that during calm times, investment mistakes are caused by greed or FOMO, and during crisis times, they are often caused by panic.'

This observation is particularly relevant when viewed through the lens of the Covid-19 pandemic. During the calm periods before the pandemic, markets were generally on an upward trajectory, buoyed by a sense of stability and optimism. Investors, driven by greed, were eager to capitalize on this growth. This greed led many to take on excessive risks, pouring money into overvalued assets, speculative stocks or sectors that were experiencing unsustainable growth. For example, the tech sector saw a significant influx of investment as companies like Zoom and Peloton surged in popularity. While some of these bets paid off, others were driven by unrealistic expectations and a fear of missing out. Investors were caught up in the euphoria, ignoring fundamental valuations and the potential for a market correction. This greed-induced overconfidence resulted in many portfolios becoming heavily concentrated in high-risk assets, setting the stage for significant losses when the calm was inevitably disrupted.

Then the crisis phase hit, as the world grappled with the unprecedented challenges of Covid-19. The sudden onset of the pandemic triggered widespread panic, sending shockwaves through global markets. Fear became the dominant emotion, causing investors to make hasty and often irrational decisions. As stock markets plummeted in March 2020, many investors rushed to sell off their holdings, desperate to preserve whatever value remained. This panic selling, driven by fear, led to significant losses for those who exited the market at its lowest point, only to see prices rebound in the months that followed. The fear of further losses overshadowed long-term strategies, leading investors to abandon well-thought-out plans in favour of immediate, short-sighted actions.

One illustrative example of this was the massive sell-off in sectors like travel, hospitality and oil, which were among the hardest hit during the early stages of the pandemic. While these industries undeniably faced severe challenges, the fear-driven exodus led many investors to sell at rock-bottom prices, clocking in losses that could have been mitigated had they held their positions and waited for the eventual recovery. Those who were able to maintain their composure during the crisis and resist the impulse to sell in fear were often rewarded as markets rebounded.

Conversely, in the calm that followed the initial crisis, greed once again reared its head as investors rushed back into the market, sometimes without fully assessing the ongoing risks of the pandemic's long-term economic impact.

Sundaram's insights highlight a timeless truth about investing: emotions like greed and fear are powerful forces that can lead to significant mistakes, whether in times of calm or crisis. The key takeaway is that understanding and managing these emotions is crucial for effectively navigating the market during both calm and crisis periods.

Recognizing and admitting to errors

In the early stages of Sundaram's investment journey, much like many other beginners, the mistakes he made were not immediately evident. He candidly shares how it was only when the results turned unfavourable that the true nature of these errors became clear to him. This realization was particularly stark during the period from 1993 to 1995, when the consequences of poor decisions began to manifest, haunting his portfolio through the subsequent years of 1996 and 1997.

It was a time of reflection and self-examination, and it became painfully apparent that these mistakes were primarily of his own making. However, recognizing these mistakes was only the first step. The more critical part was to ensure that the lessons learned were not lost, but rather deeply embedded in both the discipline and behaviour that would guide future investment decisions.

This introspection led to a significant turning point for Sundaram in 1996, when he made the tough but necessary decision to bite the bullet and overhaul his portfolio. The goal was to eliminate any holdings that did not meet his fundamental investment criteria or had been purchased during periods of market hype, driven by emotions rather than sound analysis.

The first step in this rectification process was ruthlessly eliminating the deadwood from his portfolio. This meant taking a hard look at every investment and being brutally honest about its potential. Companies that lacked strong fundamentals or were bought during a wave of market euphoria, without proper due diligence, were promptly removed. While admitting past mistakes and taking losses on underperforming assets was undoubtedly difficult, it was a crucial step in setting a new foundation for his portfolio, one that was free from the baggage of poor decisions.

Next, he focused on adhering to clearly definable and measurable quality in the businesses he purchased. This meant establishing strict criteria for what constituted a worthy investment. Businesses with strong financial health, competitive advantages and sustainable growth prospects became the cornerstone of Sundaram's portfolio. By following these well-defined metrics, he ensured that the likelihood of repeating past mistakes was reduced.

Finally, Sundaram paid specific attention to the entry price of investments. The importance of buying at the right price became a key lesson from the previous years' missteps. Overpaying for even the highest quality businesses could lead to poor returns if the price was not justified by future earnings potential. Therefore, the disciplinarian in Sundaram took the obvious approach, where he ensured patience played a crucial role. Investments were only made when the price was right, aligning with the potential for future growth.

These three steps—ruthlessly eliminating underperforming assets, committing to investing in high-quality businesses, and being meticulous about the entry price—were instrumental in rectifying the situation for Sundaram. They marked a turning point in his investment strategy, transforming it from one that was reactive and emotionally driven to one that was disciplined, strategic and focused on long-term success.

By learning from past mistakes and implementing these corrective measures, the foundation was laid for a more robust and resilient investment approach, one that would serve well in the years to come.

Spiritual tools and investing

We belong to the land of self-realization through vipassana and various other forms of meditation. Could these practices serve as tools in one's quest to invest better, especially when investing money that belongs to others? I pose this question to Sundaram, and his answer, once again, reflects his ability to focus.

Many others, when faced with this question, might dive into the concepts of meditation and link them to the discipline of investing. Sundaram, however, does not. Instead, he says that in times when there is uncertainty and vision is fuzzy, he believes in relying on a referral board composed of individuals with considered opinions that differ from his own.

Listening only to opinions that are in agreement with one's own is a recipe for confusion, overconfidence and hubris, with all their attendant consequences. For Sundaram, it is important to accept the fact that even after all this, one cannot be sure of achieving success.

Mistakes: Then and now

Sundaram draws a clear distinction between the mistakes he made during his earlier investment years and those in more recent times, observing that the frequency of mistakes of commission has significantly diminished in recent years. This shift, he notes, is largely due to a much greater emphasis on adhering to a disciplined investment process.

In his earlier years, the pursuit of being 'the best' or achieving the 'highest returns' often led to impulsive decisions driven by the desire to outperform the market at all times. This relentless chase for peak performance, however, frequently resulted in costly errors, as the focus was more on the outcome than on the process. Over time, Sundaram came to realize that this approach was not sustainable and often led to mistakes that could have been avoided. This realization marked a pivotal change in his investment philosophy. Instead of aiming for the highest possible returns at every opportunity, he began to prioritize consistency and discipline, focusing on being 'good' rather than trying to be the absolute best.

This shift in mindset brought about a more measured approach to investing. Sundaram placed greater emphasis on following a well-defined process that involved rigorous analysis, strict adherence to investment criteria, and a commitment to long-term goals rather than short-term gains. By focusing on maintaining a consistent standard of 'good' investment decisions, he has been able to avoid the pitfalls that come with chasing extreme outperformance.

The reduction in mistakes of commission in recent years is not just a result of experience, but a fundamental shift in philosophy. It is a recognition that in the long run, striving to be consistently good—by following a disciplined process—is more effective and sustainable than constantly chasing the highest returns. This change has not only improved the quality of investment decisions but also brought a sense of clarity and purpose to the investment process, allowing Sundaram to navigate the complexities of the market with greater confidence and fewer errors.

Managing ego

Sundaram shares more of his investment insights: Do not compromise on the quality or competitive ability of the companies that you chose to invest in, and do not buy when the hype surrounding them (as reflected in their valuations) is much higher than their long-term averages. He adheres to the practice of buying a stock only when its valuation is not much higher than its long-term averages. This often means purchasing a stock after it had substantially corrected. However, he acknowledges that the stock could fall further even after he begins buying it.

Another important point Sundaram emphasizes is that there is no rule—man-made or divine—that stipulates a stock must rise the moment one buys it. He underscores that a stock will generate returns only when others in the market, who were previously indifferent to the stock, begin to show interest, a process that may take time.

In the business of investing, a decision is acknowledged as a 'mistake' only when both the process and the outcome are unfavourable. Sometimes, when the process is flawed but the outcome is favourable, few investors are willing to admit it was a mistake. There have, of course, also been occasions in the past when a favourable outcome arose from a less-than-perfect process. As a seasoned investor, Sundaram acknowledges, 'Luck does play an important part in investing.'

Sticking with winners

Sundaram has an open mind about teams and who to work with on investment selection and doesn't have any particular favourites. He emphasizes that a single favourable outcome does not guarantee that the next one will also be successful. The key is to clearly articulate an investment process and philosophy, and then stick to it, regardless of whether it is currently favourable or unfavourable. While doing so, it is advisable to listen to alternative viewpoints before reaching a conclusion. If one is right in six or seven cases out of ten, then the outcome will be favourable.

Avoiding fatal mistakes

Exuberance and hubris are, more often than not, the causes of serious mistakes, Sundaram warns. Hubris creates a false sense of invincibility, which in turn undermines effective risk management. For Sundaram, 'fatal mistakes' in investing occur when there is a permanent loss of capital. One must therefore seek to reduce the chances of permanent capital loss.

Sundaram explains that permanent capital loss typically stems from several factors. These include investing in a weak or a deteriorating business, investing in a business where minority shareholders do not receive their rightful due, investing at too high a price, and being overly concerned about how much money others are making.

To address these risks, Sundaram advocates for a disciplined process that reduces the chances of these errors. By doing so, the likelihood of permanent capital loss and consequently, fatal mistakes in investing, is significantly reduced.

Managing people's money: Errors of omission vs errors of commission

Sundaram emphasizes the importance of always remembering that it is the investor's money being managed. If, for any reason, the investor wants to pull out of the portfolio, then that decision must be respected, he notes. A portfolio manager's responsibilities include clearly articulating the investment process, consistently adhering to it, and periodically providing evidence to the investor that the process is indeed being followed. Sundaram says, 'In investing, errors of omission are far more acceptable than the errors of commission.'

He explains that the sheer number of listed and traded companies makes it impossible for any investor to have exposure to all of them. Even after filtering for quality, around 250 to 300 companies might qualify for inclusion, but one cannot have all of them in one's portfolio. Inevitably, some good companies will be omitted. Sundaram admits to having missed several opportunities over the years—either because he chose another company in the same sector or avoided the sector altogether, only to see the omitted company's share price rise significantly over the next few years. These, he classifies as errors of omission, where the cost is a missed opportunity rather than a loss of money.

On the other hand, errors of commission—caused by negligence, lack of care or hubris—are far more detrimental. These cause actual damage to the portfolio, unlike errors of omission.

Experience and mistakes

Sundaram's ambition is simple: he aims to be proven right in seven out of ten cases, which he believes is sufficient to generate decent returns for his clients. In years when he is right in eight out of ten cases, clients have seen excellent returns. However, he acknowledges that achieving nine out of ten consistently is challenging, and he does not think a perfect ten is possible, as such outcomes often rely on pure luck.

To achieve consistent success, Sundaram follows two key principles. First, he emphasizes never compromising on the quality or competitive ability of the companies you choose to invest in. Second, he avoids buying stocks when the level of hype around them is much higher than their long-term average.

Despite these principles, Sundaram acknowledges there are times when one must bite the bullet and let go of a position, if one's hypothesis does not play out as expected.

For him, the typical waiting period is three years. If a stock does not perform satisfactorily within this timeframe, and if there is no significant, measurable improvement in the company's fundamentals, he will let it go. He explains, 'This waiting period of mine is three years—there is no science behind it. It's just that, in my opinion, it is a reasonable period that an investor would want to give to a portfolio manager.'

Democracy in investing

Sundaram firmly believes that while teamwork and open discussions are essential when managing a portfolio, democracy should stop at the stage of penultimate discussions. The ultimate decision regarding the inclusion or exclusion of stocks in a portfolio should rest solely with the portfolio manager, as accountability for errors cannot be shared by a committee or group.

Sundaram emphasizes that while checks and balances are crucial—such as periodic reviews of the portfolio manager's performance and adherence to the investment strategy by a board of trustees or board of directors—portfolio decisions are best made by an individual. However, it is important that the portfolio manager listens to different viewpoints and seeks opinions that challenge original assumptions before arriving at a conclusion.

Sundaram credits Edward De Bono's book *I Am Right, You Are Wrong* as a valuable resource for investors. He explains, 'The essence of the book is that there is no need for rigidity in thinking. If argument A is right, that does not necessarily mean that argument B is wrong. Both can be right in different situations. The same is true in stock-market investing.'

Mistakes and motivation

When asked under what circumstances mistakes can become demotivating, Sundaram responds emphatically, 'I hope this never happens!' and goes on to explain. 'If you are traveling by road and find too many potholes, are late to work repeatedly, find problems in the office such as your lunch getting messed up due to infrastructure, you are getting late to the airport for a flight, all this negativity around India still makes me bullish on India'. Sundaram does not believe that there is any country where there are no problems. If the problems are not infrastructure-related, they would probably be other kinds of problems.

To stay motivated despite challenges and mistakes, Sundaram avoids comparing one country with another that appears more developed in terms of infrastructure or one situation with another that seems less catastrophic. Instead, he focuses on progress over time, comparing the current state of India's infrastructure to what it was a few decades ago. Similarly, he evaluates new mistakes made today against repeated errors from earlier cycles. By adopting this perspective, Sundaram finds enough reasons to remain encouraged.

Mistakes of others: The loser's game

The inimitable and ever-quotable Warren Buffett once remarked, 'What gives you opportunities is other people doing dumb things'.[1]

Sundaram believes that the excessive greed, fear, hubris or trepidation of market participants lead to opportunities for those who manage to avoid such mistakes.

To capitalize on this, he feels one needs a temperament that resists the pull of hype. By avoiding stocks or sectors with excessive expectations, reliance on uncertain favourable news, businesses with poor performance or weak management, one can reduce the likelihood of disappointments later on.

Fewer mistakes lead to better overall results. Could something have been done differently to reduce the chances of mistakes and increase success, whether through education or allocation, I ask Sundaram. His response, not surprisingly, echoes what he has shared earlier in this chapter: 'Quite contrary to popular perceptions, success in investing does not have a high level of correlation to the educational qualifications of the investor. It does need a basic understanding of mathematics and accounting, but more importantly, it requires a temperament that stays detached from the overwhelming sentiments of greed and fear.'

Public image and rational decision making

Sundaram recognizes that as a public figure, the scrutiny can be harsh, with media and investors often focusing on mistakes rather than successes. He views this as 'very much part of the game', and takes it on the chin. To address this, Sundaram and his team conduct regular portfolio reviews with clients, discussing both stocks that have performed and those that have not. For the latter, Sundaram believes in revisiting the original rationale for the investment and explaining whether those reasons are still valid. However, he acknowledges that recognizing a mistake in the present does not prevent future mistakes.

'We live in a dynamic world,' he says, 'and circumstances change all the time. The stock market is a function of hundreds of variables, which keep changing.' While previous mistakes may push one to be more cautious, new circumstances will inevitably lead to new errors. For Sundaram, the role of an investment and risk manager is to mitigate the impact of such mistakes when they occur.

Reflecting on mistakes, Sundaram says he is amazed at the similarities in their causes across various fields. The most common cause, he notes, is the desire to always be the best. This classic mistake of making the best an enemy of the good inevitably leads to severe disappointment later.

In a world that often glorifies high-risk, fast-reward strategies, Sundaram's investment philosophy and approach stand as testaments to the merits of patience and thorough research, proving that sometimes, the best way to get ahead is to take your time—and perhaps, not take yourself too seriously along the way.

CHAPTER 14

JYOTI JAIPURIA

The investment pioneer and deep diver

JYOTI is a seasoned market veteran with thirty-seven years of outstanding experience, yet he maintains a low profile, letting his fund, Valentis, speak for itself through its performance and newsletters to investors.

Of his thirty-seven years in the industry, he spent twenty-one leading at DSP Merrill Lynch and eight at ICICI, and was recognized as one of India's top strategists by leading foreign institutional investors. An alumnus of IIM Ahmedabad, Jyoti believes the best learnings come from having skin in the game and focusing on research rather than market noise. He advocates a scientific process involving screening, modelling for fair valuations, incorporating sentiment and psychology into decision-making and avoiding market noise and herd mentality.

Jyoti is greatly inspired by Benjamin Graham's quote 'buy not on optimism, but on arithmetic', which teaches the importance of not being swayed by market moves on prices and highs, and focusing instead on deciphering data to understand a company's intrinsic value.

He focuses on balancing stock risk with reward, aiming to find companies where the potential returns can be significantly greater than the risks taken.

Jyoti begins our conversation by emphasizing that education and upbringing can play a significant role in shaping a person's psychology. He believes that most investment mistakes stem from psychological factors—primarily fear and greed. He points out that the fear of equities declining in the short term often drives people to stick to fixed deposits, thereby eroding their wealth over the long term.

On the topic of greed, Jyoti remarks, 'Trying to get rich too quickly makes investors take unnecessary risks, such as speculative trading or buying stocks that are rumoured to move up quickly. Invariably, these poorly researched positions lead to losses.' He highlights a common mistake many investors make: chasing the dream of becoming rich quickly instead of focusing on consistent growth, without realizing that speed may thrill, but it also kills.

Emphasizing that mistakes are not a one-size-fits-all phenomenon, Jyoti elaborates that fewer mistakes are typically made when buying stocks during a crisis.

He attributes this to three key reasons: First, valuations are generally cheap during a crisis, so most stocks are bought at low rates. Second, with the economy under stress, investors tend to stress-test all assumptions and are, in general, more conservative in their future outlook. Third, since stock prices do not rise quickly during a crisis, there is more time to do thorough research on potential investments.

The opposite often happens during bull markets. Jyoti, therefore, emphasizes that crises can be an investor's friend, offering opportunities to buy at low valuations. However, this should only be done after conducting careful research as no two companies will tackle a crisis or seize opportunities the same way.

I ask Jyoti how he typically realizes when a mistake had been made, and whether this awareness comes from intuition, results, revaluation or another factor.

Smiling, he replies, 'There are two ways to recognize mistakes—one is when the share price performs contrary to your expectations, and the other is when the business does not perform in line with your expectations.'

He explains that one should always focus on the business itself—this includes everything from management's vision, capital-allocation policies and long-term strategies to current margins and sales performance. If a stock price declines while one is positive about the company, the key is to evaluate whether the mistake lies in the initial assessment of the business. If the fundamental analysis remains sound, it is not necessarily a mistake. However, it is also possible that an investor paid too high a valuation for the company, which warrants re-evaluation.

Jyoti highlights a common investor error: focusing on a stock's fifty-two-week highs and lows or its decline relative to the current market price, rather than looking at the business's current condition and future potential.

He further adds that the focus should be on understanding whether the mistake lies in the assessment of the business or the promoter rather than the stock price. He shares some key rules he follows:

If the promoter's vision deviates from what was originally discussed or expected, the stock is sold. A common mistake investors make, he notes, is becoming attached to the stock price rather than the vision of company.

When the capital-allocation policy appears unsound, for example, there is unrelated diversification, the first step is to engage in a discussion with the promoter to understand their rationale. If the promoter cannot convincingly justify their actions, the stock is sold.

Long-term growth prospects becoming unclear is another critical factor. This itself could be due to mistakes in analysis, such as being too optimistic on demand, or external changes like shifts in government policy, the entry of new competitors, or the launch of new products that reduce the addressable market for the concerned company's product. In such cases, the entire investment thesis is re-evaluated. If the results of the analysis are unfavourable, the stock is sold, even at a loss.

Jyoti's approach emphasizes the importance of continuous evaluation and re-evaluation of investment decisions. Decisions should be based on facts rather than being influenced by biases such as attachment to a stock or its price. An investor should be pragmatic, selling even at a loss if the facts turn unfavourable.

He elaborates on another rule: If cyclical factors have weakened near-term earnings but the long-term outlook remains intact, then no immediate action is taken. In fact, if a significant drop in share prices occurs due to weak earnings, he may consider buying more. He therefore believes in evaluating a business rather than fixating on the stock price. Many investors, he notes, make the mistake of averaging down despite a deterioration in fundamentals. He, however, advocates averaging down only when the fundamentals remain intact or improve.

I ask Jyoti if there are tools such as meditation, quantitative analysis or a referral board that help minimize mistakes.

Pausing for a moment to gather his thoughts, Jyoti responds, 'We review all our holdings regularly to assess how the business is performing.' He elaborates by explaining his approach, which entails analysing multiple aspects, including: high-frequency data such as industry and company volume numbers; dealer discussions, focusing not only on current volumes and price trends but also on shifts in strategy and market share of all players in the industry; and meetings with competitors and customers.

He stresses the importance of looking beyond a single company and engaging in competitor analysis. 'If your company is gaining market share and profitability, there may be a shift worth noting. And if it is losing, that too should be examined.'

I ask Jyoti if there were instances where judgements he thought were mistakes ended up yielding favourable results. If so, why did he classify them as mistakes? Or were there changes in circumstance that turned those mistakes into a bonanza? This is akin to Raamdeo Agarwal's decision on Eicher, which he admitted to buying for its Volvo business but ultimately benefitted from its motorcycles.

Jyoti explains that he considers four possible outcomes to an investment decision. One, the process is right and outcome favourable, which is the ideal situation. Two, the process is right but the outcome is unfavourable, which is disappointing but not disheartening as the process was correct. Three, the process is wrong but the outcome is favourable, which is a lucky break, but one must work to rectify the flaws in the process. Lastly, the process wrong and the outcome is unfavourable, in which case one should gracefully accept that one got what one deserved and focus on improving the thought process to make it more efficient.

He delves into his further, noting that the third situation might not seem like a mistake to most people, as the outcome is favourable. For example, an investor buys a stock and it appreciates. However, this success is attributable to luck rather than skill. For example, the market might have risen, lifting the stock with it, or government policies could have changed for the better, or a competitor might have faced issues.

Jyoti thus emphasizes the importance of not only a sound evaluation process but also of distinguishing between skill and luck in investment outcomes. Taking credit for an outcome that was due more to luck than skill can be misleading. Instead, one should work towards improving processes to ensure better outcomes that are based on skill.

I ask him if he has a process in place to prevent mistakes from becoming fatal.

He responds thoughtfully, 'Our philosophy rests on assessing where the business and its earnings are going over next three years and aligning our investment decisions accordingly. Our constant endeavour is to focus on whether this is changing. Cyclical upturns and downturns are part of any stock's journey, and we try our best not to get perturbed by a single bad quarter as long as the future outlook is good.'

He elaborates further, explaining how their 360° philosophy plays an important role in keeping abreast of company fundamentals. 'We are in regular touch with a company's dealers, as well as those of its competitors and suppliers, who typically give you the first signs of a liquidity crunch. These interactions help us detect early signals of trouble in the industry or company, enabling us to exit the stock if necessary.'

He further adds that another key principle he follows is to exit if there are problems with the company's capital allocation unless he is convinced of the reasons for such a divergence. For instance, unrelated diversification or fresh equity raises must have a favourable outcome ahead for him to continue holding the stock.

I ask Jyoti if he believes he has evolved over time by learning from his mistakes or the mistakes of others, or if he considers the human mind to be too captivated by greed, fear and excesses to avoid revisiting the same mistakes.

He shares that he has indeed evolved, learning from both his own mistakes as well as those of others. However, he acknowledges that every few years he hears the phrase 'this time it is different'. 'That is the most dangerous phrase—it is never different,' he emphasizes.

He then explains, 'I work on the principle that we cannot eliminate mistakes. What I focus on is the risk–reward equation—how much we bet on the stocks where we were wrong versus how much we bet on the stocks where we were right'.

When I ask Jyoti how he differentiates between errors of commission and omission and what he does to improve his thinking, he is quick to respond. It is clear that his philosophy of investing is a deep-rooted process.

'There are five types of investment mistakes we focus on,' he explains. 'Not buying a stock that has shot up, not seizing enough of a stock, buying but selling too early, buying too early and losing time value, and buying a stock that goes down.'

He highlights how most investors tend to consider only the last one as a mistake. 'The general tendency is to keep holding the stock that has fallen till it comes back to the purchase price. However, in this process, we tend to lose significant opportunity cost elsewhere'.

I ask Jyoti about instances in his career where he might have taken an investment bet that seemed to be a mistake, resulting in a drawdown, yet he persisted—either leading to a bigger mistake or a turnaround. I was curious about how he managed to balance ego and commitment bias for a better outcome.

Jyoti shares his experience. 'We have seen that most of our multibaggers went down first before they went up. We typically tend to focus on the fundamentals rather than the share price. If we believe earnings are likely to go in the right direction, we continue to hold the stock or even add more.'

He admits, 'More than ego, there is often a bias to give the benefit of doubt to the company once you have bought its stock. For example, if a sudden court case causes a downturn in the stock, we may tend to believe the company will win the case.'

To handle such scenarios, Jyoti explains that they follow the 'what if' rule. This involves analysing what would happen in terms of return expectations if the company wins the case versus the potential impact if it loses. The goal is to minimize subjectivity by basing the process to objective rules.

I ask him how he navigates differing opinions within his team, especially if some prove right and others wrong. I wanted to know how he balances contrasting views within his camp to arrive at a favourable or intended outcome.

He explains that their investment process ensures every team member has a voice in decision-making. He strives to create a team that shares the same fundamental thought process yet differs in perspectives and approaches. For instance, some members focus more on the bigger picture, while others look at the finer details of numbers and ratios. Some have a more value-oriented perspective while others lean towards growth-oriented strategies.

He elaborates that the goal is to incorporate all views during the analysis phase. The final decision is then made based on the base-case scenario for the stock, weighed against potential risks and the probability of those risks materializing. 'There is no perfect stock where no one can identify any risks,' he shares, adding that he gets more concerned if the team thinks they have found such a stock.

Most of the time, they have a clear rationale for buying the stock and a set of risks they identify. He emphasizes the need to balance new stock additions with the existing portfolio, which may require selling something to fund the new position.

He also highlights their practice of reviewing both successful and failed investments in an endeavour to derive lessons for the future.

He notes, 'Accepting that nothing is perfect in investing and overcoming an overconfidence bias if we believe we own the best stocks is a great learning from mistakes.'

I ask Jyoti whether, if an outcome is favourable, he tends to persist with the team members who got it right, even though the next outcome could be different.

He is quick to respond, defending his confidence in the process. 'We pride ourselves more on the process than the people.' He explains that as a rule, the entire team is involved in all decisions. As some sectors are better understood by the team, the comfort level is higher when buying in those sectors and backing the analysts who cover them. He acknowledges, 'It's not like we will never go wrong in those sectors, but the probability of getting it right is much higher given our knowledge of the sector.'

This reflects the importance of knowing what one is buying and avoiding the common mistake of favouring complexity over simplicity or buying into stories rather than facts.

I ask Jyoti about the role of exuberance and hubris in eliminating bad decisions, particularly whether the comfort of being very large enables a mistake to go unnoticed or if the codification of a process and its transparency justifies making a mistake.

He notes that bull markets often lead to hubris, where investors tend to attribute their returns to their intelligence when in reality, it may simply be a case of rising tides lifting all boats. He observes that more mistakes are made in bull markets as people get caught up in the exuberance, unlike in bear markets.

Jyoti explains that his team typically underperforms slightly during the last phase of a bull market because they tend to become cautious early. While this may seem like a mistake at the start, he shares that it has served them well over the past couple of decades. He offers a pertinent quote from Benjamin Graham: 'Even the intelligent investor is likely to need considerable willpower to keep from following the crowd.'

I ask Jyoti about the impact of his personal life on his decision-making and whether he separates the personal and professional spheres to make better investment choices.

Jyoti thinks deeply before responding. He explains that he strives to keep his personal and work life distinct. To achieve this, he spends time every day on activities like yoga, swimming or walking, which help de-clutter his mind and reduce stress. He also emphasizes the importance of his process-driven, team-based investment approach, which helps mitigate the impact of personal challenges on his investment decisions.

I ask Jyoti whether mistakes can become a source of motivation. He shares that he believes the goal should always be to use mistakes as a motivational factor. His team regularly reviews both their winners and losers to gain lessons for the future. This ensures they do not focus solely on what went wrong, which can be demotivating, but instead look at all mistakes positively as opportunities for improvement.

He also acknowledges that there are times when one hits a bad patch—when stocks go contrary to expectations, and the team begins to have self-doubt. At such times, he stresses, it is important to reassure everyone that 'this too shall pass'. As the team leader, it is especially important for him to believe this, and he often draws on history, pointing out that similar bad patches have occurred before, but they have always bounced back.

I ask Jyoti about the impact of external shortcomings beyond the market on decision-making. I reference common frustrations, such as encountering potholes during a commute, repeatedly being late to work or missing a flight due to poor road infrastructure. I ask how such negativity influences his bullish outlook on India.

Jyoti reflects that the glass can be half full or half empty, depending on one's perspective. He elaborates by giving the example of China, which has seen spectacular GDP growth over the last twenty years due largely to spending on infrastructure. However, he says that he now has a negative view on China, as he believes it has overbuilt its infrastructure—with highways without cars and townships without residents. Markets, he explains, move on 'delta' changes, that is, bad infrastructure getting less worse, which is the case with India currently. This lays the ground for his bullish stance.

He continues, 'First, building infrastructure can cause GDP to rise, similar to what China achieved over the past twenty years. Second, the current profit margins of Indian companies exist despite the poor infrastructure. Can margins improve as infrastructure improves is what I ask myself, and this reflects in lower logistics costs and reduced working capital through "just in time" ordering.'

Before concluding, I ask Jyoti what, on reflection, he would like to change if he could go back in time—whether in terms of education or allocation or any other aspect to reduce mistakes and increase success rates.

He candidly admits to two areas he would change. First, he would have sized some of his positions better in the early stages. 'I was probably too risk averse, and though we identified many multibaggers early, in hindsight, we didn't buy enough.'

Second, he shares, 'Selling winners too early is another mistake I would like to change.'

When managing public money, mistakes can also be caused by the public itself—for example, when investors pull out at a time when they should be putting more money in. Yet, the result reflects poorly on the portfolio manager. I ask Jyoti how he balances public perception and rational decision-making.

He explains that their guiding principle is the understanding that they are unlikely to get money when they most need it (when there is 'blood on the streets') and will instead receive funds when they least need them (at high valuations after a sharp rally in stocks). To mitigate this, they maintain higher cash levels in portfolios when they believe valuations are high and encourage investors to invest through systematic investment plans (SIPs).

He emphasizes their efforts to educate investors on their goal, which is to get superior risk-adjusted returns over a three-to-five-year period. Despite these efforts, Jyoti acknowledges that investors do question every stock that underperforms. In such cases, the team patiently explains two points: first, to focus on the overall portfolio returns, and second, the rationale behind buying the stock in question. If they do go wrong, then Jyoti and his team admit the mistake to all investors, but often have to urge them to be patient. Regardless of whether they got it right or wrong, the process of learning and improving continues.

I want to understand, with all Jyoti's wisdom on mistakes, his extensive experience and the many market ups and downs he has navigated, why he continues to make mistakes.

He patiently explains that mistakes are an inherent part of the investment process. 'Firstly, when we buy stocks, we are forecasting the future of the company. This can be influenced by many factors, including management strategy and execution, decisions of competitors, government policies and so on—none of which are in our control. We try to forecast these to the best of our abilities, but some things can change, which can lead to errors. Secondly, we predict share prices based on the expected fundamentals of companies. While we believe earnings and share prices move hand-in-hand over the long term, in the short term, many factors can make share prices go in different directions, such as the monetary policies of central banks or changes in interest rates. Thirdly, our job is not to eliminate risk or the chances of going wrong. Our job is to get asymmetric returns for every unit of risk we take. Thus, we can reduce mistakes by buying low-risk companies, but then the returns will also be low. In fact, our 'three U's' philosophy—undervalued, under-owned, under-performing stocks—acknowledges that while the chances of mistakes may be higher, the returns when we are right can be huge.'

He elaborates further, discussing two types of mistakes they constantly strive to learn from to avoid repetition. The first type, he explains, involves errors in the fundamental assessment of a company or industry.

He emphasizes the importance of staying abreast of the latest technological changes that could render an industry or company obsolete, noting that moat erosion often comes from unexpected sources. He cites Kodak as an example, where the digital camera eroded its moat—not because of competition within the film space, but because the demand for film itself reduced drastically. To address this, they try to closely monitor technological trends, while recognizing that most changes follow a 'hockey stick curve'. As a result, they try to exit early. For instance, while electric vehicles may take a long time to become mainstream, they focus on assessing how significantly such a shift could impact a company and assume a low terminal value for them.

The second type of mistake, he continues, arises from behavioural aspects, which are often more difficult to control. 'As a general rule, we prefer investing in segments that are not the flavour of the market—our three U's philosophy naturally takes us there. We are also very valuation conscious and are willing to walk away from a stock early if need be.' He goes on to acknowledge that, as a result, they tend to underperform during the last phase of a bull market when euphoria takes over.

Another key insight emerges: don't make the mistake of confusing a falling bull market with the assumption that it is not justified. Euphoria may mark the end of a bull run and cause a reversion to the mean. It is important to recognize that there will always be a bull market and a bear market depending on the stocks one focuses on.

With this, I thank Jyoti for a beautiful dialogue and leave with many thoughts to revisit my own thinking.

CHAPTER 15

VIRAJ MEHTA

The rising innovator with an unconventional approach

VIRAJ Mehta, well regarded for his astute investment acumen and strategic insight, has carved a remarkable niche for himself in the Indian financial landscape. Hailing from Ahmedabad, Viraj was serving as managing director at Equirus Capital at the time of this interview, with a phenomenal investment track record over the past decade. An alumnus of the prestigious Management Development Institute (MDI), Gurgaon, his fascination with numbers began early. As this book goes to print, Viraj has transitioned to a new venture, with the announcement of his new fund eagerly awaited.

A seasoned veteran in Indian financial markets, Viraj is widely respected for his sharp analytical skills. However, like every accomplished investor, his journey has been shaped not just by his successes but also by the mistakes he has encountered along the way. His willingness to reflect on these errors and learn from them has been integral to his growth as an investor.

I ask Viraj whether investing mistakes could be linked to upbringing, including factors such as education and exposure. He responds that during the early years of his investing journey, he did commit mistakes, such as selling stocks too early.

He acknowledges that upbringing plays a significant role in influencing one's approach to handling initial success. Viraj explains that given his middle-class upbringing, he was unaccustomed to managing significant sums of money. As a result, he made the mistake of selling early in his initial investments, a misstep he only understood at a later stage.

Viraj emphasizes that the value of holding investments in the stock market is an important learning. Holding investments over the long term is a proven approach that offers several key advantages. As investments grow, the returns earned also begin to generate their own returns, creating a snowball effect that can significantly increase one's wealth over time.

Historical trends show that despite short-term dips, the stock market generally trends upward over the long term. Successful companies often see their stock prices appreciate significantly over time, rewarding patient investors with substantial capital gains.

I next ask Viraj to share his thoughts on the likelihood of making mistakes during calm markets compared to crisis-driven situations such as Covid-19, 9/11 or similar events. Viraj is of the view that mistakes made in calm times are often fundamentally different from those made during extreme events like Covid-19.

He believes that tough phases do not give you the time to buy back the same or better opportunities. The recovery in such cases is often quick, across the spectrum and unpredictable. In contrast, calm periods provide more time to reflect on opportunities.

Viraj's insights highlight the delicate balance investors must maintain between the dangers of complacency in calm markets and the pitfalls of panic during crisis. Both environments present distinct challenges, but the overarching message is the importance of discipline, preparation and emotional control.

Lessons learned

Discussing the first realization of mistakes, Viraj explains that this awareness typically emerges through business results over time, which leads to a revalidation of the original thesis. He prefers to give management with a strong operational track record at least eight to ten quarters before deciding to exit a position.

Business results, he notes, offer critical insights into the company's actual performance compared to expectations, helping investors determine whether their assumptions about growth, profitability and market position were accurate. However, he acknowledges that there are instances where management consistently delivers strong operational performance over a business cycle, but due to a poor entry decision, the position might need to be sold before reaping meaningful returns. He cites his personal experience with TCPL Packaging as an example.

This is a sound approach, enabling an investor to make comprehensive assessments and thus avoid premature judgements that could lead to missing out on the company's true long-term potential.

Rectification of mistakes

When I asked about admitting mistakes and rectifying them, Viraj candidly acknowledges having identified errors during his investment journey. To course correct, he stopped buying incrementally in new client accounts and focused more on conducting thorough due diligence on the business, analysing the fundamentals, growth potential, management quality and industry trends before making decisions.

Viraj has a small team of five people who maintain constant communication on any decisions taken to reduce mistakes or quickly rectify them to mitigate their impact. He strongly believes that having complete trust in his team is the most important part of the process.

Fortunate misjudgements

Reflecting on decisions that initially appeared to be mistakes but ultimately led to positive outcomes, Viraj recalls his position in Alkyl Amines Chemicals, which was his largest holding at the start of 2020. A sudden surge in demand for one of its products, Acetonitrile, led to a significant expansion of spreads, which completely changed the company's margin profile within a couple of quarters. Margins peaked at 38 per cent, up from 20-22 per cent—a scenario he had never considered during his initial analysis. He describes the event as a lottery that he could not capitalize on. It was an instance where initial doubts or concerns resulted in unexpected success.

Viraj also shares his magic formula for avoiding fatal errors, emphasizing the role of position sizing to control the financial impact of mistakes. He tends to allocate only a small portion of capital to companies that are borderline investment cases, and he doesn't mind averaging up once the thesis plays out successfully. This approach helps balance potential returns with acceptable risk levels, ensuring no single position can cause significant damage to the portfolio if it performs poorly.

By carefully calibrating position sizes, investors can optimize their portfolios for growth while minimizing the impact of any losses.

Mistake-driven learning

Viraj mentions that while investing in stocks, he strives to avoid greed, which he believes is essential for long-term success. He explains that greed can lead to impulsive decisions, such as holding on to a stock for too long in the hope of higher gains or chasing investments without proper analysis. He highlights how easy it is to become captivated by an increasing stock price and emphasizes the importance of critically evaluating your initial decision to pass on a stock. With more years and grey hair, Viraj acknowledges the effort he puts into maintaining objectivity and preventing emotional biases from clouding his investment strategy.

Experience, he notes, teaches investors the importance of patience, discipline, sound research, analysis and emotional control—all crucial for making sound decisions in both bull and bear markets. The experiential learning builds confidence and sharpens judgement, ultimately leading to more informed and successful investment choices.

Errors of commission and omission

Viraj is of the view that in the context of financial reporting and investment analysis, only errors of commission are reported in the books, while missed opportunities are not publicly reported, making it harder to assess their impact. He says that as a policy, he tries not to anchor to a specific price level in either type of error.

Viraj's insights highlight the need for investors and analysts to be aware of the limitations of financial reporting and to consider the possibility of missed opportunities when evaluating a company's performance. This could involve examining industry trends, strategic decisions and competitive positioning to gauge whether a company is seizing or missing growth opportunities.

Balancing ego and making decisions

Managing and balancing ego bias and commitment bias are crucial for making rational and effective investment decisions. Both biases can lead to suboptimal investment choices if not addressed properly. Viraj stresses the importance of making decisions based on data rather than individual opinions. He sets a certain time frame, such as twelve quarters, before making a judgement on a business. He notes that being more than two years early is equivalent to being wrong. As a team, they focus on long-term outcomes and are not swayed by short-term news. He encourages discussions where people agree to disagree, as this helps in making better decisions. Involving multiple team members reduces the influence of individual biases and provides a more balanced view.

This demonstrates how, by managing ego and commitment biases effectively, investors can make more rational decisions, avoid common pitfalls and enhance their long-term investment performance. Balancing these biases involves a combination of self-awareness, disciplined processes and external validation to achieve better outcomes in investment strategies.

Viraj also remarks that his decisions are based on data and not on preconceived notions. 'We believe risk–reward should be favourable,' he states. 'In fact, a lot of times businesses that have survived tough times come out stronger.' Reliance on personal beliefs, hearsay or market rumours exposes individuals to significant risks, as these factors can cloud judgement and lead to irrational choices. On the other hand, a data-driven approach involves analysing financial statements, studying market trends, understanding economic indicators and evaluating company metrics. This method helps investors identify opportunities and risks more accurately, leading to more informed and strategic decisions.

On managing hubris, Viraj comments that being large is a problem. He explains that with smaller capital, the impact cost of being wrong and selling is much lower.

Balancing challenging periods in life

Speaking about his approach to personal challenges and how he separates his personal and professional life to make sound decisions, Viraj recommends making key decisions after discussions within the team. This helps eliminate personal biases or circumstances.

This highlights an important lesson: individuals are often reluctant to communicate with others. However, during challenging periods, such as health issues or personal problems, it is crucial to adopt a structured and mindful approach to ensure that business decisions remain unaffected.

Mistakes: Motivation or demotivation

Viraj views investing as an unemotional, math-based business. He doesn't take profits or losses personally, acknowledging that there are many variables that can affect stock outcomes. Mistakes can act as motivation or demotivation, depending on how one lets it affect their mindset. The more unemotional one is, the better they are as an investor.

This perspective offers a valuable lesson: mistakes in investing are inevitable, but it is how you respond to them that ultimately determines your success. The most common error that individuals, especially young investors, make is allowing emotions to dictate their decisions. When profits and losses are taken personally, there is a higher likelihood of making impulsive choices driven by fear, greed or frustration, which can derail long-term goals. It is critical to approach investing with a calm, unemotional mindset in order to transform mistakes into valuable lessons rather than setbacks.

An unemotional investor sees losses as part of the journey, not as personal failures. They don't celebrate profits with reckless abandon nor do they mourn losses with self-doubt. Instead, they focus on analysing their decisions and moving forward with a clear mind. One should remember that the market does not care about one's feelings; it rewards discipline and patience. By detaching emotionally, you not only minimize the impact of inevitable mistakes but also position yourself to capitalize on opportunities with a level-headed approach.

Bullish on India

Viraj remains bullish on India despite the everyday challenges associated with the country's development. He believes the negativity around India in this regard is irrelevant as such basic problems persist even in developed countries. He strongly believes that India is delivering on all the aspects that matter, despite its massive scale. He feels lucky to have been born in a country like India, given the country's dynamic economic landscape, abundant opportunities, booming IT sector, diverse investment sectors and strategic advantages.

Converting what looks like a mistake into a favourable result

I ask Viraj how he manages to balance his temperament to convert what initially looks like a mistake into a favourable result.

Viraj believes that finding a better opportunity helps maintain balance. 'Recently, in one of our large positions, the government decided to change the taxation methodology, which essentially meant the complete disruption of the business model.' Viraj and his team immediately exited the position at a significant drawdown and focused on deploying the capital in better opportunities.

This highlights the value of mastering emotional discipline, learning from both one's own and others' mistakes, and continuously adapting one's strategy. A long-term perspective also helps one stay grounded and reduces the emotional impact of temporary setbacks. One should regularly review their portfolios and investment decisions and reflect on what has worked and what hasn't. This ongoing assessment helps one identify patterns in the decision-making process and fine-tune strategy over time.

Balancing public image with rational decision-making

I also ask how he balances public image with rational decision-making, especially when managing public money. Mistakes can sometimes be caused by the public itself, for example, investors may pull out when it is actually time to invest. Yet the results of such actions are often attributed to the fund manager publicly. Viraj responds that choosing the right kind of clients and earning their trust are the two most important parts of managing external capital. If done properly, it is not difficult to balance public image with rational decision-making.

This offers an important lesson: it is crucial to choose clients whose values, risk tolerance and financial goals align with one's investment philosophy. While no one can guarantee returns, consistently applying a rational and disciplined investment approach that aligns with a client's goals helps earn their trust over time. Making well-researched, data-driven decisions and avoiding speculative or aggressive strategies that could harm one's reputation are key factors to consider.

I also ask Viraj about his approach to handling situations where his portfolio is performing well, but as a public figure, the media, investors or potential investors focus only on mistakes to showcase a wrong result. I was whether, in such times, Viraj dilutes this as part of overall performance, or goes into second-level thinking to treat the mistake as a learning opportunity.

Viraj explains that his focus remains on the performance of the portfolio as a whole. He acknowledges that there will always be some positions where he will lose capital, but as long as the strike rate is maintained and the overall portfolio performance is strong, he tends to ignore such cases.

Continuing to make mistakes

Viraj's final take on mistakes is that errors are a part of life, not only in investing but also in general. He also underlines that the endeavour should be to make new mistakes and not repeat old ones. Being an avid reader and observer of the world, he incorporates lessons learned from mistakes into his investment process.

Over time, investors learn how to improve future decisions and minimize errors. As mentioned earlier, it is crucial for market investors to conduct thorough research and analysis on the asset, industry and overall market conditions. Developing a clear investment strategy is equally critical to developing a well-defined plan that provides a roadmap to stay focused.

When it comes to learning from mistakes, it is advisable to keep a detailed investment journal where one records the rationale for each investment, the outcome, and the lessons learnt from it. Regularly reviewing this journal can provide insights into patterns of behaviour that may lead to mistakes. This might involve adjusting your risk-management practices, altering the research methods or changing the decision-making process.

One should remember that mistakes are part of the learning process, and with the right approach, they can be transformed into valuable lessons that can guide one towards better investment outcomes.

CHAPTER 16

PRASHANT KHEMKA
The experienced portfolio navigator

PRASHANT Khemka, the founder of Oak Capital Group of Companies, needs no introduction. He is perhaps one of the very few fund managers to have opened offices simultaneously in three countries—India, Singapore and Mauritius. Prashant then expanded Oak Capital to London and Switzerland. Remarkably, he managed to start and expand the firm within just seven years, between 2017 and 2024.

Undoubtedly, such a feat requires confidence and calculation in equal measure. He gained this confidence by working at Goldman Sachs Asset Management (GSAM), where he started as an equity analyst, then co-chaired an equity fund worth $30 billion before moving to the Global Emerging Markets (GEM) division at Goldman Sachs. Under him, GEM's equity grew from less than $500 million to over $2.6 billion.

During his tenure as the chief investment officer (CIO) of GEM, the fund he ran was accorded the rare AAA rating from Citywire and an Elite rating from Fund Calibre, among other achievements. As a result of working in both local and global markets during his stint in Goldman Sachs and beyond, Prashant brings a unique perspective that benefits both himself and those who invest with his company.

Successful careers in investment banking are often backed by a strong education from reputable institutions. A mechanical engineering graduate from Mumbai University, Prashant pursued an MBA in finance from the renowned Vanderbilt University, where he was awarded the prestigious Matt Wigginton Leadership Award for outstanding performance in finance. Beyond education, Prashant is a fellow of the Ananta Aspen Centre, India.

Mistakes and investments are two words people do not want to see together in a sentence. However, no investment banker has ever achieved success without making some mistakes along the way. Prashant opens up to me about what mistakes mean to him and how his journey with them has made him who he is today.

I begin our conversation by asking Prashant about the role of education and upbringing in investing. He immediately responds, 'I would say your success as well as your mistakes are bound to be impacted by your education and upbringing.'

He notes that these factors profoundly shape one's ability to make informed investment decisions. While this influence may not be deterministic, it is undeniable that it affects risk tolerance and decision-making processes, ultimately having an impact on one's investing career.

An important factor in determining why a mistake was made is examining when it was made. Time, therefore, is an important factor, according to Prashant. He explains, 'One of the differences could be that in times of crisis like Covid, decisions might have to be made under time constraints, whereas in so-called ordinary times, there might be less of those time constraints.'

Elaborating further, Prashant points out that when decisions are made with limited information and analysis, one can never fully grasp their potential impact. He notes that decision-making in times of crisis involves less of futurism or predictability, whereas in normal times, one must take future growth prospects into consideration.

Prashant explains, 'In India's context, in usual times, future growth prospects for the economy over the next decade or two, whether they are ultimately right or wrong, can be reasonably assumed in a certain narrow band of a few percentage points.' However, in a crisis like March 2020—the start of the Covid-19 pandemic—an investor has to make a decision to act or not with the knowledge that it is irrational to have any forecast of national or global economic growth over the next decade or two. When it is irrational to have such forecasts, it is more irrational to have any confidence in forecasts for individual companies, he elaborates.

He says, 'In ordinary times, you can rationally assume a certain normal distribution curve for outcomes such as economic growth and individual company forecasts. But in times of crisis like Covid, these normal curves start becoming flatter than in usual times. This is how it can be quantitatively explained.'

I move on to the question of realization. In the high-stress world of investment banking, timely recognition of mistakes is an important aspect. Prashant observes, 'The biggest mistakes, those involving substantial financial loss and opportunity cost, are generally realized over long period of time, and it is, I would say, a realization that comes from observation and reflection.'

However, he acknowledges that realization often comes too late, after significant damage has already been done. He notes that this realization can come about through various mechanisms, including noticing negative results, revalidating decisions and their consequences, intuition or reflection.

Prashant emphasizes that rectification involves avoiding or mitigating similar mistakes in the future. The first step towards admitting and rectifying a mistake is recognizing the error, which often involves acknowledging a significant financial loss due to an oversight, such as underestimating misgovernance or weak corporate governance within a company. Upon realizing the mistake, one should immediately exit the investment to minimize further losses.

Next, reflection on the mistake is crucial to learn from it and identify areas for improvement. This involves analysing the overlooked governance issues and understanding the importance of alignment between management, controlling shareholders and minority investors.

I ask Prashant if he uses tools like meditation or quantitative analysis to keep his mistakes in check. While acknowledging that he has tried meditation, he notes that one must have a clear mind, free from thoughts of mistakes while meditating. He feels that although meditation serves as a valuable practice for maintaining mental clarity, it is not directly used for analysing past errors. Instead, he emphasizes a more reflective approach to understanding mistakes.

Prashant explains that reflecting on his past—meticulously reviewing both failures and successes—provides profound insights into his decision-making process. He shares that he has invested significant time in contemplating his journey from the 1980s, when he began as a novice, to today. This reflective process has often revealed that learning from mistakes has been more beneficial than merely focusing on successes.

He highlights an important distinction: not every financial loss is inherently a mistake. Sometimes, what initially appears to be an error results in unexpected gains, which he describes as a 'lucky mistake'. There are occasions when a mistake leads to significant profits, which, in retrospect, might be deemed a stroke of luck rather than an actual error. Conversely, sound investments might not yield immediate results, but, in the long run, they are likely to prove rewarding.

Prashant then explores the importance of understanding the rationale behind mistakes. The key is not just to assess financial losses but to evaluate whether, with improved insight and experience, the same investment would be made again. If the answer is yes, it implies that the decision was not erroneous at that time. Conversely, if the answer is no, it signifies that the initial choice was indeed a mistake, prompting a thorough review of the lessons learned from that experience.

Taking the discussion further, I ask Prashant whether he has ever made decisions that were initially considered mistakes but ultimately turned out favourably. I was curious why he might still view them as mistakes despite their positive outcomes. Prashant explains that mistakes, which initially seem like misjudgements, can, due to changing circumstances, evolve into a bonanza.

He shares that it is often the case that one might make more money from errors than from meticulously planned investments, a recurring theme in his experience. Reflecting on various investments, he observes that even if a decision appeared profitable initially, a deeper analysis might reveal that the investment should never have been made in the first place. To illustrate, he adds, 'The company goes down by 20 per cent or more, or has gone nowhere for two or three decades, which is a huge loss as well. There have been such instances in my experience.'

Prashant's reflections underscore the importance of not only celebrating successes but also critically assessing mistakes. Even when mistakes yield favourable outcomes, the underlying decision-making process is scrutinized to understand and learn from these experiences, ensuring better future investment choices.

When I inquire whether he employs a particular thought process to prevent a mistake from becoming fatal, Prashant responds with characteristic clarity: 'In investing, there really are no mistakes that are truly fatal.'

He elaborates by explaining that he no longer uses leverage. However, he admits that he did take on leverage in his earlier days, which could indeed lead to a situation where one's investments could diminish to nothing. However, with no leverage, the risk of going to zero is significantly mitigated. Prashant also notes that concentrating all funds in one, two or a handful of stocks poses another risk of catastrophic loss. According to him, the key to avoiding a fatal mistake lies in diversification and avoiding excessive exposure to any single sector or market segment.

When I ask Prashant if he has evolved over time by learning from his own mistakes or those made by others, he responds, 'I have, and I think most investors—in all seriousness, all investors—do learn from their mistakes. I have definitely learnt a tremendous amount from the mistakes I have made.'

However, he notes that while personal mistakes contribute significantly to one's growth, observing and understanding the missteps of others can be equally enlightening, enriching one's investment wisdom and decision-making capabilities.

Prashant distinguishes between two types of errors in investment decisions: errors of commission and errors of omission.

Errors of commission, he explains, occur when a person invests money in a company or opportunity that ultimately turns out to be a poor choice. In other words, it's a mistake the person made by choosing to invest.

Errors of omission, on the other hand, relate to missed opportunities. These are situations where a person did not invest in an opportunity that later proves to be highly successful. This type of error is more about the cost of missed chances. Both types of errors are interrelated and illustrate the unpredictability of investment outcomes, says Prashant. Sometimes, a person might encounter a windfall, while at other times, they might face a setback. Even with sound decision-making, change can render previous choices less effective.

According to Prashant, if one evaluates a company and decides not to invest, but later realizes that, given the same circumstances, they should have invested, the missed opportunity is also an error of omission. This occurs when negligence, procrastination or other reasons lead to a missed investment opportunity that, upon re-evaluation, would have been worth pursuing, he says.

When asked how he manages ego and commitment bias, Prashant shares that he learned long ago that the stock market is indifferent to our ego and emotions. For successful investing, it's crucial not to let these factors influence decision-making. He acknowledges that while he may have made other mistakes, ego and emotional bias have not been significant issues for him personally.

When I ask Prashant how he navigates differing opinions within his investment team, he explains that even the best investment teams and investors are wrong about 40 to 50 per cent of the time, so it's important to accept that being right 100 per cent of the time is unrealistic.

The key is to focus on minimizing mistakes. For instance, he says, if a person is making the right decisions 45 per cent of the time, the aim should be to improve that to 43 per cent. This involves recognizing the inherently probabilistic nature of investing and continuously integrating probabilistic thinking into the decision-making process.

According to Prashant, investing is about understanding and managing uncertainties while striving to make more informed and accurate decisions based on one's own analysis and experience. He acknowledges that favourable outcomes in investing can sometimes occur even when mistakes are made, resulting in unexpected windfalls. However, according to him, investing is inherently non-deterministic. To accurately assess performance, he advises evaluating results over a longer period rather than basing judgements on just one or two years.

Prashant notes that performance measurement is a complex science, blending both skill and an element of luck. Over time, if an investor consistently achieves favourable outcomes, it is reasonable to give them the benefit of the doubt. He feels that long-term results provide a more accurate picture of an investor's ability and effectiveness.

Prashant, the seasoned investment banker, addresses the impact of exuberance and hubris on mistake management. He explains that exuberance—whether it manifests as overconfidence, excitement about a theme or complacency—can be detrimental. Overconfidence doesn't help in eliminating mistakes; rather, it often exacerbates them by increasing the likelihood of making errors without due intent or awareness. Understanding and managing exuberance is crucial to avoiding pitfalls.

Prashant elaborates on how, in the world of investing, overconfidence is a significant risk. Staying vigilant and consistent is crucial to maintaining performance and avoiding the pitfalls of complacency. He uses cricket as an analogy to illustrate his point. Even in a seemingly secure position, where a team is performing well with a substantial lead and few runs to win, overconfidence can lead to complacency. This can result in a sudden slide in performance if key players become careless or take unnecessary risks, ultimately jeopardizing the outcome.

He also points out that overconfidence can lead to failures in other areas, such as politics, where it has sometimes caused politicians to lose elections. The overarching lesson is that overconfidence and complacency are often the root causes of mistakes and performance decline.

Regarding the impact of mistakes, Prashant notes that the significance of a mistake depends on its size relative to the portfolio. For instance, a Rs 1 crore mistake in a Rs 10 crore portfolio is proportionately more significant than the same amount in a Rs 1,000 crore portfolio. In the larger portfolio, the Rs 1 crore mistake is a smaller percentage and might receive less scrutiny. However, it's important to recognize that a large mistake in absolute terms, regardless of the portfolio size, should still be addressed seriously.

Prashant also emphasizes that while many mistakes are made in investing, not all will yield valuable insights. Thus, focusing on the most significant errors is more productive. Codification of processes and transparency should ensure that mistakes are properly assessed and addressed. In Prashant's view, a well-defined process should facilitate the identification and correction of mistakes, rather than allowing them to be overlooked.

While mistakes have an immediate impact on one's psyche, they can either motivate or demotivate a person depending on their nature. When discussing the question of when a mistake becomes demotivating, Prashant explains that if a person learns from a mistake and can extract valuable lessons, it tends to be less demotivating, even if the mistake is significant. This learning, he believes, provides confidence that similar errors will be avoided in the future.

On the other hand, Prashant notes, if a person fails to derive any lessons from the mistakes they make, the experience can be quite demotivating. The larger the mistake, the more it can impact motivation, especially if it leads to frustration or an inability to identify actionable insights. Ultimately, he emphasizes, the key to maintaining motivation lies in the ability to learn from and address mistakes effectively.

Bullish on India

Speaking on why he is positive about India, Prashant notes that while India's infrastructure may lag behind more developed countries, the critical factor for equity market returns and economic growth is not the current state but the direction and pace of change. He emphasizes that India's recent advancements, even if they start from a lower baseline, can drive substantial growth and returns due to the significant improvements over time.

Prashant explains that investment returns are driven by market dynamics rather than by infrastructure alone. He notes that while Japan boasts some of the world's best infrastructure, it has not consistently delivered exceptional returns or growth. According to him, while strong infrastructure contributes to a high standard of living and reflects stock market wealth, equity returns are more influenced by change and the pace of that change than by the existing infrastructure stock.

He points out that in India's case, although its infrastructure is less developed compared to many countries, the rate and direction of change have been significant. This dynamic—where rapid improvements occur despite a lower starting point—can be more impactful on economic growth and equity market returns than the absolute level of infrastructure. He cites the example of Indian Railways over the past decade, noting that the progress in this sector has been notably rapid compared to the incremental improvements in Swiss Railways, which, while still among the best globally, have seen slower advancements.

Prashant also mentions the Vande Bharat trains, which represent a leap forward in Indian rail infrastructure. Despite being far from Swiss standards, the rapid progress in India's railway system illustrates how significant improvements in infrastructure can occur quickly, which can positively influence economic growth and market returns, he explains.

Sharing his perspective on turning a mistake into a favourable outcome, Prashant suggests that instead of waiting for the market to correct itself, investors should take proactive steps to address their mistakes. If an investor believes the market is undervaluing a company or making an error in its assessment, then it is their role to act on that conviction, he notes.

According to Prashant, an investor's goal is to identify opportunities where they believe they can achieve outsized returns because they see potential that the market has overlooked or underestimated. The hope, he explains, is that either the market will eventually correct its mistake and appreciate the company's value, or that the company will outperform expectations, validating the investor's thesis.

However, Prashant acknowledges that if an investor realizes they have made a mistake in evaluating the company's prospects, it is also reasonable to expect that the market may have similarly erred in its assessment. In such cases, he notes, addressing one's own misjudgements and adjusting their strategy is crucial. At the same time, expecting the market to correct itself is also part of the investment process.

I ask Prashant what he would change, in terms of education and allocation, to reduce mistakes if he could go back in time. He reflects that for a seasoned investor, education alone might not fully address past errors. Instead, he believes that deeper and more reflective analysis of mistakes at an early stage could have significantly reduced subsequent errors.

He explains that it's not just about one-off mistakes, such as misjudging a company's governance standards, but also about missed opportunities. These missed opportunities, whether they happened twenty years ago or more recently, represent both a personal and strategic loss. While it's impossible to completely eliminate mistakes—given that everyone, even the best mentors, will make around forty significant errors over their lifetime— focusing on understanding and learning from them can help reduce their frequency and impact.

Managing public funds is a serious responsibility, demanding both a deep respect for the investors' hard-earned money and an acute sense of accountability. Investment bankers often face pressure from various investors to make specific investment choices, but when these investments fail, the blame often falls on the bankers themselves.

When asked how he balances maintaining a positive public image with making rational decisions, Prashant responds that it's crucial to critically examine and learn from one's own mistakes. While it's important to address and understand these errors, the focus should be on the lessons learned rather than solely on correcting them to satisfy specific investors.

He acknowledges that performance relative to other investments and the actions of investors have limited influence on the internal mistakes made by the investment team. The responsibility of learning from these mistakes ultimately lies with the investors themselves. Investment managers can and do provide guidance, but each investor must also learn from their experiences with any fund manager.

When asked how he handles situations where the media focuses on a single poor investment among many successful ones to tarnish his reputation, Prashant responds that his investment team and he have a deep understanding and access to detailed information about their portfolio. The level of analytics and insight they have is far beyond what the media or outsiders can possess. Given this, they do not place significant weight on media portrayals or isolated incidents. Even if the media's portrayal were accurate, Prashant believes it would not impact their long-term assessment of mistakes. The focus remains on their thorough and informed evaluation of the portfolio's performance over time, rather than on external criticisms.

Despite his success and experience, Prashant acknowledges that mistakes are an inherent part of investing. Once again, he compares investing to cricket, where even top players make mistakes. They might get bowled out, misjudge a delivery, or face other mishaps despite being at the peak of their game. In cricket, the distinction between top players and others lies in how they manage their mistakes. The best players make fewer errors and score more runs in between those mistakes, which results in higher averages and better performance. Similarly, in investing, even the most skilled investors will make mistakes. What sets them apart is their ability to make more successful investments and achieve higher returns between those mistakes.

Just as cricket players aim to score more runs than their opponents, the goal for investors is to generate higher returns for their clients compared to others in the industry. It's about balancing the inevitable mistakes with achieving superior overall performance.

CHAPTER 17

SUNIL SINGHANIA

The market whisperer with a passion for trends

SUNIL Singhania's investment journey began about twenty-five years ago, and today he helms Abakkus, an asset-management firm managing approximately Rs 26,500 crores invested in Indian listed companies. At the time of our conversation, his new fund was on the verge of launching, with plans to invest in mid- to late-stage/pre-IPO companies.

Sunil says he has learned well from his errors and believes success is determined by the number of wins versus the number of mistakes one commits.

Childhood and mistakes

Sunil holds a traditional view on the value of education, seeing it as an important foundation that shapes one's decisions and actions. Citing his own example, he notes that as a chartered accountant, his accounting background taught him the importance of cash flows and has helped him greatly in his career as an investor.

Sunil acknowledges that beyond formal education, one also learns informally from one's environment. He shares that he has learnt from his family, friends and surroundings, which has been of great value, as 'most investment is about learning'.

Emotions

Sunil believes that investing is not just about rationality; emotions play a significant role as well. Over time, investors learn, to some extent, how to manage their emotions. When times are challenging and things are uncertain, one must try not to panic or assume the worst. He emphasizes the importance of not acting impulsively out of fear as decisions made in a state of panic often end up as wrong calls.

Sunil suggests that during uncertain times, inactivity could be better than reacting to negativity. One should try to remain calm and wait for the situation to unfold. You may discover a week later that things are more settled. Instead of rushing to sell in panic at distressed valuations, one could evaluate whether it is the right time, instead, to buy for a longer term. Events such as the Covid-19 pandemic or the subprime crisis can cause fear and panic, but it is how one overcomes these emotions that determines performance.

From Sunil's insights, we learn the importance of avoiding extreme reactions. One should strive to balance their perspective, considering both short-term as well as long-term impacts, provided the fear can be rationally conquered and buying is not subject to immediate measurement that dissuades you if it seems to go against you for a while more.

Realization of errors

Having been an investor for over twenty-five years and managing public money, Sunil says he has learned a lot from his mistakes. For him, the biggest lesson is to avoid committing the same mistake again. One should analyse mistakes by asking, are these new mistakes or am I making the same ones all over again? As long as the mistakes are of a different kind, they are a part and parcel of investing and its learning process.

Sunil classifies his mistakes into four types: the first are mistakes where something was bought, but it didn't work out and lost in value. The second is not buying something despite having developed or begun to develop conviction about it. The third are mistakes where you had conviction and bought but did not buy enough—even over time—despite continued validation of the conviction. And the fourth is when you buy a stock and sell it for a profit, but the lure of that profit pushed you to sell too early, before the full run is justified.

He adds that one must reflect on all four types of mistakes to re-evaluate one's investment process. Making a loss is not the only criterion for a mistake. Missing an opportunity or not making the most of a correct decision also constitutes a loss. While it is true that one cannot maximize every investment, the question one must ask is, why am I exiting? If the answer is based solely on returns made, it is akin to driving while looking in the rearview mirror, ignoring what lies ahead.

'It is easier to analyse the first type of mistake—why a stock you bought did not perform as well as expected. There can be multiple reasons for this. For example, you may have been carried away by a robust market, where a particular sector or company was doing exceptionally well. You may have wrongly presumed that this performance would continue over the long term. This type of mistake is easier to identify because the stock is in your portfolio and you can see that its price is either stagnant or moving downward.

The other three mistakes, according to Sunil, require more effort to identify. For example, if you do not buy a stock and it subsequently moves up, you need to reflect deeply on what you missed. To extrapolate if the upmove is already in the price or does the company have more value left.

For stocks you owned but sold too early, you need to evaluate what made you sell. Did you misread the company's ability to grow? Were you overly fixated on the stock's price movement and returns, or even taxes, rather than on the company itself? You need to ask yourself whether the company is likely to grow, and if so, to what extent.

Sunil acknowledges that mistakes are bound to be made, in both the listed and private equity markets. In listed markets, there is likely to be more realization of the price movement than otherwise, so one should reflect deeply on the actual reason for the error. More often than not, mistakes are a result of fundamentals not playing out as envisaged, getting carried away in a flow or the role of momentum.

He cites an example, noting that recently, several themes—such as defence, railways, EMS, digital and IPOs—have played up. People have made errors of judgement, either not buying when they were attractively priced, buying too late or selling too soon. Such mistakes, he explains, are often realized only over time, and one must learn from them.

Coping tools

A key insight Sunil shares is the importance of maturity and learning from the markets, which includes the humility to accept when an investment isn't playing out as expected. Many people, upon realizing this, continue holding on in the 'hope' that it will work out. This, however, often leads to disaster, as by the time they admit their mistake and take action, it is too late, and they have lost both time and money.

Sunil shares that he has been able to reduce this type of mistake, and he is continuously working to minimize them even further.

He elaborates that he tries to analyse mistakes arising from changes in a sector or company's outlook, recognizing that investing happens in a dynamic world. He explains, 'Gone are the days when we could take a company or sector call with a twenty-to-thirty-year perceptive. Now we are in disruptive world where things change even more dramatically. What is favourable may become unfavourable or vice versa.'

As an example, he cites the changes in the automobile sector, particularly in passenger vehicles. Electrification is being heralded as the future, compressing the valuations of the traditional automobile sector globally. However, as I write this, leading automobile companies are already moving away from electric to hybrid models.

Sunil emphasizes that is it important to evaluate why a hypothesis about a company is not playing out. The problem may be company-specific rather than sector-wide, such as a problem of execution or stronger competition entering the field.

To resolve mistakes, he believes the 'worst mistake is sticking with losers just because you don't want to sell a stock at a loss.' Many make the mistake of confusing themselves between a loss that has happened and the perception of it not being so in the wrong illusion of recovery, which is taken for granted even in cases where it is not to be.

Sunil shares that one of the tools he uses to avoid mistakes in the equity markets is maintaining a calm mindset, which he links to meditation. He stresses the importance of remembering that human emotions such as jealousy, greed, fear and anger often lead to errors in decision-making.

Here Sunil draws an analogy from the movie *3 Idiots*, where Aamir Khan's friends, upon not seeing his name in the exam results, say, '*Dost fail hota hai toh bahut dukh hota hai, but first aata hai toh bahut zyaada dukh aata hai*' (It is painful to see a friend fail, but if he comes first, then it is extremely painful'). Sunil finds inspiration in this dialogue, noting that our actions can reflect a similar sense of jealousy or the desire to be one-up on others.

He advises striving to rise above these emotions and to act with a calm mind. To achieve this, he suggests utilizing quantitative tools, regularly reviewing which stocks are doing well and why one doesn't have them in the portfolio, and evaluating the performance of the stocks one owns. Keeping track of global events is important as the world is becoming increasingly interconnected. As a result, stocks in the same sector cannot trade at drastically different valuations across countries.

Citing recent examples, Sunil highlights Indian subsidiaries of multinationals that have traded at many times the valuation of their parents, leading to poor returns due to overvaluation. Similarly, global developments have impacted the returns of certain IT majors.

Sunil acknowledges that there may be times when a mistake yields a favourable result. This can happen in sectors like commodities. Avoiding them may not be a mistake though the outcome may be different to what you envisaged as there was a sudden jump in the price of a product or in some case, you had to deal with a news flow that impacted the company but was beyond your process. Then you think, the outcome could have been good had you invested in it.

There can also be cases where one invests in a company expecting the stock to double or triple over two to three years, but it shoots up in a year, perhaps because the market took notice of something or the results were much better than anticipated. In such situations, Sunil and his team re-evaluate whether the outcome exceeds what the fundamentals warrant and, if needed, they sell.

Avoiding fatal errors

Sunil has learned valuable lessons from his twenty-five years of experience. In his new avatar at Abakkus, he ensures that he does not invest in loss-making companies and places significant emphasis on return on capital (ROC) and return on equity (ROE). He believes a visible ROC/ROE of at least 14 to 15 per cent is important.

Sunil prefers investing in the listed space and therefore avoids what he calls 'B-kind' investments. He typically will not invest in companies that, while having great business models, need to constantly raise capital to survive. He is willing to provide capital for a company to grow, but not to build its business or to survive.

Dealing with fear and greed

Sunil acknowledges that it is difficult to completely overcome mistakes, as well as the emotions of greed and fear, because we are all human. At times, one may be tempted to act against their fundamental beliefs. However, he believes that with time and maturity, one is able to better manage such challenges.

He emphasizes the importance of adhering to one's core belief system, even though it can be difficult given the momentum of the market. While one may feel their stance is conservative, it is important to resist the lure of deviating from one's principles. The market is a great equalizer and a great teacher, and one must endeavour to keep learning from it.

Kinds of mistakes

Sunil believes that every investor has a different perspective, philosophy and style of investing. Some investors are great at momentum investing, while others focus on fundamentals, as his fund does. Some chase high growth, others deep value. Some invest based on dividend yields while others chase commodities.

Therefore, it is important to adhere to one's core beliefs and investment philosophy, rather than copying the strategies of the current stars of the market. One should ask oneself what has worked for them as by staying true to one's strengths and avoiding areas of weakness, the likelihood of errors is significantly reduced.

Sunil stresses that errors can arise when investors don't adequately track companies or lose sight of the rationale for buying them in the first place. The Indian economy is exciting, with numerous opportunities across sectors. It is therefore very difficult to track each and every company, every earnings report and every call, and an investor may miss out on opportunities because their bandwidth is choked.

He also reflects that sometimes, investors question whether their decisions were correct, especially when the market does not react as expected. In the short term, the market may overlook what an investor perceives, but if in the long term things don't work out, there could be a flaw in their understanding.

Dealing with mistakes

If one is driven by ego in investing, it often leads to more mistakes and losses. There are times when an investor must take a call. If something is not working out but conviction remains high, Sunil believes there is no harm in waiting. However, there are also situations where one holds a perspective that doesn't materialize, and the stock corrects. In such cases, holding on to the stock could prove fruitful, but sometimes it may not.

During Covid, Sunil recalls, he sold many stocks in response to the dramatic change in the environment. While he later regretted selling some of them as their prices moved up, there were also instances where his decision proved right as those stocks fell further. As he says, decisions are usually taken based on what seems appropriate at the time, and getting it right or wrong is simply a part of the process.

Taking the decision

Portfolios cannot be built by consensus, says Sunil. Final decisions must be taken by the portfolio manager, based on their expertise. Sometimes, an analyst may push for a certain stock, but if the portfolio manager feels it's better to wait, the call is ultimately theirs to make as they are finally responsible. Sunil emphasizes that just because one outcome is correct or incorrect, it does not mean every outcome will follow the same pattern.

Over time you may discover that certain individuals have a knack for being more right than wrong. Recognizing this can help identify a person's strengths, such as picking themes, stocks or value, or understanding the direction of the market, the microeconomic environment or global trends. The key is to figure out over time what you can rely on and what you should avoid.

In decision-making, Sunil advises balancing exuberance with caution as exuberance often goes hand in hand with greed and momentum. One should question what can happen if the market discovers that the exuberance can at times last long and go to extremes. Sunil feels in the past, the big corrections or underperformances have happened because the markets went into an exuberance zone and then reacted to mean.

Personal life and judgement

Sunil highlights the importance of family support and a stable home environment for maintaining a calm and peaceful state of mind. He considers a serene mind and an encouraging environment at home to be a blessing, especially in the intense profession of investing, which requires constant awareness of what is happening in the world. He acknowledges that investing also often involves taking calls at odd hours or even during holidays, making work-life balance essential. However, Sunil believes that if one loves their work, then a work-life balance is automatically achieved.

He emphasizes the importance of having the motivation to excel. A key source of motivation for him is the commitment to 'not repeat your mistakes'. While mistakes can weigh one down, one should focus on the many opportunities that lie ahead and move on.

Reflections

Sunil reflects on living in Mumbai, acknowledging that the city needs improvements in many areas. He mentions how his commute to the office, which used to take just twenty-five minutes, now takes over an hour for a mere twelve-kilometre ride. While such things can be frustrating, they should be seen in the context of the bigger picture. Growth in India is certainly higher than before, and the increase in traffic reflects the fact that more cars are being sold than roads being built. Although cities have started working on improving infrastructure, the scope for improvement is huge.

He points out that life offers both positives and negatives. For example, he shares that when he was in Europe, the air quality index (AQI) was 11, compared to levels of 300 in Mumbai and 700 to 800 in Delhi. Such things can be frustrating and impact one's investment outlook. Good air is critical, and he hopes the government addresses the issue. Yet, when he goes to Europe, he sees stagnation, whereas in India, there is plenty of growth. It feels like a long festive season—the malls are full, flights are booked and hotels are bustling. Sunil emphasizes the need to balance short-term frustrations with the realization of how fortunate one is to be in India during a time of significant growth.

Mistakes to miracles

Sunil recalls an instance when he held a large stake in a reputable pharmaceutical company. Unfortunately, the company faced its first-ever US Food and Drug Administration (FDA) issue, causing the stock to fall by 50 per cent. Such incidents, he explains, cannot be anticipated and can disrupt one's performance and mindset. In such situations, Sunil believes the best approach is to accept the fact that while all the right steps were taken, the event itself was unforeseeable.

He reflects on similar scenarios during events like Covid-19 and the Ukraine-Russia war, where markets corrected sharply due to factors beyond anyone's control. Stocks fell by 35 to 40 per cent within days, with some halving or losing even more of their value. In such situations, one should let time pass, collect one's thoughts and avoid impulsive actions or make use of the fall to salvage what became of greater value. In both cases, you won. By letting time pass by. Then by selling the panic.

Sunil next talks about reversing mistakes. He admits that he has missed out on many stocks due to being overly conservative, a mindset he hopes to overcome. He adds that while conservatism has its merits, he has missed many opportunities because he tried to time them and was unsuccessful. Another mistake he wants to correct is being too conservative when buying. He notes that he is working on addressing both these issues.

Role of communication

Sunil feels that Indian investors have matured over time. He emphasizes the importance of maintaining clear, regular and open communication with investors. He is upfront about mistakes, opportunities and potential market volatility. He makes it a point to explain that small percentage fluctuations are bound to happen and should be expected. The goal is not to outperform short-term volatility but to deliver outperformance over the long-term.

Effective communication helps in dealing with misaligned expectations. Sunil believes that presenting granular data and clear metrics helps maintain a balance between inflows and outflows. He also ensures that the fund is not over done with one-two investors or one-two companies. Efforts are made to reduce the impact of volatility in both funds and companies. He also uses a matrix of not going beyond a particular percentage of the free flow of any company. He says with inflows, he does not want to make the mistake of only buying our own companies and not newer ideas.

Making mistakes

Mistakes are inevitable, and Sunil shares some key strategies he employs to mitigate errors.

First, he avoids discussing his stocks in public. If people know he is a large investor in a stock that does not perform well, he is likely to be trolled, which can negatively impact his mindset. Sunil believes it is best to focus on investing with conviction rather than be influenced by public opinion.

He draws an analogy with cricket, saying that just as a top player might be trolled for getting out cheaply but is applauded by the very same people when he scores a century, investors too should be prepared to face both criticism and praise. 'If we can take claps, we should be prepared to take flak,' he notes, adding, 'It's all fine as long as you do more right than wrong.'

Second, Sunil acknowledges that mistakes are bound to happen as no one is infallible. Mistakes can be of multiple types. One, external factors can turn a decision one has made into a mistake. Second, one may invest in a great company whose stock price fails to move. Third, a stock one has invested in may not move the way one expected due to the dynamic nature of business. He stresses that mistakes are a part and parcel of life. What leads to success in the long run is ensuring that wins outweigh the mistakes.

Learning from others

Sunil stresses that no one makes mistakes deliberately. He explains that the definition of a mistake is different for different people. While one individual may not see an error, someone else could perceive it to be one. In the profession of investing, this perception is largely because of price movement. Sunil recalls that during Covid, some stocks fell by 40 per cent, while others dropped by 50 per cent or more, but everything fell, everything looked like a mistake. He adds that while some were smaller and others bigger, everything was nonetheless perceived as a mistake.

Buying right is important

Sunil emphasizes the importance of buying at the right price, noting that even Warren Buffett has famously said, 'It's far better to buy a wonderful company at a fair price than a fair company at a wonderful price.' He explains that while companies have moats, their returns will not align if earnings fail to reflect valuations. P/E corrections can occur, or there may be no expansion of that and returns may be suboptimal even in companies perceived to have a 'moat'.

He avoids highly valued companies where he sees either growth or P/E will suffer. He says, 'I am a little bit of a value conscious investor—investors have to understand that a good company or a good team is not necessarily a guarantee of good stock returns.'

He concludes our conversation by emphasizing the importance of keeping things simple and maintaining a disciplined approach to achieve decent returns. He advises against trying to 'maximize returns every single day, urging investors to remain patient' and not deviate from their stated disciplined strategy. He highlights the importance of aiming for decent returns rather than extraordinary ones. He believes 'India has some great times ahead.' He encourages investors to learn well from their mistakes, avoid repeating them and set up a sound investment process.

CHAPTER 18

K. SARATH REDDY

The daredevil with a strategic edge

IT is not every day that you hear of an investor who started their journey at the age of fifteen. It makes me wonder how lucky his friends and colleagues might have been if they had benefitted from his wisdom of starting early—something even Warren Buffett and the late Charlie Munger endorsed. Buffett famously said: 'Charlie's always said that the big thing about it is we started building this little snowball on top of a very long hill. We started at a very early age in rolling the snowball down. And, of course, the snowball—the nature of compound interest is it behaves like a snowball of sticky snow. And the trick is to have a very long hill, which means either starting very young or living very—to be very old.'

Sarath Reddy is a natural-born investor, driven as much by intuition as by logic.

Imagine selling your stocks to fund your MBA degree.

Sarath's story of buying Titan stock at Rs 16 and later selling some of those shares to finance his MBA at Utah State University is a sparkling, yet lesser-known tale. While some might argue in hindsight that he could have held on to those shares, one mustn't forget both his foresight in buying them and the immense return on investment from a high-quality, self-funded education.

As a teenager, when his peers were likely more interested in comic books, Sarath Reddy was already investing in IPOs. Perhaps because he lost his father when he was only four, Sarath learnt the value of making money and building wealth early. The determination to win and stand on his own feet is what shaped much of his success in later years.

Today, as the founder and managing director of Unifi Capital—a company he established in 2001 in Chennai—Sarath has carved a niche for himself in the Indian investment landscape with his unique approach to capital management and investment strategies. Unifi Capital today is a boutique investment-management firm with an incredible track record of managing over Rs 25,000 crore in AUM and consistently outperforming the market. This success has drawn many towards him, myself included.

Sarath's approach has always been different from traditional asset management firms. He emphasizes niche investment strategies, focusing on under-researched and under-valued opportunities in the market.

He has grabbed many spin-off opportunities, capitalized on arbitrage opportunities and invested in high-yield, low-credit-quality securities often overlooked by mainstream investors. He has also invested in holding companies that trade at significant discounts to their intrinsic value, unlocking value through strategic investments.

As we begin our conversation on evaluating investment mistakes, Sarath highlights two often-overlooked dimensions. First, the frailty of availability bias, and second, the importance of distinguishing losses caused by investment errors from those arising due to the inherent randomness of equities.

Availability bias, he explains, occurs when one overweighs easily accessible information and underweights undiscovered information because it is unavailable. In the world of investing, this bias runs rampant due to the structural invisibility of data on certain types of mistakes, namely, errors of omission. Charlie Munger explains it best: 'The mistakes that have been most extreme in Berkshire's history are mistakes of omission. They don't show up in our figures. They show up in opportunity costs.' This observation, Sarath notes, highlights the fact that investors can be misled into viewing investing mistakes solely as picking losers, when in reality, the bigger mistake lies in missing winners. Both errors of omission and commission should be treated as equally serious mistakes.

Sarath considers errors of commission to be by far the biggest danger to a portfolio over the long run. Addressing these mistakes occupies more of his research team's mental space and causes more anguish than any other issue. He notes, 'It's what our analysts work on every single day when they go into work. They begin and end their day asking, "What are we missing?"'

However, he clarifies that not every missed profit is an error of omission. Errors of omission pertain only to those investments where the facts were available and Unifi had the skillset to appropriately evaluate them before the stock price ran up. For example, not taking advantage of the sudden approval of a drug by a small pharmaceutical company would not count as a mistake. On the flipside, there is substantial opportunity to discover value in sectors that are not well understood by other investors. By leveraging expert assistance and committing research resources, he aims to build competence in sectors that others are not willing to put the effort into—this, he believes, is a key contributor to his investment returns.

Sarath also emphasizes that, in pursuit of outperformance, it is part of his job to take investment risks and get some wrong. Not getting a few calls wrong indicates a lack of independent instinct and will inevitability lead to investment underperformance. He stresses that when reflecting on loss-making investments, it is important for investors to differentiate between mistakes arising from poor judgement and losses due to the inherent unpredictability of equities. The latter, he explains, should be limited and controlled through diversification, not by risk avoidance.

In pursuit of investment outperformance, he counsels, investors must have the courage to take contrarian bets at times. However, this is often tough in a culture that is averse to renegades and doesn't allow them to be creative, avant-garde or daring. 'The world would rather fail conventionally than be successful unconventionally.'

Sarath warns against this mindset and encourages investors to build a corporate culture that breaks free of those chains. For example, creating a mistake-review process that makes analysts feel like they are standing trial will destroy their contrarian instincts. Instead, Sarath consciously works to de-stigmatize mistakes, making it clear that errors are a routine part of the investment process. He mandates—not just encourages—the open discussion of investment ideas from inception to exit. This fosters a free-flowing critique of all ideas, enabling Unifi to detect mistakes early. This is why a good corporate culture is important; it directly translates into better investment performance.

With a laugh, Sarath points out that in contrarian investing, one can be right about a stock pick for the wrong reason. Instead of confusing luck for skill, a humble and clear-eyed investor would accept he was wrong and critically review the investment error.

To put it simply, successful investing requires finding the delicate balance between offence and defence. Merely playing it safe to curtail errors of commission exposes a portfolio to too many omission errors. These nuances—where not making enough mistakes is also a mistake, and where losses are not always errors—can cloud the evaluation of investment mistakes and make learning from them difficult. After all, if it were easy, we wouldn't keep making mistakes.

Having finished the primer, we delve into Sarath's reflections on his long list of mistakes spanning thirty-five years. Despite his unusual talent, Sarath believes that his mistakes are not unusual. Intrigued, I ask if mistakes are influenced by personality, upbringing, education or life exposure.

Mistakes often emanate from the views and biases people hold, which lead them to prejudge situations. He asserts that with experience, one learns to reflect on their mental processes to guard against such dangers. However, some biases are so deeply embedded in our personalities that they act on the subconscious. 'We're so inseparable from our deepest views that they virtually form our instincts,' he remarks.

He goes on to add, 'There's no doubt childhood and adolescent experiences lay the foundation of who we are; education and experience add layers on top, but it's very hard to re-lay the foundation of one's life.' At the same time, he notes that the exposure, decisions and experiences one has as a young adult can condition thinking and attitudes, influencing the decisions one makes as an investment manager.

For example, Sarath recounts how he has observed that analysts from large companies tend to be great communicators but weaker entrepreneurs compared to those from smaller firms. The enterprising ones are more persistent and innovative and do better in less structured situations.

Another example he cites is how analysts working in Mumbai, the market's epicentre, receive similar inputs and tend to draw similar conclusions, whereas those working in less central locations, such as Chennai, must fend for themselves, making them more independent in their thinking. These individuals gravitate easily to contrarian ideas and are less focused on what their peers in other firms are thinking. This aptly captures how one's environment shapes their understanding of their trade. I am reminded once again of Warren Buffett, who said he prefers staying away from the noise of New York by living in Omaha. This distance helped him make investment decisions to buy and hold companies without overreacting to every market up and down in the early years of his career.

As discussed in other chapters of this book, the same pattern is followed by three ace investors who have chosen to stay away from the mainstream noise and base themselves in other cities.

Sarath next expands on how decisions one makes as a young analyst can help one avoid mistakes as an investment manager. A young investor, he says, has more scope to create differentiated value not through hard skills (such as financial modelling or accounting knowledge) but via soft skills like making friends in different industries (who you can turn to for sector advice), working well as a team (to attract and collaborate with the best analysts), celebrating diversity (to gain access to different viewpoints), perseverance (to keep the faith through low cycles), self-confidence (to go against the grain) and honour (to gain the trust and respect of clients and colleagues so you can act independently from popular street views).

These essential tools are cultivated by an analyst even before they apply to college, through the tough challenges that life throws at one early on. In fact, Sarath believes the foundations of one's investment career are laid even earlier, during childhood. He explains how an upbringing that values sports (which teaches teamwork, confidence, the hunger to win and determination in the face of poor odds), duty to family (which imbibes honour and trust), good academics (which fosters disciplined hard work), loyalty to friends (which provides a support network and the ability to build professional relationships later in life) and niche or unique interests (which encourages creativity and free-thinking) is highly conducive to building the qualities of a successful analyst.

Sarath's assertion leaves me in awe. I feel I have learnt a beautiful lesson about the philosophy of life although I came to discuss investing with him.

He concludes by cautioning that one's background only does so much; a great deal of personality shaping must still happen in adulthood. For example, deep personality traits—such as humility, the ability to take and give constructive criticism, and most importantly, the capacity to change one's mind—are typically developed on the job, not during one's childhood or formal education.

In the course of our conversation, Sarath notes, 'The timing of the mistake can sometimes be worse than the mistake,' while explaining the difference between mistakes made during normal times and those made during a crisis. Mistakes made in calm waters can be corrected relatively easily and at a moderate cost, provided they are detected early and corrected efficiently. However, a decision made during a crisis is likely to coincide with extreme price swings, and its impact cost on a portfolio can be significant. It is these actions, he adds, that change the trajectory of a portfolio's performance.

While cautioning about the greater risks of mistakes made in uncertain times, Sarath does not fail to highlight the potential rewards of taking well-calculated risks during such periods. He views uncertain times as the bearers of hidden treasures, when one's investing skills can truly shine. By navigating through the thick smoke of uncertainty and emotions with experience, agility and independent research capabilities, an investor can act before the smoke clears. In his words, 'It's in times of crisis, when the market's efficiency is hamstrung, that one's investing skills can shine and have the biggest impact.'

He illustrates this by pointing out the disparate performance among portfolio managers in the twelve to twenty-four months following Covid. 'The magnitude of realignment triggered by Covid-19 led to dramatic changes in the market cycle; events that would normally take years were crunched into a few weeks,' he explains. 'The market's prevailing narrative was hijacked overnight by health and medical drivers that required analysts to understand and interpret without skipping a beat. Sector leadership changed hands in a single day, with pharma taking the lead, followed swiftly by technology and internet sectors within a few weeks, and then financials a few months later. A portfolio manager who got it reasonably right during those twenty-five weeks from the latter half of March 2020 on earned profits equivalent to what he would have earned over five normal years.'

Sarath believes that apart from learning from self-reflection and identifying bias, the most powerful defence against mistakes is the quality and bandwidth of one's team. He explains how collaborating with a team of highly competent analysts brings a diversity of thought that helps catch errors by patching the holes in any analyst's thinking.

He believes that a combination of experience, process and a talented team helps reduce the number of flawed investments. However, even the best analysts have both great insights and blind spots, making it crucial to avoid personalizing decisions. Sarath believes in letting facts and data drive objective views rather than being overly influenced by an analyst's personality or track record.

Unifi's approach combines scheduled, structured team-wide research meetings with more frequent, informal, small-group discussions. These impromptu sub-meetings ensure a relaxed and comfortable environment, encouraging even the younger or quieter team members to voice their views and concerns. This fosters a richer intellectual mix and enables better reflection. Even the most experienced analysts receive a lot of food for thought from these debates, especially those who have trained themselves to filter information while remaining open to varied perspectives.

Despite these measures, mistakes may still slip through. Sarath is often alerted by signs such as a sudden dip in the stock price, an unfavourable change in the price of a key raw material, or other mishaps such as fires, accidents, regulatory orders, customer issues, product recalls, keyman exits or poor quarterly results. While such incidents are part of normal business operations and are typically resolved by the management, if they occur repeatedly, then one needs to re-evaluate one's judgement.

To catch such errors early, his team maintains the same 360° look-out for red alerts as they do for opportunities that offer value. They constantly test their initial investment thesis by asking themselves if they would still buy the shares at the current price today.

He recounts how only experienced practitioners truly understood George Soros's anecdote about exiting certain positions when initiating them coincided with him developing a specific back pain. Sometimes, even after diligent research, favourable expert opinions and consensus amongst investment committees or analysts, certain investments just don't feel right. Sarath believes this is the gut or sixth sense guiding one. He pays attention to this gut feeling—now referred to as the 'second brain'—as it often alerts him to any mistakes in the making. He clarifies that this is not about being guided by emotions but acknowledging one's subconscious thinking. As he aptly puts it, 'Professional instincts honed over decades count for something.'

Whether the red flag is identified through ongoing due diligence or professional instinct, it pays enormously to be vigilant and act early. Early detection of leading indicators of potential trouble have helped Unifi avoid substantial losses. This approach enables him to nip disappointments in the bud before they bear the fruit of failure. However, he recognizes that money is not the only asset being wasted—time wasted while waiting for an incorrect thesis to play out is often the bigger loss.

Sarath employs several methods to limit mistakes. As widely acknowledged in financial academia, diversification is the key to superior risk-adjusted returns. By capping individual stock exposure at 10 per cent—even for their highest conviction bets—he ensures no single mistake can be fatal. To further reduce their downside from 10 per cent to a more reasonable 4 per cent, Sarath strictly adheres to the growth at a reasonable price (GARP) investment philosophy. This value-oriented approach creates a margin of safety that helps limit losses.

However, diversification alone cannot compensate for bad investment decisions. Sarath relies heavily on Unifi's research team and investment process to minimize errors. He believes that nothing limits investment failures more effectively than a robust understanding of the investee business and industry. This understanding can only come from having the internal capability to execute in-depth, bottom-up fundamental research. Conducting market-leading research is, in his view, the surest way to limit the number of wrong calls.

One refinement Sarath has found particularly helpful, especially in niche sectors, is seeking independent counsel from experts who have spent their entire careers in a specific sector. The depth of their experience brings out the essence of that business and draws attention to important drivers that might otherwise be overlooked. For example, sectors such as fertilizers, paper and sugar are considered dull and have limited analyst coverage, making insights from industry experts a significant competitive advantage. However, Sarath understands that finding the right expert can often be time consuming and cautions against inadvertently choosing the wrong advisor, which could lead to inheriting their biases and making critical investment errors.

He reiterates that there is no substitute for building strong in-house knowledge to the extent feasible. This enables proper identification of the best experts, ensures the right questions are asked and pursued, and helps identify which factors will impact the stock price and which factors can be safely ignored.

When it comes to rectifying a mistake in investing, speed is everything. Sarath emphasizes that the scope of rectification is limited since, once a stock is bought, its cost price is permanent. They either like the stock at its current market price, or they don't, but either way, whatever action can be taken to rectify an error hinges on the speed of execution. He explains, 'If the logical solution is to chop a limb to save one's life, then the best time to do it asap! It's much better to book a loss and bear the pain now than to live in denial nursing the wound, praying it will heal.' Speed in decision-making also applies to acting fast when a stock-price decline presents a buying opportunity.

In addition to curtailing loss-making positions early, speed in accepting a mistake allows them to quickly redeploy this capital with a fresh perspective, recovering lost ground.

Preparedness, effective processes, constant monitoring and adequate research bandwidth are essential for enabling organizational speed. Before any investment is made, his team prepares a written investment thesis, which is circulated and accepted. As part of their maintenance diligence (ongoing research and tracking of investees), assumptions, beliefs and estimates are constantly re-tested. The team quickly identifies any new developments, often within minutes of them becoming public. Sarath attributes their ability to respond rapidly, often faster than others, to this constant state of preparedness and scrutiny.

Being a small team, they are people-oriented rather than hierarchy-oriented. Analysts have immediate access to decision-makers with minimal checkpoints in between. This means a decision can be made instantly by just the CIO and the analyst tracking the stock, enabling them to react swiftly to market developments.

On rare occasions, an investment may falter due to unethical or incompetent actions by an investee's management. To address such situations, Unifi employs activism as a rectification strategy. Sarath believes that as fiduciaries of thousands of clients, it is their duty to fight to protect their clients from being cheated. For example, Unifi might write to independent directors to highlight the transgression or rally other shareholders to form a strong voting block against a corporate action. They are not hesitant to ruffle feathers, neither do they buckle under intimidation tactics.

'It's critical to understand—while we forgive mistakes as learning opportunities, we have no mercy for repeated mistakes. Learning from mistakes is the only way to survive,' Sarath emphasizes. Over the course of his career, he has optimized his research team's processes to institutionalize learning from other's mistakes.

During the initial investment proposal, every member of the investment team—from the most junior to the most senior—sits around the same table and is actively involved in deliberations. This fosters team—not individual—ownership of each investment idea, encouraging each analyst to critically apply their knowledge and pool their unique perspectives for the company's benefit.

Although Sarath acknowledges that investing is a highly competitive field where the glitter of the top honours can be blinding, he believes that maintaining a philosophical foundation and a sense of studied humility have guided some of the smartest investors in differentiating between aggressive opportunism and hubris.

Sarath illustrates with an example how he and his team navigate drawdowns while managing and balancing ego and commitment for a better outcome.

He presents the following scenario: After a great deal of research, and with some reservations, you make a large investment in a secular growth business. The firm has grown profits at a compound annual growth rate (CAGR) of 21 per cent over the past five years, and you believe it can sustain a CAGR of 15 per cent over the next five years. The stock had already tripled in market cap prior to your investment, and you were concerned at the outset about buying into a strong performer, not wanting to risk being in a momentum play. However, you were reassured by the long-term governance track record and the capital allocation and intended to stay for the long term.

A few quarters later, the business hits a bump. Margins drop sharply, profits fall by 25 per cent and the CEO quits (reportedly at the behest of the board). The stock declines by 20 per cent. After speaking with the chairman and CFO, you believe they acted sensibly and swiftly. A new CEO is appointed within two months. While his track record is credible, he is an unknown quantity and may be out of touch with current market conditions. With quarterly results due in two weeks, there's concern that if the new CEO makes a poor impression in his first conference call, the stock's slide could worsen significantly.

Would you take advantage of the sharp dip and raise your exposure? Would you exit fully, disappointed in yourself and the company for this deeply worrying situation? Or would you hold your position indecisively, potentially missing an important opportunity to act and protect your outcome?

Sarath shares his wisdom on addressing such challenges.

As a first step, investment team members are discouraged from sharing views on public platform such as TV, newspapers or the internet. Taking a public stand can create resistance to changing one's opinion due to bias and ego.

Second, in their notes to clients, team members avoid the overuse of adjectives, keeping the tone factual and objective. This ensures that if the facts change, they can reconsider the view.

Finally, within his team it's clear that the buck stops with the CIO. While investment decisions are an intensive team effort, the final call is the CIO's responsibility. The CIO must take full ownership of each crisis and prioritize time to revisit the thesis, meet with company management and make the final decision. The CIO should have the experience and discipline to manage emotions, make the decision and take full accountability.

Sarath adds that as an additional measure, when an analyst is under severe stress, they are given the space to think, review and construct their view.

Requiring them to handle anxious clients during an emotionally charged time could make them susceptible to bias or ego-driven responses. Unifi, therefore, ensures that experienced relationship managers interface with clients, providing a buffer that allows the investment team to think calmly and act objectively.

The treachery of fear and greed is well known to any investor, but these emotions are so deeply pre-programmed into our biology that breaking free of their influence, even slightly, requires an experience powerful enough to counteract them. Simply being told to watch out for fear and greed doesn't work. It takes moments of tremendous pain, where one is betrayed by their own emotions, to engrain a distrust of these feelings deeply enough to reduce their hold. Losing money, being wrong, being embarrassed, being afraid enough to internalize the danger of fear and greed is part of what investment managers refer to as 'investment experience'.

Experience is not only knowledge of markets but also knowledge of oneself. Good judgement is built not just by sweat, but also, unfortunately, tears. After one recovers from a mistake, the lingering memory of the pain instils a fear that keeps one constantly on guard against repeating it. Fear, while unglamourous, 'is probably the strongest visceral defence against making or repeating mistakes—as long as it isn't overwhelming. The markets, after all, can be a dangerous place.

When I ask about the impact of personal events and circumstances on making a mistake, Sarath explains that the ability to compartmentalize personal emotions and health from professional focus and energy varies from person to person. Professional stress is par for the course and can be addressed logically. However, personal stress, Sarath admits, can significantly impact one's ability to function effectively. He does all he can to create conditions around him that are conducive to maintaining balance.

He believes that the harmony and health of key relationships, both at home and work, combined with one's attitude towards money and success, lay the foundation for a balanced life. One's personal philosophy and values play a defining role in how we relate to those close to us and how we prioritize our most valuable resource—time. For one to be emotionally available and professionally effective, the whole equation has to be balanced from the foundation upwards.

As this book focuses on mistakes, Sarath shares one more learning: in nine out of ten scenarios, mistakes feed our learning cycle and motivate us to sharpen our craft. For him, the path from initial pain to integrating its value into the process code is not one of natural progression. It takes conscious effort to create the circumstances for the learning cycle to thrive.

For example, a slow and long leadership journey of building a culture that encourages open discussion and documentation of mistakes is necessary to sustain a feedback loop. If mistakes are denied, forgotten or hidden, the process falls apart.

Sarath's pragmatic approach highlights his understanding that imparting a culture goes beyond slogans or decorating the office with posters of corporate values. For the team to truly internalize a culture, it must permeate every facet of the firm. It must be visible in senior management's behaviour, in compensation and performance appraisals and in hiring and firing decisions. Each member of the team must truly believe that their supervisor and peers seek to learn from their mistakes and that they will be rewarded, not reprimanded, for documenting them.

Sarath believes that the CIO must take responsibility for mistakes from an external perspective to protect his team, particularly younger analysts. Internally, identifying the source of the mistake and communicating with the concerned analyst must be handled sensitively, so the individual and the team are motivated to do better rather than retreat into a defensive fear of reprisals. He candidly acknowledges that if a team member clearly lacks the right attitude, one must let them go without hesitation. Acting fairly and decisively to maintain the team's competitive edge and its confidence to win is a huge motivator.

There is only one type of investing mistake that personally demotivates Sarath: unethical practices. Over his thirty-five-year career, he has honed his ability to 'smell the rats'—those with unethical motivations and methods that conflict with the interests of other market participants and regulators. He employs a range of methods, including reference checks, governance scoring and plant visits, to identify unethical players, but once in a while, a very smart one manages to slip through the cracks. To him, this is personally demotivating as it reflects a market dynamic that allows such bad apples to continue contaminating the water we all share.

To balance it out, the risk-taker in Sarath has a fun side. He enjoys listening to 'The Gambler' by Kenny Rogers and sailing on the open ocean. His comfort food is the humble rasam and rice, and he enjoys the occasional rum and coke.

Lastly, when I ask him about being bullish on India, Sarath, ever the realist, acknowledges the problems of lag in terms of economic and social indicators. However, he also recognizes the efforts being made to address these issues and notes that for an entrepreneur or an investor, such conditions provide great opportunities for growth. 'The road to glory is often mired in potholes,' he quips. Despite the numerous impediments in India, Sarath is confident that the superhighway to growth will be fixed. He observes, 'When one looks at our country, one can either see everything that's wrong with it, or all the opportunity it has before it. Every year in India is better than the year before. There's not a doubt in my mind that, at some point, all our infrastructure—physical, social and institutional—challenges will be overcome. It may take until the end of my life, but I am certain that at some point, every pothole will be fixed, every airport built and every pavement cleaned. And the journey until then will not be a sacrifice—we will have been part of one of the greatest national developments in human history, and a part of the accompanying investment opportunities.'

It is this perfect mix of pragmatic thinking and aspirations of a tomorrow beyond our imagination that makes Sarath who he is. This ideology is well reflected not only his approach to life but also in his approach to investing.

CHAPTER 19

AMISHA VORA

The limitless data-driven leader

AMISHA, a chartered accountant and equity expert by profession, is one of the most sought-after opinion makers in the market. She is also one of the leading women entrepreneurs in India's financial services sector.

After starting her career with JM Financial as an analyst in the late eighties, Amisha joined Prabhudas Lilladher (PL) in 2000 as the vice president of foreign institutional investor (FII) sales. By 2006, she had become a key shareholder (co-owner) and group joint managing director at PL. In 2022, she acquired a 96 per cent stake, becoming the chairperson and managing director of the eighty-year-old financial services powerhouse.

With over thirty-five years of experience in the financial services sector, Amisha has been determined in her opinions and honest in her views. Under her leadership, PL has won several awards and accolades, including being recognized as one of the best banking, financial services and insurance (BFSI) brands in India in 2022 and 2024 by the *Economic Times*. PL was also recognized as 'One of the Most Respected Brands' by Asia Award for two consecutive years and won the 36th Jamnalal Bajaj Award for Fair Business Practices in 2024.

Her ascent to the pinnacle of leadership, assuming the mantle of chairperson and managing director, stands as a testament to her unwavering dedication and visionary prowess. Amisha embodies not just leadership, but stewardship, driving PL Capital towards unprecedented heights of success and distinction.

Amisha, a powerful woman leader in the dynamic financial services landscape, has emerged as an emblematic figure and has been acclaimed as the 'Most Iconic Woman of the Year 2024' by Women World India and the Business Leader of the Year by CMO Asia. Her list of awards includes the Rashtriya Udyog Ratan Award for Corporate Leadership and the Annual Impact Creator Award from the Governor's office and Government of Maharashtra in 2021. She was also honoured with the prestigious Women Empowerment Principles Leadership Award 2019-20 by the United Nations.

With a distinguished educational background in chartered accountancy and profound expertise in equity, Amisha is highly respected as one of the country's most influential financial opinion-makers. Her passion for work, attention to detail, astute understanding of business models and action-oriented work style have enabled PL to scale new heights consistently. Within six years of taking the reins of PL's institutional business (2002–08), Amisha grew the business thirty-six-fold.

In addition to her roles on the institutional side, she also spearheaded the formation of corporate advisory services and helped corporates raise approximately $1.8 billion between 2005 and 2008. She took over the reins of the group's retail broking business in 2012, achieving 10x growth in ten years. She has strengthened PL's presence in key markets, apart from spearheading a complete transformation in how the retail business operates, led by technology and quality advisory services. Besides driving growth in existing businesses, Amisha played an instrumental role in diversifying the group's businesses. She launched the NBFC (2006) and the investment banking businesses (2007), as well as the portfolio-management services (PMS) business (2005).

Her mindset of consistent innovation has also made PL one of the pioneers in quantitative investing in India. Her unwavering ethical standards fit in perfectly with PL's founding principles of trust, transparency and integrity.

Amisha is a member of the CII Capital Markets Committee and has received several accolades in the past few years. She is also a board member of the Association of Portfolio Managers in India (APMI).

I remember her very recent interview with NDTV Profit, where she shared her perspective on the prevailing market sentiment. With markets becoming nervous after the 2024 Lok Sabha polls outcome, Amisha emphasized the importance of strategic stock selection amid volatility.

In my conversation with Amisha, which of course focused on mistakes and learnings from them, she begins by emphasizing that, at their core, markets and investing are all about the emotions of greed and fear. According to her, emotional quotient (EQ) is as important, or perhaps even more important, than IQ in investment decisions.

She shares from her own experience that a solid educational foundation, exposure to financial concepts and a supportive environment can equip individuals with the knowledge, skills and confidence needed for sound financial decision-making.

However, it is EQ that helps one ride both upcycles and downcycles, control the urge to book early profits and make the right investment decisions.

Amisha firmly believes that a good EQ enables one to remain calm and rational—even in the face of market volatility and sentiment swings—a mindset that is crucial for long-term success in the stock market. She emphasizes that understanding one's behavioural response patterns, critically evaluating the outcomes of these patterns, and developing an objective plan to mitigate the errors caused by behavioural biases are important in investing. Staying calm and rational, she stresses, is the key to navigating the ups and downs of the stock market.

Market volatility can be unsettling, but maintaining a clear perspective helps in making informed decisions rather than reacting emotionally. Long-term success often hinges on a well-thought-out strategy and the discipline to stick with it through various market conditions.

Trying to time the market—buying low and selling high based on short-term predictions—can be risky. Instead, one should focus on a consistent investment strategy. It is also very important to periodically review and adjust your portfolio based on changes in goals, risk tolerance or market conditions.

However, she advises against making frequent changes based on short-term market movements.

Elaborating, Amisha believes that human beings react differently in calm times compared to crisis situations, and the nature of mistakes can vary. In calm times, complacency can set in, leading to a more relaxed attitude towards risk. This may result in critical aspects of the investment process being overlooked, such as vendor and reference checks, competition mapping or accurate valuation.

She cites the dot-com bubble as an example, noting that during that time, many tech stocks were significantly overvalued without a solid understanding of their underlying fundamentals, leading to substantial losses for investors when the bubble burst.

According to her, the focus should ideally be on improving future outcomes or gains. Instead, people anchor to past prices, current profits and losses, making decisions that aren't aligned with the forward-looking nature of the markets. During crises, she adds, the 'risk-off' mode dominates, where perceived risks often appear exaggerated. The natural human response is to be risk-averse when it comes to losses, as the pain of losing a certain amount is felt more intensely than the pleasure derived from gaining an equal amount.

Investing is about being rational, but usually, Amisha says, most people don't respond to profits or losses rationally or equally.

She adds that investors often want to hold on to losses or avoid booking a loss but are in a hurry to book profits, which can be a big mistake. Such behaviour deviates from rationality and can lead to panic selling, impulsive decisions and the failure to consider long-term investment potential. She mentions that the 2008 financial crisis and the Covid-19 pandemic are two instances where investors reacted hastily to the crisis at hand without fully evaluating the long-term prospects of their investments. This is why it is important to maintain a balanced and rational approach to decision-making regardless of market conditions, she claims.

Investors often overestimate their knowledge or ability to predict market movements, leading to risky behaviour. Fear of losing money can cause them to sell in a downturn, while greed during a market rally can lead to overexposure and high risk. Cognitive dissonance occurs when there is a conflict between an investor's beliefs and their actions. For instance, individuals who invest might hold on to losing stocks to avoid admitting they made a bad decision, hoping the stock will rebound.

To counteract these emotional biases, investors can adopt several strategies. These include developing a clear investment plan with set goals and rules. Adhering to this plan helps avoid emotional decisions during market fluctuations. Investors should also periodically review their portfolio and make adjustments based on the long-term goals of the investee company, rather than short-term market movements. Additionally, when faced with negative news about a company, it is important to reassess the company's moat, market opportunity and the execution capacity of its management over three to five years.

Recognizing emotional biases and implementing strategies to manage them can improve decision-making and contribute to long-term investment success.

Amisha adds that during her career, she has encountered various types of mistakes, from missed investment opportunities to investments that didn't unfold as expected. She believes that the first realization of these mistakes typically occurs not through intuition but through observing the actual price behaviour or investment results. When the price behaviour deviates from initial expectations, it serves as the trigger for a more in-depth analysis. Amisha believes that the results and outcomes of one's actions and failures always guide one to introspect and revisit the decision-making framework.

In such situations, Amisha likes to dig deeper to identify the factors she may have missed while considering the investment or to determine whether it is simply a genuine delay in the growth strategy materializing, and the business remains on the right track. She then decides whether to rectify the mistake or ride it out.

Listening to Amisha's personal experiences during her investment journey prompts me to ask if there are tools she employs to help minimize mistakes. Amisha candidly shares, 'Maintaining composure in the equity markets is paramount for making well-informed decisions. To achieve this, I prioritize three facets of well-being: physical, emotional and conscious fitness.'

She emphasizes that incorporating meditation and mindfulness practices into her routine significantly contributes to better decision-making by mitigating stress and enhancing concentration. Her daily regimen includes dedicated time for guided meditation, which improves overall well-being and strength.

This leaves us with a valuable lesson: Mindfulness practices improve one's ability to focus on the present moment and filter out distractions. This enhanced concentration allows one to analyse information more thoroughly and make better-informed decisions. By reducing mental clutter and increasing awareness, meditation—or any other methodology based on personal interest—can help achieve a clearer mindset, which is crucial for evaluating investment opportunities and making strategic decisions.

Beyond this, she firmly believes that quantitative signals and frameworks help reduce significant investing errors arising from style, emotional and behavioural biases by the process of elimination. Well-tested and researched quantitative strategies and models developed by PL help adapt the asset allocation, sector and style mix of the portfolio, while keeping them away from no-go areas. This helps in dynamically navigating the changes in the market landscape.

I ask Amisha to share instances where what she thought was a mistake ended up with a favourable result. And, if that was the case, would she still qualify them as mistakes, or was it a change in circumstance that converted the mistake into a bonanza?

Amisha explains that external circumstances and changes often help convert mistakes into success, with luck sometimes playing a factor. These cases are typically the result of evolving circumstances or unforeseen market dynamics. For example, there have been times when a stock she invested in corrected more sharply than anticipated, or a company's financial performance fell short of expectations, making her judgement appear flawed. In response to such situations, she adopts a methodical approach. She delves deeper into the specific case, conducting a thorough analysis to determine whether the issue is a structural problem or a temporary setback in the company's growth trajectory. This analysis is instrumental and helps her make an informed decision about whether to maintain her investment position or exit.

I then ask her about her process for ensuring that a mistake doesn't become fatal. She shares that for her, having a structured thought process, being systematic and adaptive to changes, and focusing on incremental delta helps her balance risks. The principle of delta ensures that she looks at incremental risks, opportunities, growth, rerating or derating. She emphasizes the importance of maintaining a forward-looking perspective to act rationally. Understanding financial risk and reward, which itself is a moving goal post, helps her stay nimble in dealing with fatal risks. Additionally, staying informed and monitoring the impact of her decisions helps her deal with any deviations promptly, ensuring that a mistake doesn't become fatal.

This brings us another important learning: making sound investment decisions involves having a clear, organized framework for analysing and addressing problems or opportunities. It helps break down complex issues into manageable parts, ensuring that decisions are based on a thorough understanding of all relevant factors. By being systematic, one follows a structured method or process, and by being adaptive, one adjusts the process based on new information or changing circumstances. Combining both ensures one stays on course while remaining flexible enough to pivot when necessary. By examining incremental risks, opportunities and adjustments, one can make more manageable changes and continuously improve while keeping a close eye on the impacts.

I then ask Amisha to share how she has evolved over time by learning from her own mistakes and those of others. I also enquire whether she thinks the human mind tends to become too captivated by greed and fear, leading to the repetition of the same mistakes.

Amisha shares, 'In the thirty-five-plus years I have spent in the financial services industry, I have evolved and learned from both my own mistakes and the mistakes of others. I always remain vigilant against the pitfalls of greed and fear. While human psychology can tempt one to repeat errors, I put in a conscious effort to learn and adapt. It's not always easy, but I believe that only by overcoming these psychological traps can I become a more resilient, adaptable and informed decision-maker.'

She goes on to explain how to incorporate these principles effectively:
- Learn and review
  - Review and reflect: Regularly review investment decisions and outcomes. Analyse what went wrong or right and why. This reflection helps you understand your mistakes and avoid repeating them.

- Document lessons: Keep a journal or log of your investment decisions, including the rationale behind them and their outcomes. This documentation provides valuable insights for future decisions.
- Seek feedback: Engage with mentors or peers to gain different perspectives on your investment strategies and decisions. Constructive feedback can enhance your learning process.

- Avoid greed
  - Set clear goals: Define your investment objectives and risk tolerance. Having clear goals helps you stay focused and prevents you from chasing after quick gains.
  - Diversify: Avoid putting all your money into a single investment. Diversification reduces risk and helps manage the impact of any one investment's performance on your overall portfolio.
  - Stick to your strategy: Develop and adhere to a disciplined investment strategy. Avoid making impulsive decisions based on short-term market movements or sensational news.
- Manage fear
  - Understand market cycles: Recognize that markets go through ups and downs. Understanding these cycles can help you stay calm during market downturns.
  - Maintain a long-term perspective: Focus on long-term goals rather than short-term market fluctuations. A long-term perspective helps you stay invested through volatility.
  - Use stop-loss orders: Implement stop-loss orders to automatically sell investments when they reach a certain price. This can help limit losses and manage fear of significant downturns.
- Develop emotional discipline
  - Follow a plan: Create an investment plan and stick to it. A well-defined plan reduces the likelihood of making emotional decisions.
  - Practice mindfulness: Develop mindfulness techniques to manage stress and maintain a balanced perspective. This can help you make more rational decisions.

Balancing the lessons from past mistakes with the ability to manage emotional responses like greed and fear is essential for long-term investment success. By adopting these practices, you can make more informed and disciplined investment decisions.

I next ask Amisha how she differentiates between errors of commission and errors of omission, and her approach to becoming a better thinker. Reflecting on the question, Amisha explains that errors of commission involve taking action that results in a mistake, while errors of omission are missed opportunities or not taking action when one should have. However, it's usually the errors of commission that stay with one, impact one and teach one. Errors of omission do lead to short-term regret, but that typically disappears quickly.

She adds that to become a better thinker, she embraces continuous learning, stays updated with market trends and conducts in-depth research. She reviews both successful and unsuccessful decisions for valuable lessons. What also helps her is focusing on a long-term vision, resisting the temptation of short-term gains, and maintaining emotional control to make rational decisions.

I then delve into Amisha's approach to balancing ego and commitment bias. She explains that often, the rationale doesn't pan out as anticipated, but it is important not to let ego and commitment bias come in the way. 'I always prioritize objective evaluation of investments and assess whether the original thesis remains intact. If not, I take corrective measures immediately.'

Amisha acknowledges that since her early days in this profession, she has learnt the importance of research and risk management. With predefined exit strategies, she limits potential losses. She also maintains a learning mindset and adjusts her strategy based on new information. This helps her make rational decisions that lead to a better tomorrow, even in the face of initial investment setbacks. She reiterates that the principle of delta, and being adaptive and objective, helps her navigate investment mistakes by rising above biases.

I next ask her how she creates a balance between two sets of views in arriving at an outcome. Amisha emphasizes the importance of open communication among team members, fostering an environment where every opinion is valued. She explains that she encourages data-driven decision-making, ensuring that choices are based on objective analysis rather than personal biases. She appreciates differing views as this allows her to get a holistic picture before making a decision. She notes that diversity is good, both in investments and in the workplace, and the ultimate goal is to build consensus, drawing from different viewpoints to arrive at a decision that reflects the collective wisdom of the team.

She does not trust someone blindly just because they have achieved favourable outcomes in the past. What worked previously may not yield the same results in the future due to changing market conditions, regulations or other factors. Processes drive performance and having a data-driven process approach helps achieve sustainable and repeatable outcomes. She adds that one gets favourable outcomes when talented people are driven by robust processes.

This offers an important learning: incorporating a data-driven approach ensures that decisions are based on concrete evidence and analysis, leading to more predictable and repeatable outcomes. It supports systematic evaluation and improvement, making it easier to achieve sustainable success.

I then ask her to share her thoughts on the role of exuberance and hubris in making bad decisions, such as whether the comfort of being very large allows a mistake to go unnoticed, or if the codification of a process and its transparency justify making a mistake.

Amisha acknowledges that when an individual or organization becomes overly confident or complacent due to its size, it can lead to a false sense of security. In such situations, mistakes may occur because of a belief that past success guarantees future success, even though one knows that isn't true. She believes that no entity, regardless of its size or previous achievements, is immune to making mistakes. Transparency and a clear process should serve as tools for learning and accountability. It's crucial to encourage a culture where individuals are empowered to question decisions and processes, even when things seem to be going well. This helps identify potential issues and address them before they escalate into significant mistakes. Also, an attitude of continuous improvement and a cautiously optimistic culture help in dealing with complacency.

My next question to her is about the impact of personal life and the circumstances surrounding it on decision-making, specifically asking how she maintains a distinction between her personal life and business life to arrive at a good decision.

Amisha smiles as she shares that over the years, she has learned to maintain a clear separation between her personal life and professional responsibilities. As work is of paramount importance to her, she does not let her personal emotions or challenges impact her clients' trust and financial well-being. This commitment serves as a driving force, ensuring that personal emotions or challenges do not influence her decision-making.

She adds, 'I personally think that at times, maintaining separation between personal life and professional responsibilities can be a bit challenging but that definitely helps ensure that you can be fully present and focused in both your personal and professional life, leading to greater satisfaction and effectiveness in each area.'

I ask Amisha if she believes mistakes can become a motivation, to which she responds that rather than dwelling on past errors, she uses mistakes as stepping stones for personal and professional growth. 'The recognition of my mistakes encourages me to analyse what went wrong, why it happened, and how I can avoid similar pitfalls in the future,' she says. She uses mistakes as a motivation to remember that there's always room for improvement, and each mistake is a chance to become a more astute and resilient investor and leader. Simply put, learning, evolving and becoming more tactful with each mistake helps one grow.

I move on to ask Amisha about situations when she feels mistakes become demotivating. She replies, 'It is said that if you find yourself in a hole, don't dig deeper. Find a way out of it! I take inspiration from these words and always accept and learn.' She further explains that mistakes become demotivating only if she doesn't identify and accept them and take measures to rectify them. 'Or if the outcome is large, irreversible, and has a significant and permanent negative impact on many people, I always try to avoid such circumstances by constantly monitoring the impact of my decisions—whether in the markets or in the business—and course correct as needed with agility.'

I ask Amisha how, despite all the negativity surrounding India's infrastructure, she remains bullish on the country.

She emphasizes that while these issues are pertinent, they are minuscule compared to the ocean of opportunities that lie ahead for India. 'We are among the fastest growing economies and are in truly what I believe is India's golden decade.' Because of this, she remains bullish on the country's long-term prospects. Her view is simple—every challenge is an opportunity. For example, as the country addresses infrastructure and logistical problems, these sectors will witness significant development. The government's infrastructure push is not only improving infrastructure but also creating jobs and investment opportunities. Moreover, obstacles drive innovation and entrepreneurial solutions, contributing to the nation's growth.

She adds, 'The way I see it is, the more the problems, the more the solutions there will be, and the higher the growth opportunities will be.

I next ask Amisha how she balances the mindset required to convert what initially appears to be a mistake into a favourable result.

She shares that being agile is an important quality for a successful investor because things don't always go as planned. She approaches the challenge of converting mistakes into favourable results by focusing on adaptability and robust risk management. This approach helps her make the most of the circumstances, whether the mistakes are self-caused or influenced by external factors. She also firmly believes in having a solution-oriented mindset, not a problem-oriented one. 'The principle of delta and theory of relativity help here. This means, I always try to find relatively better solutions, if not the best solutions. I assess what is the best solution at a given point in time for a better outcome,' she shares.

I also ask her what she would change, looking back in time, to reduce her chances of making mistakes and increase her successes, including in areas such as education and allocation. She replies, 'With the benefit of hindsight, I realize that what we've achieved at PL is something I can genuinely be proud of. There will always be regrets about the past, but I'd rather focus on the future. I always look ahead as there is no point thinking about things I cannot change. I simply learn from the past, but I don't get attached to it. It is better to invest my time in changing the future than worrying about the past.'

This teaches us that while it's important to learn from past experiences, it's equally crucial not to become fixated on them. Obsessing over past errors can lead to a negative mindset and hinder progress. One should embrace the art of detaching emotionally from past outcomes to maintain a clear and objective perspective. This helps in making decisions based on current circumstances rather than being clouded by past disappointments. One should channel efforts into activities and projects that will positively impact the future. This includes making improvements, pursuing new opportunities, and working towards goals that will drive growth and success. In short, while learning from past experiences is valuable for growth and avoiding repeated mistakes, it's essential to move beyond them and concentrate on what one can control: the present and future. By doing so, one can make more effective decisions, foster a positive outlook, and work towards achieving one's goals.

I ask Amisha about managing public money, especially since mistakes can also be caused by the public itself—for example, they may pull out of investments when it is time to stay invested. Given that the result often reflects poorly on the investor, I enquired how she balances public image with rational decision-making.

Amisha shares that first and foremost, she believes in maintaining transparency and clear communication as it is essential to keep the public, particularly one's clients, informed about the investment strategy, the potential risks involved and the expected outcomes. This transparency helps manage expectations and reduces the likelihood of a knee-jerk reaction when market conditions change. She also adheres to a well-thought-out investment strategy that considers both short-term and long-term goals. All her decisions are rooted in deep research and analysis rather than reacting to market noise. This helps her make rational choices, even when the public sentiment might be against it.

I ask Amisha about situations where, despite a successful portfolio, the media, investors or potential investors highlight a mistake to showcase a wrong result. I wanted to know whether in such situations, she views this as part of an overall performance, or whether she employs second-level thinking to learn for the future.

She emphasizes that she prefers to acknowledge and learn from the mistake rather than diluting it as part of overall performance. Mistakes are an inherent part of investing, and even the most successful investors have made them. By delving into the specifics of the mistake, she aims to understand what went wrong, why it happened and how to prevent similar errors in the future. Simply put, it's not about dwelling on the mistake but rather using it as a stepping stone for improvement.

She adds that she continues to make mistakes because, in the world of investing, no amount of experience or education can completely eliminate the possibility of errors. Even a legendary investor like Warren Buffett admits to making mistakes. Investing is a constant journey of learning and improvement, and she stresses that it is important to recognize, admit, rectify, learn, introspect and prepare a mental and emotional framework to avoid the same mistake in the future. Even a wise person makes mistakes, but only a fool repeats his mistakes. The endeavour must be to learn from mistakes, reduce them as much as rationally possible, and constantly conducting risk–reward analyses to stay rational.

Before ending my conversation with Amisha, I ask her about her personal interests. She shares that she loves listening to the latest Bollywood dance numbers, as they always lift her spirits. When it comes to entertainment, her favourite singers are Rahat Fateh Ali Khan, Kailash Kher and Arijit Singh, and her all-time favourite song is '*Main jahan rahoon, main kahin bhi rahoon, teri yaad saath hai*'. Her favourite movie is *Hum Tum*, while her favourite actors are Shah Rukh Khan and Ranbir Kapoor.

Another activity she really enjoys is spending time with nature—whether on the beach or amidst the mountains. Talking about her childhood memories, she shares, 'I was really playful as a child. On Saturdays, we had morning school, and I used to find it difficult to get up early. I would somehow convince my mother to allow me to skip school. Instead, I would get ready by 11 a.m. and spend the entire day reading a book borrowed from the school library. My aim was to finish one book every Saturday. I used to be so engrossed in reading that my mother would have to call me several times to even just eat lunch!

She also has a strong interest in sports, even those traditionally thought of as being only for boys. She adds that she was particularly good at marbles, accumulating a huge collection through her wins. Every time we played, I used to lend them to my guy friends and charge them interest in terms of extra marbles for lending. At one point, all the marbles in my entire society belonged to me!' she shares.

Amisha's favourite travel destination is Italy given her love for its history, rich culture and emphasis on family values.

Amisha also expressed that she is quite a foodie and at home nothing spells more comforting to her than bajre ki roti and dahi and when it comes to outside cuisine, then it would be Lebanese food. In drinks, Amisha enjoys having fresh fruit juices.

When I asked her about favourite restaurant, she said, 'I find true joy in eating home-cooked meals; so, my favourite restaurant is home!'

Amisha's favourite quote is 'Small things make it perfect, but perfection is not a small thing.' She shared that it explains the significance of even the smallest elements in creating something truly exceptional.

Jain scriptures hold a special place in Amisha's heart, and she finds immense value not only in their teachings but also the theory of karma makes her feel fearless, focused and centred.

CHAPTER 20

MADHUSUDAN KELA

The investing mastermind with a heart of gold

THIS chapter focuses on the journey of the well-known strategic investor and mentor to passionate individuals and entrepreneurs, Madhusudan Kela, or Madhu, as we affectionately call him.

Reflecting on his past, Madhu shared in one of his TV interviews that, for him, the stock market was a means to achieve a better living, as had he done something else, he wouldn't have earned as much. He emphasizes that the stock market is 'not a means to make income, but a medium to create wealth.'

With over thirty years of experience in the investment business, Madhu is one of the most eminent and seasoned investors in India's stock market industry. He shares his take on investing and mistakes, straight from his heart and enriched by his vast experience.

Early days and educational background

Madhu is originally from a small village in Chhattisgarh. Raised by a father who worked as a bank employee, Madhu learned early on the importance of diligence, analytical skills, comprehensive understanding and dedication in achieving success. Coming from a modest background, he faced numerous hurdles in pursuing his education and career goals. He earned a Master's degree in management studies from the esteemed K.J. Somaiya Institute of Management Studies and Research (SIMSR) in Mumbai. His career began in the early 1990s, and he was initially associated with a few brokerage firms and financial institutions.

With solid experience in hand, Madhu later joined Reliance Capital, where he made a significant impact and was very successful. In 2004, he was awarded the Business Standard Equity Fund Manager of the Year by Dr Manmohan Singh, the then prime minister of India.

In 2017, Madhu founded MKVentures, his proprietary investment vehicle. With close to three decades of experience and learnings from the Indian capital markets, he comes across as a man who can speak to you as if you were a next-door neighbour, explaining ideas, visions and opportunities with ease. He is an inspiration to many investors, and has earned the admiration of market players for his ability to make wise, practical and simple investment decisions.

Personal interests and motivations

I start by asking Madhu about his childhood and the memories he cherishes, and whether these had any impact on shaping his mindset in later years.

He shared that as a child, he was a simple boy with persuasive ability, which he says he still possesses. Despite coming from a small village, he was always keenly interested in business. This orientation led him to take up various small business ventures during his higher secondary school days through college.

Madhu says he loves listening to music as it brings him peace and joy. For many, music serves as a backdrop to their cherished moments. He adds that one of his favourite singers is late Mukesh, one of the most iconic voices in Indian music. One of his favourite songs, which resonates deeply with Madhu's philosophy, is '*Sab kuch seekha humne na sikhi hoshiyari*' from the movie *Anari*. Translated roughly, it means 'I have learnt everything, except how to be smart'.

Perhaps, Madhu is hinting at the idea that while you can learn many things, you can't learn it all and consider yourself truly smart.

Passionately, he says, 'Mukesh ji's voice in this song carries a poignant sense of vulnerability and sincerity, making it a masterpiece that continues to resonate with listeners even today. His ability to evoke such profound emotions through his singing is what makes him truly legendary.'

Madhu goes on to share that family gatherings have always held a special place in his heart—a chance to connect, share laughter and create lasting memories. He enjoys dressing in Indian casual wear, finding comfort and style in traditional attire that reflects his cultural roots. He also has an insatiable craving for pani-puri, savouring each tangy bite with delight. When it comes to drinks, nothing pleases him more than red wine, which he enjoys during quiet evenings or with family and friends. His favourite restaurant is Wasabi by Morimoto, well known for its Japanese cuisine.

Among all the places he has travelled, Europe stands out as his favourite destination. He is fascinated by the rich history, diverse cultures and stunning landscapes of the continent. Madhu is a lively individual with a deep love for simple pleasures.

When I ask Madhu about his favourite movie, he mentions *3 Idiots*, a film that resonates with his love for wit and heart-warming stories. His favourite actor is Aamir Khan, whom he admires for his powerful performances, versatility and dedication to his craft, which have left a lasting impact.

We move on to discussing books, and Madhu shares that his favourite books are *The Psychology of Money: Timeless Lessons on Wealth, Greed and Happiness* by Morgan Housel, and *Thinking, Fast and Slow* by Daniel Kahneman.

When I ask him what he finds inspiring in these books, he elaborates that *The Psychology of Money*, to him, is a thought-provoking exploration of how people think about and manage money. Housel delves into the psychological factors that influence financial decisions, illustrating how emotions, biases and personal experiences shape our relationship with money.

As for *Thinking, Fast and Slow*, Madhu considers it a ground-breaking book that explores the dual system of thoughts that drive human decision-making. This profound exploration of the human mind examines its influence on every aspect of our lives. It challenges readers to rethink how they perceive and interact with the world, offering insights that are both intellectually stimulating and practically applicable.

I ask Madhu to tell me about his favourite quote, as I was curious to understand what inspires his philosophy towards life and investing.

He says, with a smile, 'The stock market is a place where people with money meet with people with experience. And then, people with experience get all the money and people with money get only the experience.'

He also shares another favourite: 'There is a world of difference between knowing what to do and actually doing it.'

Now, equipped with a better understanding of his personality, I explore with Madhu the subject of mistakes and the lessons they offer.

Mistakes and learnings

Madhu believes that 'It's not just upbringing, mistakes can be caused by a variety of reasons,' emphasizing that the primary causes of mistakes are usually personality and attitude. While upbringing does play a role, education is only one of the factors in anyone's success. To him, discipline is what creates the real differentiation. Discipline helps one understand the difference between knowing what to do and knowing what not to do.

He emphasizes that a person's inherent traits and their outlook on life significantly influence their decisions and actions. Education of any kind, including from experience, shapes one's ability to make informed choices and avoid missteps. Discipline, on the other hand, instils consistency, self-control and the ability to learn from past mistakes, enabling individuals to course correct and grow.

Madhu classifies mistakes as a function of how a person reacts to situations, whether in moments of calm or stress. He adds that times of crisis or significant external events amplify the vagaries of the human mind, leading to powerful domino effects and ripple shocks that make the investment landscape even more volatile. These situations institutionalize and create patterns of common behavioural mistakes. He says, 'Talk about dealing with a single deranged mind versus the entire human race!'

I remember listening to one of Madhu's TV interviews, where he shared, 'Selling a stock is a very difficult art. Sometimes you can be too early, sometimes you can be too late.'

It's ironic that there are many books and articles on how to buy stocks but very few on when to sell.

Madhu adds that, in his experience, one of the mistakes investors often make is trying to time an outsized and large opportunity once it is identified.

He explains that the correlation of a large opportunity will always leave enough on the table, and one should not make the mistake of perfecting the entry price. If the opportunity plays out as envisaged, the return will still be enormous. It's like the saying: 'don't be penny wise, pound foolish'.

According to Madhu, trading—buying or selling, not day trading—is ultimately about valuations. However, the real question is what phase of the market one is in.

He shares his wisdom: 'Value is something that should encourage you to analyse a stock more, but you should never get trapped in value.'

He firmly believes it's important to revisit one's investment strategy once in a quarter—or even sooner, depending on market conditions. This is crucial to assess whether things are going well and whether there's a need to replace something with more compelling opportunities.

Madhu here touches upon two important aspects: the revalidation of your basis for owning something and the much more complex task of evaluating the opportunity cost of missing out on something bigger that could have attracted your capital.

In terms of realizing errors, Madhu says that at the start of his career, his approach was more result-based, which later evolved into an intuition-based one.

Over time, he has strengthened and fine-tuned his approach, choosing not to wait for results but go the extra mile to ensure that he doesn't get trapped in the wrong investments.

Admitting and rectifying errors

Like some other legendary fund managers in this book, Madhu agrees that the admission or recognition of a mistake is often the first critical step in addressing it.

'What one cannot admit being wrong about cannot ever be corrected,' he adds.

Acknowledging errors, especially in public, requires humility and courage, but it can open the door to learning and self-reflection. Transparency fosters trust and respect from others, as it shows commitment to honesty and self-improvement. Moreover, by putting in the effort to correct a mistake, one demonstrates resilience and a willingness to grow, which could lead to better decision-making and a stronger character in the long run.

I then ask Madhu if he uses any tools or methodologies, such as meditation, quantitative analysis or a referral board, to help minimize errors.

Madhu answers that it is very important to remain disciplined and stick to a process, both in good times and bad.

He explains that while discipline may come from upbringing, personality, or meditation and focus, it is crucial for investors to maintain clarity and composure, even during market fluctuations.

By staying disciplined, market investors can consistently adhere to their investment plans, make informed decisions, and ultimately, achieve their financial goals.

Madhu's strategic approach to sectoral allocation and his willingness to take calculated risks underscore his ability to navigate market dynamics and capitalize on emerging opportunities. On multiple occasions, he has stressed the importance of controlling emotions and continuously learning from various sources to refine one's investment approach.

Curious, I ask Madhu why we often call something a mistake even if its outcome was favourable and produced better returns.

I also ask if mistakes that unexpectedly result in positive outcomes can be considered blessings in disguise, as they may guide one without damaging their portfolio or wealth.

Madhu opines that serendipity does sometimes work in the market. He emphasizes the importance of differentiating the process from the outcome. Over the years, he acknowledges that he has often made errors in judgement, including but not limited to bet sizing errors, timing buys or sells incorrectly, overriding his intuitive investment call and taking promoter guidance too seriously. Many of these mistakes proved beneficial in hindsight.

From his wealth of experience, Madhu identifies at least four types of mistakes one can make. The first is buying right in the wrong quantity, which means not meeting your conviction with adequate backing. The second is ignoring valuations when buying or getting carried away by momentum and the fear of missing out, or selling too quickly without analysing the potential that still lies ahead for a company or sector. The third mistake is ignoring the power of the subconscious mind and not deliberating or fact-seeking to support or dismiss it. Finally, the fourth mistake is getting overly influenced by lofty or even negative management talk, overlooking the fact that human traits like greed and fear can be extreme.

Madhu advises analysing a mistake to determine whether it is fatal like a heart attack or if it is likely to pass with little or no damage.

Fatal errors are what Madhu considers the most important to avoid in investing. He explains that while experience can help minimize the number of mistakes, one cannot entirely eliminate them. What one can control, however, is ensuring that mistakes do not become fatal. When I ask him how he achieves this, he shares that he does so in one or more of the following ways: through bet resizing and cutting positions when realizing mistakes; a disciplined, process-oriented approach to increase objectivity and reduce subjectivity; and finally, re-evaluating his investments every quarter, if not earlier.

He further elaborates that, in his experience with stock investing, effective bet sizing and position management are crucial for managing risk and optimizing returns. It is important to understand that betting too large on a single stock can expose a portfolio to significant risk, especially if the stock underperforms. Just because the result may be different if a stock performs well does not make the process of betting too heavily on a stock right.

Recognizing mistakes and adjusting one's portfolio are vital to protecting it from further losses. He stresses that investors must remain vigilant and adaptable, regularly assessing their decisions. More importantly, they must be willing to cut losses early rather than holding on to a long position out of hope or stubbornness. A disciplined approach helps maintain a balanced portfolio and minimizes the impact of inevitable errors in judgement.

Many investors suffer from the delusion that there is an aura around what they own and remain in disbelief even when facts work against them. The loss on screen appears temporary to them due to this aura, and they fail to see this as stubbornness and ego, rather than being pragmatic about it.

This reminds him of the analogy of the pigeon who shuts his eyes when he sees a cat, hoping the cat will go away, and it won't be eaten.

Greed and fear

Upon asking Madhu whether one can evolve over time by learning from one's own mistakes and those of others, or if the human mind becomes so captivated by greed or fear that it overlooks and revisits the same mistakes, he shares an experience.

Says Madhu, 'I would like to cite here the extensive work and opinion of Charlie Munger on the behavioural biases and patterns that affect all walks of society, including investing. There are clear patterns of the same basic mistakes that most people tend to commit. In my view, the litmus test for any long-term investor is to identify and avoid these mistakes on a continuous basis, almost as a daily habit, like brushing our teeth or having a bath. It is a constant exercise in restraint and judgement.'

He continues, 'To that extent, I have been fortunate to identify my own inherent biases and weaknesses early, so as to minimize the errors stemming from them; and also, to recognize and benefit from such biases and errors when I see them being committed by others.'

Errors of commission and omission

When talking about the approach he takes to differentiate between errors of commission and errors of omission to become a better thinker, Madhu shares that there are more than 6,000 stocks listed in Indian markets, with nearly 1,500 stocks having a market cap greater than Rs 500 crore. There is opportunity for every style of investing. He prefers to restrict his universe to a limited number of stocks that meet his investment criteria. He says he is happy to miss out on wealth creators that fail his screening list. The idea, he explains, is to continuously fine-tune the checklist and narrow the selection list.

This leaves us with an important learning from Madhu: the key to his success lies in staying true to his approach while maintaining discipline in stock selection. By restricting options, he ensures that each holding aligns closely with his investment philosophy and objectives. This focused approach allows for deeper research and a better understanding of each stock's potential, reducing the chances of being swayed by market noise or short-term trends.

Balancing ego and commitment bias

I quiz Madhu with a googly next. I ask him if, during his career, there have been times when he took an investment bet that seemed to be a mistake, resulting in a drawdown, but he persisted—either leading to a bigger mistake, or finding a sudden turnaround. What methodology does he employ to manage and balance ego and commitment bias to achieve a better result?

He candidly admits that he once made the critical error of letting a position become big enough to account for a sizeable portion of his portfolio.

While he didn't incur a loss on his original invested capital, he did have a large drawdown from the highs. The emotional stress and attachment to his bet forced him to hold on for longer than necessary and bear an even larger drawdown. He failed to read the changing signals on the company and the stock.

He says, 'Whatever you do, as an investor, never let an individual position affect your mind to such an extent that it becomes difficult to behave rationally.'

Here, Madhu shares a nugget of wisdom—the difference between owning a stock as a unit for returns and managing a portfolio. If a stock fails, it should not cause the entire portfolio to fail. Such maturity in stock investing requires not only financial acumen in position sizing and restriction but also strong emotional discipline.

It is important to maintain objectivity and emotional balance when making investment decisions. Allowing an individual stock to dominate one's emotions can lead to decisions that harm overall financial health. By diversifying, sticking to a well–thought-out plan and maintaining a long-term perspective, one can reduce the emotional impact of market movements and improve the chances of achieving investment goals.

Regarding Madhu's approach to balancing two sets of views in arriving at an outcome, he shares that his investment company has a culture of open-ended, free-flowing discussions within the team. Anyone is welcome to give inputs, provided they are specific in nature and not generic. He then tries to question individual biases and reduce subjectivity to the extent possible.

This response led me to ask Madhu if, when the outcome is favourable, he continues to work with the same people who got it right, knowing that the next outcome could be different.

He candidly answers, 'This question reminds me of the concept of Vaastu and positive and negative vibes. I am a firm believer in relationships and the fact that every relationship has a certain vibe associated with it.'

He continues, 'Favourable outcomes do reinforce my comfort in working with an individual. Over time, the vibes or intuition are replaced by actual judgement of the person's strengths and weaknesses, and how the partnership can be more fruitful for both of us.'

Madhu adds, 'Also, I ensure that all my important relationships are not transactional but rooted in respect and appreciation of each other's capabilities and circumstances. This also allows me not to worry about specific event-driven outcomes once I have placed my trust in the individual and the process of engagement with them.'

Role played by exuberance and hubris in eliminating bad decisions

Madhu points out that most investing decisions made when a stock is in strong upside momentum (or conversely, in a free fall) are bad decisions. However, these decisions can appear great at the time as the stock continues to move up despite poor fundamentals. He notes, 'Investors usually pat themselves on the back, assuming it is their stock selection at work, when in reality it is nothing more than a leveraged portfolio balance sheet meeting the right environment for froth!'

Impact of personal life and circumstances on making a mistake

Madhu admits that he would be lying if he said personal life, health and similar factors do not impact decision-making at work (or vice versa). However, he shares that over time, he has managed to be disciplined and focused on his work, while keeping it separate from his personal life. He emphasizes that having an understanding family and a strong, trustworthy core team at work have played a big role in providing him the mental peace and space to think clearly, enabling him to focus his energies on what he loves doing—investing.

Through great effort, Madhu believes he has reached a point in his career and life where he can handle bad days at work or in personal life with relative ease, without allowing hubris to dominate on the good days. A rational, balanced mind allows him to make better decisions.

He also believes that making mistakes is acceptable, but not learning from them or failing to fine-tune one's process is unacceptable. Every mistake he has made in the past has taught him a lot and motivated him to overcome similar errors in the future. He shares that mistakes often become demotivating at the absolute peak or bottom of a cycle. As he puts it, 'Night is usually darkest before dawn.'

An important thing to avoid, according to Madhu, is committing a 'flagship error'—publicly committing to a particular style of investing.

Madhu prefers to be opportunistic yet rational in his investment decision-making. This allows him to identify and profit from patterns or deviations when others stray from their stated, publicly committed investment styles. According to him, one of the best ways to avoid mistakes and balance public image with rational decision-making is to work only with serious, discerning investors who have a strong sense of engagement and skin in the game.

Typically, observes Madhu, investors who commit large sums of money are more patient with their capital and more likely to focus on understanding the process rather than just concentrating on market outcomes.

'It is our constant endeavour to find and engage with such investors,' he says.

To have a growth-oriented mindset, Madhu emphasizes the importance of learning and self-improvement. Mistakes are a natural part of life and an inevitable aspect of any learning process, whether in personal development, professional growth, or any other area. What distinguishes successful individuals and organizations is their ability to learn from these mistakes and use them as a foundation for future success. Simply acknowledging a mistake isn't enough; understanding the underlying causes is key. This might involve analysing external factors, examining internal biases or reconsidering assumptions. Embracing mistakes as learning opportunities rather than failures can lead to greater innovation, resilience and a deeper understanding of oneself and the world.

Additionally, factors such as harsh self-criticism, external pressure, lack of support and a focus on failure can contribute to demotivation. However, by fostering a more supportive, growth-oriented mindset and viewing mistakes as opportunities rather than setbacks, it is possible to overcome challenges and maintain motivation, even in the face of errors.

Being bullish on India

Madhu is bullish on India, and the setbacks do not bother him much. 'I see all this as an opportunity, and it reinforces my bullish stance and conviction. Potholes, traffic jams and poor infrastructure all mean there is huge scope for development and growth,' he says. The fighting spirit and passion of people to prosper despite all the challenges make him bullish about the Indian story.

An investor's public image

Madhu says that despite his popularity, he has never been carried away by media appearances. He explains that he has always spoken his mind in public interactions and has managed funds with the 'utmost sincerity,' without worrying about looking good in front of investors. Despite several wins, he makes it a point to understand the root causes of mistakes and how they can be avoided in the future.

'Keep things simple' is Madhu's uncomplicated formula for success.

Over the years, he has developed a clear and focused approach to investments. He sticks to the basics, usually focusing on familiar sectors. Along the way, he tries to avoid profiteering whenever he comes across a known pattern of bias or mistake. He is also happy to let go of opportunities and clearly states that it is not possible to participate in every party in town. He needs to stay focused and disciplined.

I ask Madhu what he would do to reduce mistakes and increase strikes.

He would like to learn from the mistakes made by others, read more books and spend more time on understanding the companies in which he invests. He reflects that during his last role as head of AMC, he spent a lot of time on non-investment-related activity, which, in the hindsight, he should have avoided. When asked about continuing to make mistakes, he replies, 'To err is human ... to forgive, divine!'

Talking to Madhu showcases his skill in investment. Learning from his mistakes can be a blueprint for making informed investment decisions. Madhu credits the legendary guru, Rakesh Jhunjhunwala, for shaping his investment acumen. True to his philosophy of diversification, his investment portfolio reflects his ability to balance risks with opportunities.

CHAPTER 21

RAMESH DAMANI

The lessons on mistakes and the role of humility from a true blue-blooded veteran

RAMESH Damani is a name synonymous with India's equity markets. Known for his sharp investment insights and strategic vision, he has earned respect as one of the country's most influential market veterans, with over three decades of experience. He is currently managing director of Ramesh S. Damani Finance and chairman of Avenue Supermarts (DMart).

Mr Damani is also well recognized for guiding both beginners and seasoned investors. His journey began in the early 1980s when he completed his MBA at California State University. Returning to India in 1989, at a pivotal moment in its history, he witnessed the country's economic liberalization, driven by transformative political leadership. This era of opening doors to foreign investments and nurturing an emerging stock market proved to be the perfect backdrop for Mr Damani's investment prowess. Leveraging his deep understanding of macroeconomics, business fundamentals and market cycles, he carved a legacy in equity investments—one that continues to inspire generations of market participants.

Anyone observing Mr Damani over the years would have come to recognize him for his long-term investment philosophy—he is the Indian stock market's lambi race ka ghoda (a horse for the long race).

In this pursuit, he has always emphasized the importance of identifying quality businesses early and staying invested through market fluctuations. He advocates simplicity in investing, often reiterating the power of compounding and the importance of patience. Over the years, he has been instrumental in educating the masses through his talks, interviews and participation in forums like the Bombay Stock Exchange (BSE). He has been a well-known, or shall we say 'well-recognized', face on Indian business television.

His journey is a testament to how clarity of thought and disciplined execution can yield extraordinary results in the stock market. His legacy continues to inspire a generation of investors who look up to him not just for his financial wisdom but also for his humility and unwavering passion for wealth creation.

Does this mean the veteran has made no mistakes? And if he has, how did he deal with them? Did he allow them to impact his decision-making, especially when he was handling money belonging to others? He answers this rather stoically, quoting from the Bhagwat Gita: 'There are no mistakes in life, only lessons.'

For Mr Damani, investing is not just about numbers, charts or strategies. It's deeply personal, shaped by his history, beliefs and even fears. One of India's most respected investors, he started his journey in the equity markets and has since learnt that investing is as much about understanding oneself as it is about understanding businesses and cycles.

He acknowledges that upbringing plays a significant role in shaping how one approaches risk. 'Middle-class people are risk-averse. It's hard to put money on the table,' he declares. This ingrained caution comes from a deep-seated belief in preserving what one has, rather than risking it for the unknown. For someone born into a middle-class family, the fear of losing hard-earned money can outweigh the allure of returns, making every financial decision a battle between prudence and opportunity. However, investing demands a departure from this mindset. It requires the courage to take calculated risks and the humility to accept that not all bets will pay off. For Mr Damani, overcoming this risk aversion was a pivotal step in his journey as an investor.

Like most seasoned investors, he is deeply aware of the comfort trap, or mistakes made in good times. He admits, 'Complacency is dangerous.' Reflecting on mistakes made during prosperous periods, he recalls moments when success bred a casual 'dekha jayega' attitude (we'll see what happens).

Sometimes, tax-saving considerations overshadowed better judgement, leading to investments he wouldn't have made otherwise. 'Success can lull even the sharpest minds into a false sense of invincibility, a trap that often leads to decisions based on convenience rather than conviction,' he observes.

On the other hand, while good times bring complacency, bad times can trigger fear. Mr Damani candidly shares that during market crashes or crises like Covid-19, panic takes over. 'In those moments, the survival instinct kicks in, and rationality often goes out of the window.' Mistakes made in fear—selling prematurely or exiting fundamentally strong stocks—can leave scars just as deep as those made in arrogance.

One of Mr Damani's greatest inspirations, Warren Buffett serves as a reminder to respect capital above all else. 'Buffett refuses to bet even a dollar on a sporting outcome,' he notes, emphasizing the need for discipline and restraint in all financial decisions.

Recognizing mistakes as an inevitable part of any journey, he believes the markets are relentless teachers. 'When your hypothesis doesn't play out, you know you've made a mistake,' he says. The key lies in recognizing this and acting quickly. Often, haste and overconfidence can blur judgement, leading to decisions that seem sound in the moment but prove costly in hindsight.

For him, markets demand honesty above all else. 'To survive, you have to be honest—not just with others but with yourself. Recognizing mistakes is crucial because denial only amplifies losses.' Once recognized, the first step to recovering from a mistake is admitting it. 'You can't let ego stand in the way,' he advises. For many investors, ego becomes the poisoned chalice they refuse to put down, even as they sip losses with every passing moment. 'Once you've taken a loss, you can move on. But until then, it's like knowingly drinking poison.' His metaphor of the poisoned chalice captures the essence of market mistakes: the longer one clings to a failing position, the harder it becomes to escape. It's a lesson in humility and acceptance, virtues that are valuable not just in investing but in life itself.

For Mr Damani, every mistake is a stepping stone to wisdom. The markets, with their cycles of exuberance and despair, are unforgiving but fair. They reward those who learn and adapt, while punishing those who refuse to. 'Mistakes are inevitable,' he reflects. 'But what separates successful investors is how they respond to them.' By respecting capital, shedding ego and embracing humility, Mr Damani continues to inspire generations of investors, showing that mistakes aren't merely setbacks—they are the building blocks of a resilient and enduring investment philosophy.

So, how does he navigate the investment maze? What is the wisdom he has gained from the markets? His empirical learning is that investing, at its core, is a balancing act of intellect, temperament and self-awareness. As in any journey, mistakes are inevitable, but the lessons they leave behind can be transformative. For an experienced investor, the focus is less on perfection and more on the process. After all, success in the markets comes from learning to play to your strengths, staying humble and sticking to your principles.

For him, his conviction comes from the concept of valuation of businesses. Every investment begins with a question: What is this business worth? For seasoned investors, the answer doesn't lie in complex models but in a straightforward evaluation of market cap, enterprise value and intrinsic worth. 'Buy when the difference is yawning in your favour', goes the mantra—no discounted cash flow required. Knowing the why and what behind a purchase makes it easier to navigate mistakes because there's clarity about the initial rationale. With experience, the margin for serious errors in valuation narrows.

Independent thinking is another key. He firmly believes that determining a business's worth allows you to trust your own judgement and not get swayed by the crowd. And if the investment turns out to be a mistake? Accept it with grace and move on.

Another point that Mr Damani has come to believe firmly is that markets have a way of flattering everyone in good times. 'It's important to recognize why you made money,' he reflects. Was it because of rigorous research or simply because the rising tide of a bull market lifted all boats? Remembering John Kenneth Galbraith's warning—'Everyone is a genius in a bull market'—

is crucial for keeping ego in check. Humility ensures that one doesn't mistake luck for skill.

For him, true wealth isn't built on quick gains but on the steady power of compounding. 'Diversify. Don't leverage. Be humble,' are his three golden rules. Leverage, after all, can wipe out years of gains in an instant—'anything times zero will always be zero'. That statement is so easy to understand, and this ability to simplify seemingly complex issues is what has kept him in the race longer than most in the Indian stock market.

Mr Damani's advice has always been that the focus must remain on incremental growth, on raising the compounding percentage, rather than chasing fleeting victories. Another crucial learning comes from this beautifully simple piece of advice shared by him: play to your strengths. 'How do you beat Viswanathan Anand? Don't play chess with him,' the wise investor quips. The markets are full of temptations, but success comes from staying within your circle of competence.

The moral is clear: avoid envy, and focus on an inner scorecard. Compete with yourself, not others, and build on what you already know.

Like several other investing stalwarts mentioned in this book, Mr Damani emphasizes that mistakes in investing can take two distinct forms—errors of commission and errors of omission. The former, given the sheer number of decisions an investor must make, is almost unavoidable. However, the latter—missing an opportunity that was within reach—leaves a more lasting impact. These missed chances often demand a deeper level of introspection to ensure they are not repeated.

This is where the importance of independence in decision-making becomes evident. He views investing as a deeply personal journey that requires both conviction and resilience. He advises, 'Listen to everyone, quietly, but make your own decisions.' In the solitary world of investing, there is no room for passing blame. Mistakes, when they happen, are entirely one's own to bear. Reflecting his philosophical outlook, he often quotes, 'I am the master of my fate. I am the captain of my soul.'

This blend of self-reliance and a contemplative approach is what sets him apart. His temperament—marked by emotional stability and rationality—has been instrumental in helping him avoid rash or poorly thought-out decisions. He emphasizes that the ultimate goal is not to get every stock right but to ensure the overall portfolio performs well. For him, success is rooted in a disciplined, process-oriented mindset that accepts occasional errors while focusing on long-term gains.

He also draws parallels between life and the markets, noting that both are shaped by challenges. Criticism, failure and being underestimated are far greater motivators than constant approval. One of his most memorable lessons came during a bull market when he lost money. It taught him a crucial principle: 'Drive with your eyes on the road ahead, not glued to the rearview mirror.'

He also encourages investors to confront challenges head-on, steer clear of herd mentality, and approach crowded trades with scepticism. Mistakes, though unavoidable, become invaluable lessons when paired with the right mindset and a commitment to growth, ultimately leading to sustained success.

For Mr Damani, the optimistic and seasoned investor, perspective is everything. While market cycles can be turbulent, he believes returns—not the bumps along the road—ultimately shape one's outlook. 'In returns, every crisis serves as an opportunity,' he says, reflecting on the extraordinary journey of the Indian equity market. During his lifetime, the Sensex has climbed from a modest 800 points to over 80,000—a transformation he has witnessed firsthand, naturally encouraging him to adopt a glass-half-full mindset. Optimism, he asserts, is a vital trait for any investor aiming for success.

'Great ideas are rare,' he explains, emphasizing the importance of recognizing and acting on them with conviction. He humorously refers to this as 'backing up the truck'—an act of doubling down when one is confident in a game-changing idea. It's not easy, but the rewards are often worth the leap of faith. At the core of this approach is an unwavering belief in independent thinking. 'Don't outsource your decision-making or follow the crowd's cheerful consensus,' he warns. To him, the best investment decisions come from trusting one's own analysis, not external noise.

Another step he has adopted is that of steadfast independence, which is also why he has steered clear of managing money for friends and relatives who casually seek his advice, often expecting quick and easy gains. 'They don't understand the patience and discipline required for compounding,' he laments. The process is far from easy, and he avoids the dissonance that comes with such unrealistic expectations. Instead, he focuses on nurturing his investments without external pressures, keeping his strategies grounded in long-term principles.

He also makes it a point to avoid discussing individual stock picks in the media, preferring instead to share his thoughts on sectors as a whole. While he acknowledges the media's fairness in general, he remains cautious about how specific ideas might be interpreted or sensationalized.

Mistakes, for him, are an unavoidable part of the investing journey. 'To err is human,' he acknowledges, but he views mistakes as affordable lessons—stepping stones to mastering the art of compounding. 'The best antidote to errors is successful compounding,' he advises, emphasizing the importance of learning from failures and staying committed to long-term growth. Even with decades of experience, he admits to always worrying. 'When markets are volatile, I pray for calmness. When they're calm, I hope for volatility,' he quips with a smile, embodying the paradoxical mindset of a seasoned investor who understands the cyclical nature of markets.

In essence, for Mr Damani, investing is not just about numbers—it's about maintaining a resilient and optimistic outlook, embracing mistakes as learning opportunities, and committing to the transformative power of compounding. 'With the right mindset, every crisis becomes a chance to grow, and every lesson learned adds to the wisdom that shapes lasting success.'

CHAPTER 22

PUNITA KUMAR-SINHA

The champion of breaking investment barriers

WITH an illustrious career spanning over three decades, Dr Punita Kumar-Sinha is a towering figure in investment management and financial markets. Her journey is marked by an impressive blend of deep expertise, groundbreaking achievements and a commitment to excellence in governance.

Punita's extensive experience encompasses capital allocation and financial strategy, reflecting her profound understanding of global markets. Her career began in the early 1990s, a period when she was at the forefront of pioneering foreign investments in emerging markets with a particular focus on the Indian subcontinent, a bold move that significantly shaped the landscape of international finance in the region. This early innovation laid the foundation for a career defined by vision, leadership and immense success.

As the founder of Pacific Paradigm Advisors, Punita established an independent investment advisory and management firm with a keen focus on Asia. Her leadership at Pacific Paradigm is a testament to her dedication to navigating the complex financial dynamics of the region, offering insightful and strategic advice to clients across the Asia-Pacific area on both investments and governance. She has also chaired the investment committee at the CFA Institute while serving on its global Board of Governors. She continues to contribute to her alma mater, IIT Delhi, as chair of the Investment Advisory Board.

Punita's career is distinguished by her tenure at several prestigious financial institutions. At Blackstone, she served as senior managing director and head and chief investment officer of Blackstone Asia Advisors, where she played a crucial role in steering the firm's investment strategy in Asia. Her nearly fifteen-year role as senior portfolio manager and chief investment officer for The India Fund (NYSE: IFN) further underscores her deep expertise in managing one of the largest India-focused funds in the United States.

Before her impactful years at Blackstone, Punita held significant positions at Oppenheimer Asset Management and CIBC World Markets, where she managed funds focusing on India and Asia. Her earlier roles in quantitative investing in international and emerging markets at Battery March (a Legg Mason company), Standish Ayer & Wood (a BNY Mellon company), JP Morgan and IFC/World Bank provided her with a robust foundation in global financial markets and asset management.

Such a successful career in a field like investing almost always comes from a good education. Punita earned a PhD and a Master's in finance from the Wharton School, University of Pennsylvania, and holds an MBA from Drexel University, Philadelphia. Her undergraduate degree with distinction in chemical engineering from IIT, New Delhi, adds to her strong analytical and technical background. Additionally, she is a CFA charter holder, further underscoring her expertise in finance.

Despite her impressive career, she maintains the pragmatic view that mistakes are an inherent part of the investment journey. Punita's formative years significantly shaped her investment approach. Growing up in a post-Partition family that highly valued education, she learned the importance of diligence and caution. Her middle-class upbringing, while instilling a strong work ethic, also fostered a risk-averse mindset.

These early lessons have contributed to her systematic and prudent investment style.

During times of crisis, Punita advocates for a strategic approach: either capitalize on the downturn by purchasing more assets, forecasting a potential bear market, or carefully assessing the risks before making hasty decisions. The key, she emphasizes, is to stay calm and conduct thorough research rather than reacting impulsively.

In assessing investment decisions, Punita relies heavily on results. She explains that fund managers receive daily reports that serve as a real-time validation of their decisions. Good outcomes confirm that the investment strategy is on the right track. For her, quantitative analysis is crucial as it helps mitigate biases, offering a balanced perspective amid varying investment styles.

Punita recalls a stock purchase from six years ago that, despite its strong long-term prospects, underperformed and impacted her portfolio negatively. Although the stock later appreciated significantly, this experience highlighted the challenge of deciding whether to hold on to a non-performing asset or to exit and potentially re-invest elsewhere. Such dilemmas require nuanced judgement.

Liquidity is a critical factor in Punita's investment strategy. She recounts her experience with Bangladesh Lamps, a stock that soared 1000 per cent before becoming illiquid and difficult to exit as market conditions worsened. This highlights the risks associated with investing in low-liquidity stocks, particularly in volatile markets.

Punita emphasizes the importance of humility in investing. The market humbles even the most confident investors. Hubris can lead to overconfidence and poor decision-making. She notes that managing commitment bias involves being patient with investments and recognizing the limitations of one's analysis.

When managing international portfolios, Punita values a diverse team with varied perspectives, including those focused on growth, quality, risk-aversion and risk-taking. Despite this, the ultimate investment decisions rest with one person. Effective decision-making requires balancing diverse views while ensuring clear and accountable choices.

Punita believes that a well-balanced personal life contributes to better professional decisions. When personal and professional lives are aligned, it is easier to make rational, less emotionally driven decisions. Chaotic personal situations can lead to misguided investment choices.

Looking back, Punita regrets not being more optimistic about India's growth potential in the 1990s and early 2000s. Her initial scepticism about India's market opportunities, compared to other emerging markets like Thailand, Malaysia and China, now seems misplaced. This reflection highlights the importance of adapting one's perspective to evolving market conditions.

Punita acknowledges that mistakes are a natural part of investing, driven by gaps in understanding or market misjudgements. She emphasizes the need for continuous learning and adaptation. Investors must stay informed, adhere to their investment frameworks and navigate global macroeconomic influences.

Punita's approach to investing underscores the dynamic nature of the market, where the actions and mistakes of others can impact outcomes. Embracing this challenge with adaptability and resilience defines her investment philosophy, making her journey through the market both a formidable challenge and an exhilarating experience.

CHAPTER 23

SANJAY BAKSHI
The wisdom-infused educator

PROFESSOR Bakshi, or 'Prof' as he is affectionately called, hardly needs an introduction. He has devoted a good part of his life to being a teacher to many of us investors with his blockbuster presentations, replete with anecdotes and case studies through which he analyses human behaviour as a tool for investing.

True to his nature, his blog is called 'fundooprofessor'.

Prof is a fun guy to know, and whether you're discussing fine food, coffee or racing cars, he deep dives into every aspect, from utility to trends. He imparts a wealth of knowledge in sessions that often run into the early hours of the morning, ensuring you go to bed with an incredible number of thoughts to mull over in the days and weeks ahead.

The sum of it all is that he is much loved, a man one can walk up to with doubts, and the more intriguing the doubts, the greater the probability of a session on them in the days ahead.

I recall once driving back with him after a class at MDI, Gurgaon, where he had taught earlier (he is now with FLAME University). To begin with, he offered me a rather healthy but delicious apple health bar. As we hit a red light and had 120 seconds to the next green, he promptly picked up a book from his dashboard and started reading. Not that my company was boring, but Prof has an insatiable hunger for learning and is generous to share much of that in his sessions.

He is adept with technology and uses most of the latest tools. I believe one can learn a lot about mistakes merely by going through his numerous presentations, many of which are in the public domain.

Let us now explore Prof's take on mistakes and the learnings from them.

Prof begins our conversation by sharing that one of his sources of inspiration, from whom he has learned a lot, is Richard Zeckhauser, a renowned professor at Harvard University. In the book *Maxims for Thinking Analytically: The Wisdom of Legendary Harvard Professor Richard Zeckhauser*, Dan Levy, a former student and current professor at Harvard University, presents a selection of maxims for analytical thinking formulated by his mentor.

Maxim eight states: 'Good decisions sometimes have poor outcomes.' Prof explains that although this maxim sounds simple, it is often misunderstood. He adds that this can be proven simply by asking friends to describe some of their best decisions. He admits, 'I did, and not once did I come across a friend who talked about a great decision that resulted in a bad outcome.'

Quality of decision vs quality of outcome

		Quality of Outcome	
		Good	Bad
Quality of Decision	Good	You decided well and did well	You were unlucky
	Bad	You were lucky	You decided poorly and did poorly

The table above may be familiar to many readers. Prof elaborates that it shows that a good decision-making process can produce both good and bad outcomes.

Similarly, a bad decision-making process can also result in both good and bad outcomes. The key, he emphasizes, is to focus on the process, not the outcomes. He points out that this is not a new idea. The same concept was articulated in the Mahabharata, when Krishna implored Arjuna to ignore outcomes and focus on his duty (the process).

According to Prof, two situations in the table warrant special attention: a good process producing a bad outcome and a bad process producing a good outcome. He goes on to examine each of these carefully within the context of investing.

A good process producing a bad outcome

Prof shares that this happens often in investing, no matter how careful one is. Investing is a probabilistic game, and some bets are bound to go bad, no matter how good the process, due diligence or preparation is.

So, if the outcome is negative despite having a good process in place, what should an investor do when faced with such a result?

The answer, according to Prof, is to 'do nothing', but that's not how most investors behave. Instead, they become upset when things don't work out as expected. They often incorrectly attribute bad outcomes to a bad process, which needs to be 'fixed'.

Interestingly, he adds that successful traders don't think like this. They accept that some bets will not work out well and will produce losses. They rationalize this by accepting that 'you win some, you lose some'.

Tweaking an investment process to avoid all losses would, according to Prof, be a mistake because one would then become over-conservative. One would, in effect, replace one mistake with another.

He elaborates with an example, 'Let's say you invest a small sum of money in a small B2C company. Despite the risks associated with its size and high customer concentration, you have great confidence in the management's ability to achieve strong performance. The company sells a non-essential product for which there is no close substitute due to patent protection. Earnings have been growing steadily, and the future outlook is promising. Additionally, the stock is undervalued at seven times earnings. However, with the sudden onset of Covid-19, demand for the product disappears, and the company begins to experience losses, leading to its eventual shutdown. Fortunately, you manage to sell your shares before this happens, but at a 50 per cent loss.'

He goes on to analyse this outcome: 'If you believe that the negative outcome resulted from a flawed process that allowed for investment in a promising but ultimately unsuccessful consumer discretionary business, you may decide never to invest in similar businesses again. After all, who knows what the future holds? There could be another pandemic, war or global depression that devastates consumer demand.

'However, modifying the process in this way could result in missing significant opportunities, as it would limit investments to only businesses selling essential goods or services that are not severely impacted by changes in demand. Such businesses are rare, and their stocks are often quite expensive, making them unattractive investments. Buying them at a high valuation could lead to a genuine mistake while attempting to correct a false one.'

He adds, 'In such situations, it is not wise to change the process as the negative outcome was due to bad luck, not a flawed process.'

Similarly, he shares, 'If you are a skilled insurance underwriter, you may still encounter negative results. The most important factor is maintaining consistent underwriting discipline over time, rather than focusing on individual cases. The same principle can also be applied in banking.'

He explains that if you are overly cautious and aim to avoid any loan losses, you may end up making less than optimal lending choices.

The same logic applies to investing. While you can make changes to your investment process to increase your success rate, you should be mindful that some adjustments may have a negative impact.

The role of diversification is important in reducing the overall harm to a portfolio caused by bad luck.

As Benjamin Graham states in his book *The Intelligent Investor*, there is a close logical connection between the concept of a safety margin and the principle of diversification. One is correlative with the other. Even with a margin in the investor's favour, an individual security may work out badly. For the margin guarantees only that one has a better chance for profit than for loss—not that loss is impossible. However, as the number of such commitments increases, it becomes more certain that the aggregate profits will exceed the aggregate losses.

That is the simple basis of the insurance-underwriting business.

A few years ago, Prof recalls, he invested in a B2C e-commerce company with a unique business model. The company had a significant cost advantage and earned exceptional returns on invested capital, giving it a durable competitive advantage. Its operating cash flows were excellent and more than sufficient to fund growth without needing to issue new shares or take on additional debt, which in any case was negligible. The business was growing rapidly, and the stock was available at an attractive valuation.

However, after a few quarters, he says, his investment hypothesis failed when a competitor with a significant cost disadvantage was able to raise money from private equity investors. These investors instructed the competitor to take market share without considering profitability, causing the company to offer discounts, free shipping and interest-free loans to industry customers. As a result, the industry's profit pool collapsed. He candidly adds that his portfolio company was faced with two choices, both of which were unfavourable. It could either join the competition and suffer financial losses, or refuse to join and lose market share. Initially, the company chose the latter option. However, due to high fixed costs, the drop in revenues led to a significant decline in profitability.

At the time, Prof wasn't sure how long the competition would behave irrationally. It was tempting to assume that it wouldn't continue, as the competitor's funds would eventually run out due to losses. But what if the competitor raised even more funds from private equity investors and continued with its irrational pricing behaviour? Meanwhile, the stock price had collapsed. He was faced with the decision of whether to give in and sell or hold on in the hope that the irrational competition would recede, and profitability would return.

He decided to sell, after asking himself: 'Given what I now know about the situation, would I want to buy this stock?' The answer was a resounding no. And so, he sold and took a loss.

A few years later, the competition receded, and the business once again became profitable, causing its stock price to multiply several times from the point where he had sold out of the position. It was painful for him to see this happen.

Despite the pain from the bad outcome, he does not believe it was a mistake to invest in the business in the first place. Neither, in his view, was it a mistake to sell at a loss.

I ask Prof if the bad outcome required him to tweak his investment process to avoid making similar 'mistakes' in the future. Again, his answer is no.

He says that bad luck is inevitable, and the quality of a decision is dependent on the process used to make it with the information available at the time. When he made the investment, there was no irrational competition. But when it did happen, he had to re-evaluate and make a decision.

Prof discloses that the name of the business he had invested in was VGL Products.

A bad process producing a good outcome

In 2013, Prof recalls, he invested in a consumer appliance business that earned extraordinary returns on capital. The company was ranked as one of the highest ROE-listed businesses in India at the time. The competition in this niche was mainly from the unorganized sector, which was losing market share to the business he had chosen. The company's business model was asset-light, as all manufacturing was outsourced, and the business operated on negative working capital. Margins were excellent, and the business was growing rapidly. The stock was available at low double-digit multiples of recent operating earnings.

Over the next few years, as earnings grew, the price-earnings multiple also rose dramatically, resulting in the stock multiplying several times from his cost price. At one point, the stock was selling at over seventy times earnings, and he decided to sell out at a huge profit. There was just one problem: he had not paid close attention to entry barriers at the time of the investment. He says, 'Basically, I ignored Philip Fisher's advice in his book *Common Stocks and Uncommon Profits*':[1]

> In today's highly fluid and competitive business world, obtaining well-above average profit margins or a high return on assets is so desirable that, whenever a company accomplishes this goal for any significant period of time, it is bound to be faced with a host of potential competitors. If the potential competitors actually enter the field, they will cut into markets the established company now has. Normally, when potential competition becomes actual competition the ensuing struggle for sales results in anything from a minor to a

major reduction in the high profit margin that had theretofore existed. High profit margins may be compared to an open jar of honey owned by the prospering company. The honey will inevitably attract a swarm of hungry insects bent on devouring it.

This is exactly what happened to the business. Soon after he had sold, it experienced significant competition from new entrants in the market. As the niche occupied by the company in question grew, many consumer appliance businesses that were not previously in that space entered it, and over the next few years, its margins, returns on capital and balance sheet quality were adversely affected. None of these subsequent developments were reflected in the high price-earnings multiple of the stock at the time. Now, many years later, the stock is back to where it was in 2014.

Prof says it is important to highlight this example because the investment world often prioritizes outcome over process. The outcome in this example was good, but the process was flawed and needed to be fixed by increasing focus on entry barriers. There are many businesses that earn extraordinary margins and returns on capital for a variety of reasons that won't last. Ultimately, competition will enter and destroy the extraordinary profitability. It's faulty to ignore this and to focus on short-term profitability, blindly extrapolating it into the future—the mistake he admits he made.

He shares that the name of the business was Symphony Limited.

Prof emphasizes that making good decisions does not always guarantee good outcomes, but that does not mean we should regret making them. In fact, if we make rational decisions, there is no need for regret, even if things don't turn out as we hoped. It is important to recognize that a decision can be wise, regardless of the outcome. On the flip side, just because a poorly made decision turns out well, doesn't mean we should take pride in it.

CHAPTER 24

RAJEEV THAKKAR

The unshakable sustainable strategist

BEFORE we delve into Rajeev Thakkar's career and the lessons one can learn from both his successes and his mistakes, let's agree that investing is a field rooted in probabilities, not certainties, making it more akin to poker than chess. An investor can see their cards but not those of others. Success in investing is often about managing risk, protecting against large swings, and achieving reasonable returns over the long term. But in this uncertain terrain, how does one define a mistake? In this chapter, we will explore Rajeev's story and benefit from his insights on the nature of investment mistakes and how to learn from them.

Rajeev points out that a common misconception in investing is that outcomes define mistakes. This is not true. An investor might bet on an outcome with a lower probability and still succeed by chance. The real mistake lies in the process. Rajeev emphasizes that when the probability of heads is 60 per cent, consistently betting on tails—regardless of the outcome—is a mistake. In such cases, the decision-making process, not the result, determines the error. Rajeev, a voracious reader, has found this approach explored in depth and perhaps validated in Annie Duke's *Thinking in Bets*,[1] which describes mistakes as being akin to unforced errors in tennis. If an investor can protect the downside against large swings and compound money at a reasonable rate (at the index returns or preferably better) at a portfolio level over the long run, that is a successful outcome. In a twenty-five-stock portfolio, one cannot expect all twenty-five stocks to do well, all the time.

I begin my conversation with Rajeev by asking whether mistakes in investing have anything to do with upbringing, education or exposure. Rajeev says he does not have a strong opinion on this. Of course, there are studies showing that traits like the ability to delay gratification (the famous marshmallow test), which also helps one avoid the fear of missing out (FOMO), correlate strongly with future success, though some recent studies have tried to debunk this. However, if one has been encouraged since childhood or early teens to develop multidisciplinary thinking and understand common behavioural biases like the anchoring effect, sunk cost fallacy, recency bias and so on, they will have an advantage not only in the field of investing but in any other field they choose to pursue.

Rajeev's philosophy is validated by his own childhood experiences. As a quiet and introverted child, his mother found it easy to keep him occupied. All she had to do, he laughingly mentions, to get him 'out of her hair' was get him a book he was interested in (typically fiction), and he would be occupied for hours. It's clear that Rajeev's multidisciplinary thinking was honed by his early and lasting love for fiction. Fiction, he explains, delves deep into the psychology of characters, exploring their motives, emotions and thought processes. This exposure helped Rajeev develop psychological insight and empathy, crucial for multidisciplinary thinking, particularly in understanding human dynamics in fields like economics and managing other people's money.

This reminds me of Leonardo Da Vinci's famous words: 'Study the science of art. Study the art of science. Develop your senses—especially learn how to see. Realize that everything connects to everything else.' The value of cross-disciplinary learning, which shows how art, science and other domains intertwine to reveal deeper truths, is best observed through books. Stalwarts of the investment world, like Charlie Munger, have embraced this approach to achieve success. To quote Munger: 'I don't have any one technique that works. I have many models, and the models all interrelate ... You've got to have multiple models, because if you just have one or two that you're using, you're going to torture reality so that it fits your models.' Here's a learning for every reader: Instead of retrofitting ideas into your existing boxes, think laterally and beyond your own disciplines, and tweak your technique to the given set of realities.

In exploring Rajeev's thought process further, I learn an interesting distinction he makes between mistakes made during calm times and those that occur in the heat of crises such as Covid-19 or 9/11. Rajeev acknowledges that the extremes of greed and fear can lead to more errors, primarily because decisions in such moments often need to be made swiftly. Taking too much time can negatively impact financial outcomes. Here, Rajeev offers a powerful strategy to navigate such turbulent waters: conducting pre-mortems.

For those new or less familiar to the world of investment and finance, a pre-mortem is a strategy typically used in project management. Instead of waiting for something to fail and then doing a post-mortem to figure out what went wrong, a pre-mortem involves imagining that failure has already occurred. You then work backwards to identify the potential causes and develop preventive measures. This forward-thinking approach helps eliminate reactive decision-making in crisis moments, creating a plan of action well in advance.

Rajeev gives an example: 'Imagine a situation like Covid or 9/11. An investor could decide ahead of time that during a crisis, they will only invest in companies with strong balance sheets, avoiding those with a high risk of bankruptcy.' By having this predetermined framework, the investor can act decisively without being overwhelmed by panic or market hysteria.

This brings to mind another real-life example I recall Warren Buffett during the 2008 financial crisis. Before the crash, Buffett had already built an investment philosophy focused on strong, cash-flow–rich companies. When the markets began to tumble and panic spread, he stuck to his plan and bought stocks in companies like Goldman Sachs and General Electric at a discount, knowing their financial strength could weather the storm. His pre-mortem thinking enabled him to stay rational and make bold, profitable decisions, rather than succumbing to the fear-driven mistakes many investors made at the time. Rajeev's pre-mortem approach aligns with this mindset, empowering investors to prepare in calm times for the uncertainty ahead, rather than reacting impulsively when it's too late.

Delving deeper, I learn that in Rajeev's career, whenever mistakes were made, they revealed themselves through various channels: financial results, stock price movements, insider stock sales, or even revalidation and intuition. Recognition and admission of a mistake are the stepping stones to addressing and correcting it: it's a cliché, but for an obvious reason. Like every other stalwart, Rajeev believes that the first step towards admitting a mistake is recognizing it. For him, once the realization dawns that a company's governance, business model or management competence is flawed, the only recourse is to exit the investment.

The reason behind this decision is that such fundamental flaws are long-term issues that cannot be easily fixed. Continuing to hold such an investment might further erode capital. Wisdom at its simplest! However, Rajeev cautions that one must make an important exception to this rule: when the mistake made is overpaying for a stock. In that scenario, if the stock price has dropped significantly—due to market corrections or misevaluation—it may actually present a fresh opportunity. The stock that was initially overpriced could now be undervalued, and it might make sense to hold on to it.

I ask Rajeev to give an example to simplify this for someone new to the investment market. Here is what I learn: Suppose an investor buys shares in a promising technology company, only to later discover that its executives have been involved in unethical practices, such as inflating financial results. In such a case, continuing to trust this company would be risky. The rational move would be to sell the stock immediately, as poor corporate governance can lead to deeper issues, including regulatory penalties or the eventual collapse of the business.

Similarly, business-model attractiveness might push an investor to purchase shares in a company that makes products sold in physical retail stores but fails to adapt to online sales trends. As the e-commerce space grows and the company loses market share, the business model becomes outdated and unattractive. Upon realizing this, the investor must exit, as waiting for the company to catch up with competitors would likely take too long.

The third example is that of overvaluation. An investor buys shares in a booming electric vehicle (EV) company during a period of high hype. However, after a short time, the stock price plummets due to broader market corrections, not because of any company-specific issues. In such a case, the stock could now be considered undervalued. If the underlying business remains strong, the investor might decide to hold, having learned that they initially overpaid but seeing future growth potential.

This approach allows investors to correct mistakes decisively while being open to reassessing opportunities as they arise.

Since Rajeev is a believer in pre-mortems, which is akin to predicting doomsday scenarios, I ask him if he uses tools such as meditation, quantitative analysis or a referral board to ensure mistakes in the process remain in check. He explains that for him, defined processes and tools help in avoiding mistakes. Some of the tools he has found useful include having a checklist. Rajeev recommends *The Checklist Manifesto* by Atul Gawande for those interested in learning more. His mantra is that no matter how expert you are, well-designed checklists can always improve outcomes.

Additionally, Rajeev uses scenario analysis, which involves separating narratives from numbers. In this method, you lay out a broad range of scenarios and estimate a value under each one. If the scenarios represent the complete spectrum of outcomes, you could even derive an expected value. For those who wish to delve deeper into this, Rajeev recommends *Facing Up to Uncertainty: Using Probabilistic Approaches in Valuation* by Aswath Damodaran.

Another tool he uses is explicitly calculating the assumptions behind the current stock price, a concept adequately hypothesized by Alfred Rappaport and Michael Mauboussin in *Expectations Investing*.

Rajeev also highlights the importance of inviting analysts and investors with contrary opinions for discussions, emphasizing the power of the voice of dissent in exposing unnoticed possibilities.

Furthermore, Rajeev values having a partner or a team to act as a sounding board, which, he notes, helps in every situation in life. Lastly, he mentions meditation as an important tool in his decision-making process.

Despite all these tools, there will always be judgements that one initially thought were mistakes but which ended up with favourable results. I ask

Rajeev if he would still consider them to be mistakes. He reiterates that many a time, the outcome of an investment decision does not determine whether the investment was a mistake or not. There are many good decisions that do not work out well, and on the other hand, decisions that were actually mistakes end up being profitable. He gives the example of an investor who bought an IT services company with obscure corporate governance and a high valuation in the late 1990s but saw the stock double or triple in a short span of time. Although the stock eventually crashed, a lucky investor could still have made serious money during that time. Rajeev chuckles while referencing the recent meme stock craze in the US.

In spite of having all the necessary tools and adhering to a process, a mistake may still become fatal. Therefore, my next question to Rajeev is whether there is a process that can prevent this. He shares a few crucial strategies that can help an investor survive mistakes.

The first is position sizing. The impact of a mistake depends on how much a position accounts for in the overall portfolio. For example, if a stock with 1 per cent allocation to the portfolio goes to zero, the impact will be minimal. However, if that same stock has a 50 per cent portfolio allocation, it will be a disaster.

Rajeev also emphasizes diversification, stating that in investing, diversification is the only free lunch. One must diversify across asset classes, sectors, market caps, business groups, geographies and so on to avoid being crushed by one single fatal mistake.

Furthermore, he stresses the importance of avoiding leverage and being mindful of liquidity and time horizons. He notes that he has seen many blow-ups by investors or investment firms involving the use of borrowed money. Another common cause of mistakes, he adds, is investors being forced to sell at the wrong time. For instance, if an investor loses their job during Covid and does not have an emergency corpus, they may be forced to exit equities despite the fall in stock prices, just to meet expenses. I chuckle as this reminds me of my grandmother's wisdom: '*Pair utne hi failao jitni chadar ho*'.

I now ask Rajeev if we can learn from the mistakes of others, or if we become so captivated by greed, fear and excess that we repeat the same mistakes. Rajeev says, 'I would like to think that I have become better over time, but that is for others to judge. The only thing that investors in a professional capacity—such as mutual fund, PMS or AIF managers—cannot control is the behaviour of end investors. If investors give us money at market tops and redeem at market bottoms, or if investors punish a manager for following a disciplined approach during market manias, the managers may unwittingly end up buying high and selling low. The takeaway for me is that when it's my own money, I can learn more frequently from other's mistakes. However, for someone operating on behalf of others, with their money at stake, the luxury of learning from these mistakes may not always be available.

I ask Rajeev how he differentiates between errors of commission and errors of omission. He explains that every investor, no matter how accomplished, will have limitations in terms of the sectors and geographies they understand. For instance, someone with a good understanding of banking may not be as good at pharmaceuticals, and someone skilled in automobiles may not be that great at software. Therefore, many investment firms have teams of managers and analysts to continuously track this heterogeneous space. However, Rajeev assures me that even the best and biggest of teams will commit errors of omission. They can never be completely eliminated. This is where an investor's ability to continuously learn from both their own and others' errors of omission bears fruit. Rajeev also advocates studying behavioural finance.

We are all human, and ego and bias are a part of who we are. I ask Rajeev about instances when an investor takes an investment bet that seems to be a mistake, resulting in a drawdown, but they persist, either leading to a bigger mistake or a turnaround. I want to know if there's a way to manage ego and commitment bias to make tomorrow better than today.

Rajeev shares that soon after he buys a stock, the news flow relating to that company starts to flood in. Policy changes, shifts in key management, competitive strategies of other companies, monthly sales numbers, prices of raw materials and finished goods, quarterly results—these are all easy ingredients for fear to set in. Rajeev emphasizes that one must learn to distinguish between signals and noise. Corporate fraud or mis-governance is definitely a signal, but other high-frequency indicators often prove to be mere noise. Typically, once Rajeev buys a stock, he tends to hold on for the medium- to long-term to see whether the investment is progressing as expected. This can have the downside of holding on to mistakes longer, but it also avoids exiting companies that are going through a temporary downturn.

Often, decisions are made by multiple people in a team, and some may prove right while others wrong. Rajeev has always believed in creating a balance between two sets of views when arriving at an outcome. While everyone in a team will have input, typically, the sector analyst or lead will have the greatest weight in the decision-making process. This theme—respect for the sector analyst or portfolio manager—is a common and important one across the wide range of investors covered in this book. If the outcome is favourable, one may continue with the people who got it right, knowing that the next outcome could always be different. Rajeev believes that over time, the sector analyst or lead must be more right than wrong. In his team, they typically do not have diametrically opposite views among members, which exemplifies the benefits of everyone rowing together in the same direction.

While talking about teams getting the right outcome most of the time, Rajeev emphasizes the importance of not allowing exuberance and hubris to set in. Bad decisions often arise from the collective comfort of being very large, where mistakes are hidden in codes and processes. However, being answerable to investors quickly reduces hubris. Additionally, media scrutiny and annual unit holders' meetings bring fund managers face to face with investors, where they are grilled on both actual and perceived mistakes.

Of course, all these factors result in a high level of stress and anxiety, which eventually impact personal life and decision-making. Rajeev is well aware of the fact that if one is going through a tough time either due to ill health or a misunderstanding with somebody, it can impact decision-making. Therefore, he considers it crucial to separate personal life from business life to maintain the objectivity needed for good decision-making. In extreme personal situations, Rajeev believes the best course of action is to take time off and let things settle down. If the mental upheaval is momentary, he resorts to listening to the quintessential Kishore Kumar. He also believes happiness = reality − expectations. 'The secret of happiness is to keep expectations low,' chuckles Rajeev.

I know that for some, a mistake can be a source of motivation, while for others it can lead to absolute demotivation. Rajeev says he has accepted mistakes as an inevitable part of the investment journey and does not rely on them for either motivation or demotivation. With his team, and over a cappuccino (Rajeev is a teetotaller), perhaps accompanied by his favourite chaat, he conducts data-based analyses of mistakes in a dispassionate manner. Once satisfied with his efforts and having accepted the outcomes, Rajeev likes to spend time with his family, watching a movie (*Sholay, 3 Idiots* and *Kahaani* are his favourites), playing board games, listening to music (Kishore Kumar) or reading a book when family members are not around. Time permitting, he loves to fly out to Greece, his favourite holiday destination.

We all know that the many issues with the country's infrastructure can lead to negativity about India. When I ask how he, as a fund manager, keeps this negativity as bay while still being bullish on India, Rajeev says that in investing, it is important to look at the motion picture rather than a still photograph. He points out that there has been a massive improvement in India's infrastructure—roads, bridges, metro rail, airports and so on—over the years. For example, the Delhi National Capital Region has a wonderful metro rail network and airport. Other cities in India are on a similar path to progress. The important thing to realize, according to Rajeev, is that nothing is ever perfect, and hence, there is that much more opportunity for improvement. He also reminds us that if we look at the woes of a city like San Francisco, we will realize that it is often the 'grass is greener on the other side' syndrome.

To survive the constant tumult of the investment world, Rajeev offers a few nuggets to the newly initiated. Some of the errors made by the investing public are well known. For example, investors often prefer stock splits, bonuses and low-priced shares. If a company announces a split, the stock will trade at an optically lower price in a few days. Rajeev suggests that it is better to sell after the split rather than before. On the other hand, if one is looking to buy the company, it may be better to purchase when the stock price looks optically high. An understanding of behavioural finance, which Rajeev mentioned earlier, helps in making such decisions.

When I ask if there are things Rajeev would like to change to reduce his chances of mistakes and increase his successes, including education and allocation, he shares that he wishes the realization that public policy is fickle and changes all the time had come sooner. Another important realization for him is that it is difficult to get returns from areas where the product is seen as a public good or a utility.

Rajeev is well aware that when managing public money, mistakes can be caused by the investors themselves. For example, they may pull out when it is time to invest. The results, however, often reflect against the fund manager publicly. Balancing public image with rational decision-making is a tightrope that Rajeev walks well by continuously communicating the importance of long-term investing and moderating return expectations, especially when the market is frothy. He explains, 'We are judged by the performance of our NAV and its returns over time. If the investors invest when the NAV is high and redeem when it is low, it harms their investment performance. However, it does not affect our published results. Where it harms us, and the industry, is that it leaves a dissatisfied investor or customer.'

There may be times when, despite one's portfolio performing well, media and investors or potential investors focus on a mistake to showcase a wrong result. Rajeev navigates this by recognizing that much of the media and investor chatter is what Annie Duke calls 'resulting'. Without understanding that investing is a probabilistic process and that not all stocks will perform well, they tend to highlight those that didn't do well. Rajeev notes that some investors have picked up on this trend. They have observed that when there are too many questions about a particular stock in one year, that stock often does well in the following year. The learning Rajeev shares here is that the analysis of a mistake is an independent process and should not be influenced by media or investor questions.

Despite his vast experience and life lessons and having been through numerous market ups and downs, Rajeev admits that he continues to make mistakes. He says that history does not repeat itself, but it rhymes. While there are patterns that seem similar, each situation is different, and one must make decisions afresh, which can still turn out to be either right or wrong. An investor who avoided the late 1990s tech boom may appear smart, but if that same investor had avoided tech altogether, they would have missed out on Google, Apple, Amazon, Meta, Nvidia and others. While past experience and education help, they do not eliminate mistakes completely.

I conclude by marvelling at the depth of Rajeev Thakkar—a man of simple tastes and grounded perspectives. His favourite place to eat is Swati Snacks, and his everyday attire consists of a formal shirt and trousers, with the occasional suit and tie. He is an avid reader, particularly fond of the book *Million Dollar Whale*,[2] and a keen observer of the world around him. Rajeev doesn't retreat into an ivory tower; instead, he draws lessons from everyday life—whether from sports, politics or people unconnected to his ecosystem.

Through his reflections, Rajeev has come to understand that mistakes, and the patterns they form, are timeless. He points out how mythology offers lessons, like Icarus flying too close to the sun, or Shakespearean heroes whose fatal flaws lead to tragedy. These stories reinforce the idea that mistakes are a natural part of the human experience. One of Rajeev's key habits is reading biographies and watching documentaries, which he believes offer invaluable insights.

'I don't think investors make full use of this opportunity,' he remarks, emphasizing the importance of learning from others' lives. I leave with a thought Rajeev shared earlier: 'History may not repeat itself, but it often rhymes.'

CHAPTER 25

SATYA PRAKASH MITTAL

The revolutionary architect of India's financial landscape

SATYA Prakash Mittal earns my endorsement as one of India's finest small-cap investors, with an impressive track record of investing and making multibagger returns over decades. He is based in Lucknow, and despite his success, remains humble about sharing his accomplishments. While he started investing early, he still believes Warren Buffett's quote: 'I started investing at the age of eleven. I was late.'

Such is his passion for the markets that when I ask him when he started, he knew the exact date: 29 December 1980. Not only did he recall the date, but he also remembered the price of his very first stock purchase. It was a company called Ambalal Sarabhai Limited, which had launched an initial public offering. He applied for 750 shares at par but was elated to find that the application money was not Rs 10 but just Rs 2.50 per share (part paid). He was allotted 225 shares, and after making the full payment, he recalls with a smile, he made his first profit of Rs 1,125.

He proudly shares that his gain of Rs 1,125 on a Rs 2,250 investment was a 50 per cent return in just three months—an outcome that awakened him to the possibility of the markets giving huge profits and fuelled his desire to discover and invest more.

To further illustrate his passion for the markets, I recall an incident to which I was privy. During his son's wedding in Lucknow, amidst the celebrations, I caught him at dinner and asked how he got started in investing. He was so delighted by my interest that he took me to his very first office, right from the function, to show me where he sat, what he read, some annual reports from his early years, and how much the surroundings had changed.

While he now sits in a large office in a modern building, he still cherishes the memories of his early days. From my conversation with him, it becomes clear that passion is an elixir for success.

Usually found in jeans and a T-shirt, with simplicity evident in everything about him, Satya is inspired by Marlon Brando and the movie *Godfather*. When I jokingly ask if he also carries a gun, he laughs and offers me the famous tokri chaat of Lucknow.

While analysing companies that many of us have never even heard of, his office often has songs playing in the background. When the song '*Chali chali re patang meri chali*' (roughly translated, 'see my kite as it flies') comes on, he shares that it is his favourite, sung by the legendary Mohammad Rafi—perhaps a symbol of this quiet legend himself. An optimist, Satya, like the song, believes that small stocks, when picked well, can soar high like kites in the sky.

Such was his fascination for numbers and business that Satya recalls changing schools in the ninth standard as his original school did not offer commerce.

As we nibble on his favourite, yet simple, meal of tandoori roti, tadka dal and kadai paneer, his team members edge closer to his room, eager to overhear every word of his experiences, as each anecdote carries many a inspiring learning.

Later, he graciously invites me to join him for a scotch, his favourite drink, at Taj Vivanta, his favourite hotel, or to come home and watch a film with his family—one of his favourite pastimes. However, as I was keen to jot down the thoughts he had shared—not wanting to miss even a single nugget of wisdom—I rushed to my room to complete my notes.

I now delve into the fascinating world of this investor and his thoughts.

Satya begins our conversation by attributing much of his success to his upbringing. 'Our upbringing can be a game changer,' he says, going on to share a personal experience.

'My father had made company deposits in Elgin Mills (Laal Imli, Kanpur) and Quality Steel Tubes (Delhi). These companies were neither paying interest nor principal. I wrote to them, and the payments started coming in! The companies were making losses and their balance sheets were not sound. These mistakes made me aware of the fundamentals of profits, price-earnings ratios, and book value, or reserves. This exposure helped me avoid a lot of mistakes in the years that followed.'

He continues, explaining that from a young age, he was fascinated by annual reports and buying and selling shares.

He recalls how his father had purchased 400 shares of Coromandel International in the 1960s, when investing in shares was unheard of. He would see his father reading *Time* magazine and the *Times of India*, as well as annual reports. This early exposure to reading and following the news made an impact.

He started participating in school fetes at the age of twelve, which helped him develop a strong business sense. He also learned about value appreciation from his grandfather, an architect and philatelist. His grandfather had a stamp collection, and Satya saw how the value of old stamps appreciated over time.

His neighbour at the time was the artist Bireswar Sen, whose miniature paintings had significant value. Through these experiences, Satya realized that when something of value is acquired early and held over time, its worth can significantly increase. Perhaps this is what prompted him to start thinking long term. He recalls, 'All these experiences taught me the value of money and the difference between a good investment and a bad one.'

He adds that his family's interest in investing has further fuelled his passion. Fondly, he mentions that both his sons, Ayush Mittal and Pratyush Mittal (also the founders of Screener) were exposed to investing at an early age. When they were able to grasp it, the family launched a public website, Dalal-street.in, to share their writings on investment learnings and tools.

It became a valuable resource, and anyone who met him was encouraged to visit the site and share their views. This created an open mind.

When I ask Satya how family unity in investing helps, he chuckles, and looking at both his sons, says, 'I think they are good investors, skilled at managing mistakes, and they share their knowledge with others so that more people can take up a second source of earnings, like they did.'

Satya believes that sharing knowledge is a great tool for learning and avoiding mistakes. He also advises keeping an open mind and listening to others. He always scouts for facts to guide his own independent decisions regarding stocks. It is clear to me that he wants others to succeed in investing, which is why he supports the open sharing of knowledge, including analytical tools—free of cost.

As he explores the subject of mistakes, Satya mentions that, in his view, there are three types of market conditions an investor may experience.

The first type is calm times. During such times, Satya explains that he likes to invest at his own pace, taking the time to acquire good stocks in a phased manner.

The second type includes abnormal upswings, such as the Harshad Mehta boom, or the software boom and bust of 1999–2000. These are times when all his small- and micro-cap stocks seem to have extraordinary potential, and it is easy to believe that every stock can become a blue chip. This overconfidence can cloud judgement, as it's unclear how long the market will continue to rise. To balance this exuberance, Satya sells his stocks either in phases or partially on every rise.

The third extraordinary situation is when the market faces a major crash, such as the subprime crisis of 2010 or the Covid-19 downturn in 2020. Satya believes such times present the opportunity to analyse and buy value picks in parts while assessing the scenario. He tends to make switches in his portfolio in a phased manner, buying more value picks at lower prices. He thus gravitates more to value than perceived safety, knowing that long-term outcomes often vary from short-term safety, and that volatility is a great tool to find long-term value.

During market crashes, Satya makes a list of all his stocks by their value and looks for opportunities to increase his holdings or even explore new options. He takes advantage of the free fall to buy what he perceives as more worthy investments than what he currently holds.

Satya explains that every market scenario presents various opportunities. It all depends on how much an investor is able to identify and explore those opportunities. Many people, however, make the mistake of reacting impulsively due to a lack of knowledge, panic, greed or fear. This often leads to losing capital, falling into debt, or even, in extreme cases, committing suicide.

Investing is a knowledge-based business where one must plan according to available funds and an understanding of the investment matrix. If one can't make the effort to learn, Satya advises them to consider joining a good portfolio-management service (PMS).

Satya next reflects on his mistakes. He shares that throughout his long career as an investor, every mistake has provided him with valuable lessons. He emphasizes that mistakes are not just about being wrong, but about the different kinds of wrongs one can make. Selling too late, buying too early, not buying enough, selling what was good and not selling enough are all different kinds of errors. The awareness of the cost of a mistake compels him to deliberate and aim to move in the right direction.

When I ask him how he avoids repeating his mistakes in the future, he is quick to answer. He explains that he focuses on managing mistakes by analysing company data instead of reacting emotionally. He also reads about businesses in depth rather than relying solely on their price ticker. Additionally, he draws inspiration from good investment books and the processes shared within them.

So, when does he realize a mistake is indeed a mistake? He highlights that mistakes often become apparent when companies report results that either exceed or fall short of expectations. If the results are better than expected, it indicates he may have underestimated the company. Price movements and company announcements—which can throw ugly surprises such as unrelated diversification, debt, misuse of funds or excessive promoter selling—also serve as red flags. Finally, intuition also plays an important role in recognizing a mistake.

Satya also distinguishes between short-term setbacks and a derailment of an investment. If the issue is temporary, he will remain invested.

He adds that as time passes, an investor gains confidence and the courage to revalidate their mistakes, rather than regretting them later. So, time in the market is a great friend of the investor.

Satya believes that value investing is the best option for creating wealth. It needs time, study, different types of strategies and full-time concentration—just like achieving success in any business.

To him, investing is the business of continuously exploring the best investment ideas. One must strive to find meaningful investments by creating a system or process that can be followed and provide benefits. When I ask him to elaborate, he explains that he makes checklists and develops a system whereby if a company gets that feature, it comes to his attention. This is perhaps why Screener, a product developed by his sons, offers so many options to screen and create alerts.

He adds that earlier, he and his sons, along with their team, had to do much of the work themselves, which was tedious. Then they created Screener.in, which has made their work much easier. Screener.in is available to everyone. It shows results in order and allows users to filter the best performers in each quarter, then analyse their value.

After reviewing the data on Screener.in, Satya recommends going through companies' annual reports, websites, conference calls, AGMs and announcements (Screener also provides much of this information, as well as credit rating reports). In his case, after going through all of this, he sometimes sends a questionnaire to the company to better understand them if he feels the need for elaboration or clarification.

Satya also recommends reading and following good investors and companies on ValuePickr and X to stay informed about their views, announcements or concerns. Keeping in touch with and exchanging ideas with other investors who share similar processes and ideas, and have a credible track record, helps in analysing mistakes and course correction. It also exposes one to new ideas and prevents the mistake of ignoring them. 'There's nothing fixed about one idea,' he adds. He admits to frequently switching every quarter. 'Mistake analysis and rectification are part of our process in such switches,' he explains, emphasizing the need to move on if a mistake is found, rather than clinging to hope without factual support.

Satya's wisdom also extends to the use of software and data tools. He agrees that tools are a great help in reducing mistakes and making investing more analytical and successful. Along with Screener and ValuePickr, he uses Basecamp for internal discussions, Dropbox for storing and sharing annual reports, and Evernote for sharing notes.

I ask him about time management, and he is happy to share: 'I try to spare some time early in the morning for a short meditation. This helps keep me in a good mood. Another important thing is doing quantitative data analysis. We check the new quarterly results and corporate announcements, go through the notes of the teams and share our thoughts.'

In essence, he likes to be prepared before the market opens (or after it closes) so he can eliminate bias to the extent possible and focus on data points rather than being distracted by the market itself. This does not mean he ignores the market. His dealers share that he even places bids at a low price on some of the stocks on his radar, especially on bad days, so if there is panic, his order gets executed.

I now ask him to share a few learnings from mistakes based on personal experience. He smiles and recounts:

'I would like to share a very interesting instance with you. I had 700 shares of DLF Ltd (old name of DLF Universal Ltd) in 1994 (thirty years back). My clients had 2,000 shares. We received letters from the company to surrender these shares and they offered a buyback twice at a price of Rs 360 against my buying price of around Rs 30. The company had applied for delisting at Delhi Stock Exchange (the only exchange where it was listed). Due to delisting fear and no possibility of further trading in future, we got scared. Me and all my clients offered most of our shares under repeated buyback letters. My two clients and I kept 10 shares each by intuition just to see the scenario afterwards and learn. To our surprise the company then offered 10:1 rights at par, followed by a 7:1 bonus and splits in 10:2 ratio. My 10 shares became 4,400 shares. I sold these for around Rs 36 lakh vs Rs 3,600 offered then. This was a change of circumstances to convert mistakes to bonanza. However, in hindsight, a huge opportunity/jackpot was lost. This brought lots of learning to me and gave me courage to explore a lot of other such opportunities and be patient.'[1]

He reflects that reacting to an offer at a seemingly advantageous price may not always be the right thing to do. Understanding a company and its value, rather than just focusing on its share price, can be far more rewarding.

To avoid such mistakes and others, one should develop a thought process. For example, he regularly studies his investments and stays nearly fully invested, trying to understand various scenarios by whatever methods are available.

On the journey of investing, he believes that there is nothing more interesting, easy and profitable. Investing becomes a passion as time passes. You enjoy it like a game and feel like a winner with every success. This spirit prevents mistakes from becoming fatal. By adopting a strict switching process, where one regularly sells a small percentage of shares in a portfolio and looks for better buying options, one can avoid mistakes.

Satya also recommends evolving by learning from both one's own and others' mistakes. Initially, he began investing with small amounts as he was uncertain about its profitability. However, after experiencing success with his early investments, he realized that investing is full of opportunities, and it became a success story he aimed to replicate.

As time passed, he poured a significant amount of his funds into investing. This happened when he realized the mistake of investing small amounts, or not finding funds and then taking the necessary steps. Eventually, a time comes in one's life when greed and fear no longer matter as you understand that long-term benefits will follow.

Satya highlights another advantage of investing in stocks, mutual funds or PMS—lower overhead expenses compared to other investment options such as gold, silver, land, farming, trading, business, industry or any type of entrepreneurship. Investing has some tax benefits (although they are now diminishing) and provides significant opportunities for wealth creation. Being knowledge-based, investing has a much lower fear factor compared to other businesses.

Often, due to the fear of losing profits, people make the mistake of selling too early. Initially, investments are based on a few key points or fundamental ratios. However, as the company grows, new factors and scenarios emerge. One needs to remain invested to maximize profits. Satya's next piece of advice is that greed becomes fatal when a portfolio is too concentrated.

He believes in investing in a wide range of companies and has a well-diversified portfolio. He quickly adds that everyone knows that shares never move in a straight line. They may dip below the purchase price, and due to the fear of losing money, many people place a stop loss or exit the investment. This fear leads to repeated mistakes.

I learnt Satya is concentrated when it comes to the fact of stocks versus other investments and diversified within stocks itself.

Satya also compares his investment returns to those of other asset classes with liquidity. He mentions that since he started investing, he has compared his performance to bank interest rates, company deposits and other investment options. Many investors make the mistake of overlooking opportunity cost, especially if they have the proficiency to find good investment ideas.

Another mistake he shares is that earlier, 'we were involved in various old family businesses. By chance, or it may have been luck, we found that our investment returns were better than our businesses, Nifty, Sensex or mid-cap indexes.' He goes on to say that errors of commission have been minimal, and that they are more serious than errors of omission. To become better investors, Satya and his team give a lot of thought to the P/E ratio, book value, dividends, profit margins and future possibilities. They also have the flexibility to add any number of scrips and currently hold more than 300. As they have such a large number in their portfolio, they have faced minimal errors of omission. Through continuous study and gradual switching, they are able to dispose of dead wood from their portfolio, minimizing the impact of both errors.

With 300 scrips, Satya consistently beats the market, mid-cap indexes and the like. This highlights the fact that, as long as one is in the top quartile of high-return companies, the number of stocks doesn't matter as much. Their diversity helps eliminate wrong choices and drawdowns on returns.

I urge Satya to share more experiences and he is happy to oblige. 'I'd like to share an instance where we made an investment, and based on price movement and comparative analysis, we felt we had made a mistake. We bought CHI Investments a long time ago. It was a holding company of the RPG group, with investments in CESC, CEAT and other companies. The market value of these investments was five times the market cap. This got me very excited, and I started buying it. From my initial buying point of about Rs 125, the stock kept falling and eventually dropped to just Rs 13. It was surprising to see more and more shares available at lower and lower prices. I kept averaging down. I was also unable to understand what was happening and often had self-doubts. I would repeat my homework, discuss it with more people, and every time, I felt the value was there. Eventually, the stock turned around, and I made a big profit.'

Hence, being fixated on a price or even a drop and exiting can be a mistake if the value only gets stronger. Satya does not believe in stop-loss. He believes in stopping only if the company's value deteriorates or if a better opportunity emerges.

To decide which stocks to buy, he elaborates on his process, adding that the analysis and discussions are conducted by his entire team, while decision-making is centralized to two individuals who operate with full independence. These individuals have established a system to share their analysis and action plans in advance, making it easier to resolve differences early on. Additionally, he has a system in place to ensure the required funds are arranged, either by selling or reallocating earlier investments, or by temporarily sourcing money from liquid funds maintained for this purpose. With this well-defined process, he faces limited differences of opinion and liquidity-related problems and is able to achieve better investing options with fewer errors. This system allows him to easily track performance and strategies and manage mistakes.

He explains that his team is responsible for researching companies, understanding their prospects and the price versus the value that they will pay for it. By doing this, one can, in his view, reduce errors of omission. When reading or exploring investment options, one can find different opportunities across different types of businesses. Hence, it is important to analyse a variety of businesses. Only then will one be able to differentiate between opportunities and focus on the better ones versus the ordinary. This understanding helps one decide whether and where to make sizable or aggressive investments. Having discussions with two or more analysts on the same platforms for small-cap and mid-cap stocks can also help. This approach has been very successful in finding and adding more growth and value-based options to his portfolio.

The role of exuberance is also good in eliminating bad decisions. 'Our stock market is very organized and systematic. It provides equal opportunities to everyone. It also has the least cost of expenses. Anyone who invests in the market gains experience and learning, making it easier to get out of bad decisions. Embracing hubris makes it difficult to eliminate bad decisions,' he advises.

'When we see large returns or profits, we tend to move into a comfort zone,' he adds. 'That's when the success level diminishes; transparency alone cannot improve things to get the desired results. One must tame complacency with the belief that a check is needed every now and then.'

Satya clearly enjoys investing. He calls it the most comfortable business. It is least affected by the ups and downs of one's personal life. He finds it easy to manage his investments even when he is busy dealing with the complexities of personal life or ill health. He notes that even if one doesn't spend any time on it, one doesn't have to worry about expenses or overheads. It is easy to withdraw money as per one's requirements. What is needed is discipline, experience and confidence.

'A change in occupation is relaxing,' he adds. 'I have many friends who are doctors, engineers or in other jobs. They have created wealth and multiplied their savings along with fulfilling their responsibilities. They enjoy investing, and it relaxes them.

'So, I recommend that everyone learn value investing,' he continues. 'Involve your children from a young age so when they grow up, they will find it beneficial in managing their personal problems along with health and wealth. They can even use this talent to manage and solve misunderstandings. Investing is the simplest and easiest way of earning and learning,' he firmly advises.

He also advises finding motivation in mistakes—or in missed opportunities. He acknowledges making a lot of mistakes, both knowingly and unknowingly, but some of strategies followed earlier are now great motivational factors/patterns to search and to invest. He also learns from mistakes by studying patterns that have worked for him.

As examples, he shares from experience that he has found great value in companies with high export volumes, such as RACL and GeeKay wires; companies that act as import substitutes, such as Poly Medicure; companies reducing costs and saving time and labour, such as Astral Poly; companies in the health sector, such as Cipla Ltd in 1990; and companies solving problems, such as DLF Ltd, which was the only real estate company known for quality and credibility thirty years ago.

Personal experiences can also guide investing, he notes, akin to Peter Lynch's common-sense investing approach. He elaborates with examples: 'When my sister was suffering from cancer about fifteen years ago, I found Shilpa Medicare, which had started manufacturing cancer treatment drugs. And when I found it difficult to find good eye doctors, I found and bought Dr Agarwal.'

He gets motivated when he sees good websites with strong presentations and then does not hesitate to invest in micro-cap companies like MK Exim, where he was impressed with their business presentation and brand associations.

He admits that he has missed opportunities to acquire good companies due to an overload of work, lack of time or bargaining biases. However, when market corrections occur and these shares are available again, it motivates him to re-analyse and buy them. He advises being prepared for downturns as well. As a word of caution, he adds that one must always be prepared for a reduction of the portfolio, even up to half of its current value. This happens in uncertain situations like the Gulf War, the software slump of 2000 or the Covid pandemic in 2020. He prepares for contrarian investing, viewing crises as opportunities to buy or procure new ideas. During the software boom, for example, he was motivated to book partial profits from software companies and invest in other sectors that were available at throwaway prices. In such scenarios, many stocks become value picks due to the price drops, and this becomes a motivation to acquire more of those stocks.

On demotivation, he shares that he is demotivated by high debts and poor responses from company management. It also becomes demotivating to keep a script in his watch list or not buy full quantities when it rises to more than two times or continuously rising and then not being able to decide what to do. So one should re-analyse and if and only if one is convinced, then one may buy at higher prices, also to forget the lower prices and to distract from price and missed factor demotivation.

Similarly, when one identifies a good stock but is unable to acquire it at that time, and it subsequently starts rising, it may then seem expensive, diminishing one's motivation to study it further or to purchase it.

In reference to this, his advice is: 'If people start learning value investing for at least half an hour daily, their lives can change. Their yield doubles, and they are able to create good resources for themselves and live a happier life.'

Satya believes that market declines are advantageous times. He notes that many people hold the misconception that falling markets are bad and one should not invest during such periods. At the time of a decline, he says that a common mistake is correlating a loss with missed opportunities ahead. In this context, Satya shares that when he began his investing journey, he encountered widespread negativity about the stock market, even though it was extremely undervalued from a fundamental perspective. Hundreds of stocks were available at P/E ratios of 5-6, with high book values of two to four times the price, along with high dividend yields of over 5 per cent.

At that time, the present Tata Electric was split into three companies: Tata Power, Tata Hydro and Andhra Valley, which had all the above-mentioned merits and were also infrequently traded on the Bombay Stock Exchange; these were referred to as 'widow's shares'.

He recalls that he started building his portfolio by procuring shares in various companies, focusing on thinly traded, high-quality stocks available at bargain prices because, at that time, the jobbing rate (the difference between buy and sell prices) was roughly as: ACC Rs 200–Rs 220, Cipla Rs 250–Rs 500 (100 per cent jobbing) for Rs 100 paid up shares.

However, investing at that time had many challenges. Shares were often stolen, jobbing was over 10 per cent, governance issues were widespread, there was a lack of transparency, and information—such as annual reports and announcements—was difficult to come by and delayed.

Over time, the facilities and systems improved while troubles, fears and inconveniences reduced. The markets have become richer and more expensive. An increasing number of investors are entering the market and more entrepreneurs are raising money. The Indian market is growing non-stop.

Even as the number of investors has tripled in the last five years to 100 million, he remains hopeful that this figure will triple again to reach

300 million in the next five years. These improvements in the system make him bullish on India.

I ask him how he approaches converting what looks like a mistake into a favourable result.

He reflects and shares: 'Many times, I have found very good shares (such as Cipla and DLF) and tried to convince other investors to invest in their hidden features. But instead of appreciating my logic, they find mistakes in my theory. They prefer to go for flashy and expensive shares lacking value. They are attracted to stocks that are extensively covered by the media or are heavily traded. Most people and analysts do not understand the importance of price-to-earnings ratios, book value and other basic metrics. The majority of investors take the easy path, following only technicals, tweets, messages or tips. They are interested in rising trends and invest in them, often overcommitting, and sudden changes in market sentiment often ruin their investing careers and diminish their interest.'

According to him, while traders often make such mistakes, these errors can be favourable for value investors. A lot of money shifts in the market, benefiting good analysts and investors. 'These investors often take advantage of favourable prices by partially or fully encashing profits, which helps in reducing their cost of investments and also generates profits for them,' he notes.

He admits that he has regrets but has also learnt from them. 'Looking back, I regret submitting 690 shares of DLF during the buyback, as well as selling Bajaj Finance, which I had acquired in large quantities for its high dividend yield, and Astral Poly and Poly Medicure. I'm still not sure why I sold those shares. These mistakes were due to exiting too early and completely.'

On reflection and analysis, he realized that earlier, he was very conservative and maintained only a minimal number of companies in his portfolio. He has since changed this strategy. 'Those shares could have added significant value to our portfolio,' he acknowledges.

Now, thanks to the lessons learnt, he says his focus is on identifying value picks and developing the skill to add his 'dream shares' to his portfolio. 'We are learning techniques and strategies to ensure that the quantities of my favourite shares are not drastically reduced. This learning process involves education and practice to refine our approach.'

When he began investing, Satya says, he observed that the market had been performing negatively for decades before he entered. Even after entering the market, on several occasions over many years, people's investments did not appreciate and sometimes even depreciated by 20 to 30 per cent. Additionally, he has often seen that when a portfolio appreciates by 20 to 30 per cent in a short period, investors become excited. However, when the market declines, they become anxious, start withdrawing their investments and are eager to exit quickly after converting the appreciation into profits, with plans to re-enter the market by getting the bottom right. While this seems easy in theory, it is not possible to implement.

To avoid such situations, whenever anyone wants to make an investment, he explains that the market is full of risks and uncertainties as most people want to join the market on rising trends. 'We try to explain that the market has already risen so much, and there are chances of a correction or unforeseen negative events that might push their investments into the negative zone. They might need to invest more so we can add more good options from time to time to their investments. And if the market goes down, we try to encourage them to remain invested.'

Despite these efforts, if someone chooses to withdraw, he advises them that they are free to do so, though this rarely happens now as investors are becoming more mature. 'So far, only a few people have left us, and they have neither returned nor have we pursued them to reinvest,' he adds.

Satya advises against seeking unnecessary media coverage. He emphasizes that their purpose is to learn, raise awareness and share techniques so that more and more people take up investing as a business or entrepreneurial pursuit. He believes that once a person achieves success or is able to grab an opportunity, the repetition of that success becomes a habit, and it becomes easy.

Satya highlights that when a large number of young investors enter the market with limited funds, their preference is for small-cap stocks and their success will also come by investing in small caps, so the small cap would get buying and small caps would appreciate a lot where we are always invested and indirectly we would continually benefit a lot.

However, Satya feels there is no advantage in publicizing his successes and attracting investors who may create a problem for his system.

Satya points out that the stock market is not a mechanized business. It is sensitive to economics, national and international politics, demand, supply, taxation and thousands of other factors that can influence market changes. One should strive to understand all the major or minor factors involved. Similarly, there are various factors related to the company in which one is invested. Continuous study and exploration of all the best possible options is essential. However, due to the many factors at play, it becomes difficult to completely avoid mistakes.

Mistakes are likely to occur, especially when one is investing aggressively. The important thing is to assess one's success rate in comparison to mistakes or underperforming investments. If one is consistently and marginally outperforming their respective indexes, the mistakes are immaterial.

Satya highlights the importance of liquidity in investing. He explains that maintaining liquidity is important for everyone, and he and his team aim to keep 5 to 10 per cent of their total investments in liquid assets. Whenever they identify a good stock, they can quickly acquire it as part of their portfolio. Since it is not always possible to arrange funds immediately, he keeps some investments in liquid funds, listed bonds and ETFs. He also takes an overdraft limit against these securities. His strategy is to ensure that no money remains idle and that every penny is in the process of earning money so that one's financial strength is not negatively affected by inflation. This allows him to invest and avoid mistakes under pressure.

Personally, he prefers small companies and explains his rationale: 'We make small bets on small companies as they are easier to understand and tend to grow faster. As these small companies grow, the bigger participants make investments in them, causing their prices to appreciate more in comparison to their growth. By following strategies to invest in small caps, we are able to invest in a variety of businesses. When we find interesting opportunities in large caps, we like to buy them in futures, where we only need to pay margin money—roughly 15 per cent in cash and shares. We keep the remaining money in liquid funds.'

He adds, 'We try to widen our portfolio, and we feel comfortable with this strategy as our portfolio is less affected by swings. We also get higher dividend yields as smaller companies are eager to grow faster and provide rewards such as rights issues, bonuses, splits, dividends and buybacks.'

Satya also invests in new issues in the high-net-worth category. He finds the process easy and often yielding good returns.

Satya next shares his long-term view. He explains that in 2014, when a stable government came into power, the market began to consolidate. After Covid, a significant bull phase began, driven by working-from-home, a surge of new investors, and increased savings entering the market. He sees this trend as sustainable due to the government's emphasis on growth, infrastructure, railways, defence, space, the 'Make in India' initiative and sovereign bonds—all of which focus on high GDP and growth.

Satya adds that currently, only 7 to 8 per cent of the population is investing, but he believes this will grow to 20 per cent in the coming years. There are strong reasons for this, including rising literacy rates, improving standards of living, and the wide reach of the internet. A lot of investment is coming into the market. Companies are doing extremely well and many entrepreneurs are launching new projects. People are eager to participate in the market, and every new issue is heavily subscribed. Foreign institutional investors (FIIs) are investing in India. Stability has led to development across sectors and prices are booming. Such times, according to Satya, are opportune for investors.

'This is a super-duper phase—something I have never seen in my entire experience. It is all due to consistent calm situations and good governance,' he remarks.

However, Satya also advises caution, saying, 'At the same time, we should be vigilant to ensure our profits are not eroded due to mistakes. In the coming days, we should maintain enough liquidity to face changes in the scenario.'

CHAPTER 26

HIREN VED

The dynamic force behind India's wealth transformation

ALCHEMY Capital's co-founder, director and chief investment officer, Hiren Ved is a leader and veteran with over thirty years of experience in Indian equity markets. A postgraduate in management and cost accounting from the Institute of Cost Accountants of India, Hiren has developed a sustainable long-term investment philosophy grounded in fundamental research and based on his experience in the markets.

An introvert as a child, Hiren prefers travelling to quiet jungles for vacations rather than bustling cities.

Hiren loves the song *'Maula mere lele meri jaan'* from the Sharukh Khan-starrer *Chak De! India* and finds comfort in the midst of chaos by listening to Mohammad Rafi and Arijit Singh. With *Sholay* being his favourite film, Hiren is an ardent Bachchan fan.

A believer in the saying 'samay balwan hai' (time is strong), Hiren's favourite book is the century-old classic *Reminiscences of a Stock Operator* by Edwin Lefevre. He prefers comfortable clothing such as jeans and a T-shirt and comfort food such as masala khichdi and buttermilk. While he loves to dine at Café Madras in Matunga, he also enjoys dining at Golden Dragon at the Taj Mahal Palace in Mumbai.

Hiren's take on mistakes

Hiren begins with the admission that mistakes, especially in investing, can prove to be costly both in the literal and metaphorical sense. Fund managers seldom have the time to recoup their losses when a mistake happens. Thus, one needs to keep learning and evolving.

Hiren, being the market veteran that he is, reflects on his mistakes, the philosophy he has developed to maintain a calm temperament, what he looks for in people, and most importantly, how long a fund manager can afford to keep making mistakes.

A strong believer in taking criticism in the right spirit, Hiren emphasizes that it is essential to have an ecosystem of parents, friends, colleagues and teachers who can critique and point out mistakes, especially when it comes to investing. The key to avoiding mistakes, in Hiren's opinion, is to develop the ability to listen to such criticism and develop a healthy tolerance for it.

I ask Hiren how he differentiates between different types of mistakes. He replies by distinguishing between impulsive mistakes and those arising from misjudgement.

He elaborates by saying that mistakes made during testing times, such as Covid-19 or 9/11, typically stem from impulsive behaviour driven by fear, greed or extreme uncertainty. However, mistakes made during calm times usually stem from misjudgements.

Hiren confesses that, though he has significantly reduced mistakes with time and experience, he still commits some due to misjudgement. He cites the example of how, during the global financial crisis in 2008-2009, he sold several high-quality stocks, assuming they would fall further owing to their higher valuations, and held on to low P/E stocks. However, he eventually realized that it was not the high or low P/E that mattered. The stocks with the strongest cashflows and highest ROCEs bounced back the fastest, not necessarily the low P/E stocks.

Hiren notes that mistakes often bring out the best or worst in a fund manager. For example, a successful fund manager's career may be defined by how quickly they realize their mistakes, especially given the pace at which markets function. Hiren explains, 'Markets hand out judgement on a decision much faster than in personal life.'

He adds that mistakes should also be measured in the context of underperformance over time rather than at a single point. One way to do so is to evaluate returns over time, and if it relates to a particular stock, then to look at adverse price action or significant underperformance over a period as an indication of a mistake. In personal life, however, the realization of a mistake often occurs due to intuition and self-reflection, the veteran remarks.

While recognizing a mistake is just the beginning, rectifying it defines the true quality of a good fund manager. Hiren believes that it is easy to rectify a mistake made in investing by simply selling the wrong investment. In real life, however, it is more complicated, as a person needs to develop the ability to overcome one's ego. His motto in such circumstance is 'accept and adapt or correct'.

I ask Hiren about the tools he uses to prevent mistakes, and he explains that a person needs both internal and external tools for this purpose. He uses reflection as an internal tool, while externally, he relies on an unbiased ecosystem of people with good judgement and objective risk-management frameworks to keep him in check.

Hiren explains that an action that initially seems like a mistake may yield favourable results over time, and hence evaluating whether it was truly a mistake requires examining the process.

He points out that while a mistake might eventually turn out right, an investor does not have an indefinite amount of time to prove themselves. Success must come within a reasonable timeframe, and hence, he advises against relying on circumstances.

According to him, if a decision proves right within a reasonable period, one could conclude that it was not a mistake, even though it initially appeared so. 'It is very important to be able to judge the extent of loss you can incur if you are wrong. It is equally important to have the ability to correct one's mistake,' Hiren emphasizes while speaking of the thought process he adopts to cut losses.

He cites the example of investing in an illiquid stock, where the inability to exit could prevent one from correcting their mistake. 'It's not just about realizing a mistake, but also having the practical ability to correct the mistake,' he concludes.

I ask Hiren whether he has evolved over time by learning from his own mistakes and those committed by others. While agreeing that he has indeed evolved, he says, 'Every evolution is a process! I can never say that I am perfect.'

Speaking about what differentiates errors of commission from errors of omission in the context of investing, Hiren says, 'When I directly pay a cost, it is an error of commission, when I pay an opportunity cost, it's an error of omission.'

According to Hiren, a practical risk-management system is an absolute must in the decision-making process. He emphasizes that the system must be designed in a way that it is objectively enforced as risk management cannot be left to judgement.

Hiren confesses to having sat on losing positions for too long, assuming they would eventually succeed or turn around. He mentions holding on to stocks like Thomas Cook and Dishman Pharma during 2018-19 for too long despite large absolute drawdowns and relative underperformance, hoping that things would improve. However, he had not factored in the opportunity cost of holding on to these losing positions.

Hiren has a straightforward philosophy on assessing people while considering their mistakes. While acknowledging that everyone can be right or wrong at times, he points out that it is important to consider a person's strike rate—how often they make the right decisions. However, he makes it clear that he does not evaluate a person based on one or two instances of success or failure. 'I evaluate the track record of individuals over time and across different conditions to determine whose judgement I can rely on more consistently,' he says.

When asked about the role of exuberance and hubris in eliminating bad decisions, the veteran asserts that hiding a mistake has no meaning if one is brutally honest with themselves. 'Frankly, in the long run, it is very difficult to hide any serious mistake,' he remarks.

Decision-making is a multifaceted process influenced by numerous factors, including personal life. Speaking about the impact of personal life on decision-making, he smiles and says that his strong emotional quotient (EQ) enables him to handle professional responsibilities without being deterred by personal setbacks. He suggests that it is important to have a process that is not too person-centric. He is also very particular about his physical and mental health.

Hiren believes that mistakes can generally be viewed as an opportunity to learn if one has a positive outlook on life. However, a mistake can become a demotivation when no one appreciates the effort, even though it was not made with any malafide intentions.

When I ask Hiren why he is bullish on India, he remarks, 'India is a runner without shoes!' According to him, if the country has progressed this far despite all the constraints it has had to face, then it will shine going forward. 'I believe in the innate ability of Indians to progress and succeed because they are born with a certain resilience,' he adds with a smile.

Reflecting on what he would change if he could go back in time to reduce mistakes, Hiren says that he would follow his instincts more and seek advice from a guru who is smarter and more successful than he is.

Handling public funds is no joke, Hiren emphasizes. 'You better understand that it is a big responsibility before you decide to manage public money. Having the maturity to handle this situation is very important. The best approach is to be honest and have conviction and faith in yourself,' he advises.

According to Hiren, a person must be able to highlight their success and performance despite having made some wrong decisions while also being open to constructive criticism on wrong decisions. He notes that maintaining this balance is an art.

Elaborating on why he continues to commit mistakes despite his education and exposure, Hiren emphasizes that the human mind is fallible. 'Sometimes, unforeseen circumstances can make a decision look like a mistake, and it is impossible to fully understand the implications of all the variables that impact the outcomes of one's decisions,' Hiren remarks.

An avid reader, Hiren makes a conscious effort not be judgemental about people even though he observes their mistakes. He reads and reflects to avoid making similar errors.

Hiren makes a deliberate and thoughtful effort to avoid being judgemental about others, even when he notices their mistakes or flaws. Instead of rushing to criticize or form negative opinions, he takes a step back and reminds himself of the importance of empathy and understanding. He recognizes that everyone has their own struggles and challenges, and that making mistakes is a natural part of being human. Rather than focusing on the errors of others, he chooses to reflect on the situation, learn from it, and gain insights that will help him grow personally. He also dedicates time to reading and deepening his knowledge, as this allows him to gain new perspectives and avoid making similar mistakes himself. Through reflection, learning, and a non-judgemental approach, he seeks to improve not only his understanding of others but also his own behaviour and decision-making.

Conclusion

MY role in writing this book was only that of a well-wisher with some decades of experience in an almost homegrown model of investing.

I am not a qualified financial advisor and am nowhere near being in the league of those who have contributed to the chapters of this book by sharing their mistakes and biggest learnings. But I am very much a part of mistakes, and many investors will resonate with someone like them.

I approach every day of my life as a learner, amplifying what fascinates me and minimizing what doesn't. To be fair, I believe (which can again be a mistake) I am a good observer, be it at the airport, while grocery shopping, when travelling, when meeting people or simply when reading newspapers, magazines, blogs or reports. It is from these observations that I get my ideas.

I try to understand why people behave in a particular way, whether as investors, consumers or policymakers, and then assess whether such behaviour can lead to long-lasting benefits or is, to my mind, irrational, even if in the moment, and can thus create an opportunity for returns.

As a student of economics, I was fascinated by the following facts:

- Resources are always limited—you can read this as money and the ability to cull out all 'relevant' information.

- Choices are unlimited.
- Choices need to be made, and do not reflect instantly if they are rational or irrational.
- Choices, when made, use up limited resources and create a bias in the mind of a right decision, atleast for the time being.
- Facts determining choices are not constant and, therefore, to get to the importance or the relevance of facts and their ability to magnify returns and not destroy capital is more important than the nitty-gritty of factors such as the dollar index, oil prices, one-off results, promoters selling for genuine money need, foreign institutional investors buying data, among others.

  For example, an unfavourable quarterly result of a company could be a small setback in the scheme of larger growth or a very good result in a quarter may actually be 'one time' and not sustainable. Line items could be positive or negative, or may be different in the short term as compared to the long term. For example, a pharmaceutical company may be spending huge amounts on research and development and report lower revenues and profits in pursuit of a transformation, which may or may not materialize. A company may be acquiring other businesses and amortizing goodwill with the aim of creating a more robust profit model in the future.
- The market behaviour itself on a certain event—when it falls a lot—could be a passing phase in a larger landscape of an economic and company growth where some companies may make the most of the adversity while the others may fall with time. We saw this during Covid pandemic when technology became so in-the-face while consumers saw temporary surge being able to run plants even during lockdown but then suffered the consequence of a slowing rural growth. Technology, after its run, saw the global slowdown impact as quantitative easing slowed consumption by their clients. Simultaneously, the rising energy and logistic costs faced by some of their clients led to budget cuts or the deferment of new IT capex. Hotel stocks crashed during the lockdown and re-emerged initially

as part of 'revenge buying' and then as a transition of the effect of everyone wanting to experience something different and being part of social media likes.
- From the pursuit of law that followed my graduation, I learnt to have a mind geared towards facts, and to believe that a decision in court will support both, rendition of facts and what is proven by evidence. Here you may draw an analogy of a decision in court with a market decision where psychology and behavioural science play a key role in impacting demand and supply of stocks at any price. While the sum of the market trade may be zero in the cash segment with a buy meeting a sell order, the sentiment may not be a sum zero as sentiments tend to sway to excess fear or greed, which eventually shows up in inflated or deflated stock prices, and only a dissection of facts decides where the final result could move. Again, consequences of facts may differ today versus a month versus a year but over time, human decisions are known to have more accuracy of predictability as many factors settle and get discounted, than in a short term where, for example, a long-term investor or institution may not sell shares but the supply of the others rattles prices downwards and sometimes causes panic-based redemptions that defy the intent of even an established fund manager to hold or buy more by forcing him to sell to meet the redemption. This is a classic example of behavioural science meeting facts to arrive at a decision to find an opportunity to buy, hold or sell.

Being an investor over time, your brain and its reaction pick up several instances that serve as aid memoir in future 'logical' decision-making, also called 'temperament balancing', though, as humans, we tend to be swayed by headlines, flashes and noise of panic or euphoria than using tools such as learning from history, 'this time is different', 'buy the stock because someone says it will go up but you have no understanding of the company' or other seemingly 'delicious doses of poison'.

With the popularity of social media and an increase in the number of TV channels and the many stock-related services and reports, one tends to fall for another behavioural trap—once a person goes on a platform and holds a definitive view of his stock or portfolio as good, repeatedly, he finds it a 'social embarrassment' to reverse the trade and face social flak, even if to the rational mind, the change of facts suggests otherwise, or even if facts did not change but the story was impacted by the discovery of 'wrong valuations' and the age-old maxim 'market (stocks) reverts to its mean average'. The most important criteria for a good stock selection is not adamance of mind (called ego) but its valuation commensurate to growth. If valuations are attractive and growth continues, stocks do get revalued and discovered while if growth falters, then your conviction may be challenged as you are bound to face stagnant or underperforming market returns.

Remember that Buffett is often misquoted as saying 'buy and hold forever', a behaviour defied both by facts and a reading of the full quote, which is: 'Our favorite holding period is forever. We are just the opposite of those who hurry to sell and book profits when companies perform well but who tenaciously hang on to businesses that disappoint. Peter Lynch aptly likens such behavior to cutting the flowers and watering the weeds.'[1]

A mistake many make is not reading between the lines. Growth is growth till it grows. And when it falters, the valuation of a company may also falter.

At events and interactions, including those on social media, people often ask me how I manage my time and cope with such a diversified portfolio in addition to being a full-time, busy lawyer.

My answer is simple: you need to cultivate the habit of reading regularly, and once you do that, the incremental effect adds up over time as facts combine with intuition and experience.

Investing is not hard, it is a habit, honed over time by a focus on reading and understanding and controlling emotions.

Do not forget that decision-making itself is a product of variables where some are fact-based, some intuitive and some aim to minimize the effect of wrongdoing. When you eliminate something that is evidently bad, you have increased the chances of good, while by sticking to the good, you cannot guarantee that good will become best.

This is why investing is a matter of discipline and time, and the more time you spend in exploring your thinking and refining the process, the better could be the outcome.

Conclusion

You may have read often that some of the more established investors significantly compound in the post fifty years of their life as, by that time, they are not focussed on novelties and candyfloss but on utilizing their experience and honed patience with validation of facts towards hitting a home run of returns.

Many people are dissuaded in the early years of their life by their corpus, or even by not getting good returns or losses. They must understand, learning takes time. And small becomes huge when compounded. Don't think any amount is small as long as it is invested from disposable income and as a discipline, first towards saving and then trying to make that saving beat inflation. Many companies and their returns blossom late but when they do, the returns are akin to the growth of a bamboo tree.

Treat markets over time

There are days when stock prices are high. This is like attempting to hit a sixer on a yorker where there is a probability that you could be clean bowled or caught or trapped leg before wicket. You would do well to just block the ball and not get out on such days.

And then there are other days when you get a full toss or a badly pitched delivery, or what is called a free hit, and by capitulating that moment, you are likely to score better. These are the days when the market decides to offer you a scrip below value, and you do your bit by accepting it graciously. Remember, though, that in any case—whether a Yorker or full toss—you have to first be at the crease, as, if you dart in and out of the market, you may do so at the cost of some percentage of your money, but never for all or nothing.

Many writings on markets show that to make returns, you cannot afford to miss the good days of the market. Even if you participate in its bad days. Since a good day does not come defined on a calendar, being invested over time has proven to be rewarding than darting in and out with all or nothing.

A mindset that has worked for me is the belief that I will be invested to try and get the good days, and, perhaps, on the bad days treat it as a yorker by avoiding being out. I usually make a list of companies that I wish to own and a price band within which I may like to own them. If, on a bad day, a company falls within this, I ask myself—can the bad become worse? As in, is it a corelated issue that is sentimental, or a cardinal problem caused by acts such as poor governance or a bad capital allocation. I may reduce the price bands if time to heal is longer or even remove the scrip from my wishlist. But if the problem looks temporary, I remind myself, returns ahead require the company to do well ahead. Not just on that day.

From the description above, it is clear that one of the mistakes that many investors make—as do I, particularly the ones in the early years of my investing career—is to believe that you, and only you, will get the best returns in the market, so that when you are not getting the highest return, you disregard some of your winners, which are seeds waiting to bloom at the mistake of chasing fads and pop-ups.

Similarly, we compromise within our mind on what we understand and can corelate to, versus buying complexities that carry jargons from other people's mouth, and convince ourselves, as if by not participating in what is trending and at that moment seems maximizing our immediate returns, we will look foolish.

Here, you may draw an analogy of why Warren Buffett avoided technology at its peak and saved himself from the .com crash, while Prashant Jain chose to be invested, literally with headphones on, in public sector units while the world at large condemned them. Both had astounding results. Albeit over time. When the time was right and Buffett saw the kind of cash reserves Apple has, he evolved his block to make it his largest buy.

When I began my investing journey, I started with a small corpus of about Rs 4,800, which was led at the advice of a reputed chartered accountant to be invested in a fertilizer company, of which I knew nothing, except its name and the fact that it was cheaper than its peers in the same segment. Here was my mistake, a trap.

First, never invest in companies that you do not understand. I tried to force myself to understand potassium, or crop enrichment, as a theme as if I was brainwashing myself to be convinced that that was it and no further.

A lawyer is not an astronaut, and an astronaut is not a manufacturer; therefore there is a scope for competency and capability that is unique to all.

You need to identify your own capability and, following the well-known principle of 10,000 hours of practice towards betterment, invest adequate time to improve your competence and eliminate—as far as possible—

the mistakes and biases. When you invest in what you are competent to understand, you will find an invisible support from your temperament to stay. And when you stay, you make returns.

Coming back to the Rs 4,800 story, since I had invested in something that I did not understand, it did not surprise me in the later years of my life to realize that that money got eroded due to my own mistake rather than to a certain belief outcome of inevitable returns. There is nothing as inevitable in the investment world. Till date, that fertilizer stock has not reached the price which I paid then with my Rs 4,800, which typically made me think what could be wrong.

Over a period of time, I realized that investing is very scientific and easy, although the outcome may not be so, especially as we sway from good processes into what not to do.

For example, there are businesses that have high return on capital employed and businesses that are purely commodities and are at the mercy of factors outside the company for profitability. It may be that the company is doing something different to keep outside factors away, but if that is not the case, it is purely at the whims of a cycle. A fertilizer company depends largely on prices fixed by the government and farming policies, and it is logical today to think that no one will allow such a company to make extraordinary gains when the farmer is also a vote bank and higher prices to him impact inflation to all. I am surprised this escaped my common-sense thinking hat way back when I started.

At the same time, it is possible that even a fertilizer company is priced way below its potential due to a sudden impact or crash in, for example, DAP prices and you may be lucky enough to ride a cycle of down-trend into up-trend.

Do you have the capability to time a cycle is something you must deliberate upon as you may end up making good returns in such a company if you do or lose a lot of money like I did at the time when I had no capability to understand the cycle.

The second learning is to never give up. I lost a good chunk of my Rs 4,800, but I never hated the market for the whip.

On the contrary, the market challenged me as if I did not know the market and thus, must pursue a passage of learning.

What better way to learn than to study, and hence I started a journey of reading books that described others' successes and actions, as well as wealth-creation reports that suggested how some companies outperformed over time while others were eradicated by obsolescence.

Left with Rs 1,300 out of the original Rs 4,800, I was determined to invest it and not make the same mistake that I had made with the fertilizer company. (Not that I didn't. I made mistakes not only with fertilizer companies but also with others, and all these made me realize that it was important to study not just a particular industry but also a set of commonalities between fads, perceived low price being value and comfort, which is not secured by these alone).

Capital was an obstacle in my mind as I had only Rs 1,300 (I was still a student), which did not allow me to buy the shares of companies that I would have liked to own.

Here, I would like to elaborate that we are often tuned to self-imposed limitations in our mind rather than exploring solutions. I was restless to find a solution but not spending time on it, and fixated by the problem. Spend time exploring solutions rather than focusing on the problem—it works like magic.

I immediately made a list of some companies that I could understand and the list read somewhat like this:

- Cadbury, which held a monopoly in chocolates. It had penetrated not more than 1–2 per cent of the entire population and was still struggling to sell to adults than to children, a problem I thought they would solve as international use was showing different trends.
- Gillette, then known as Indian Shaving Company, where the size of the market, particularly in razors that they claimed would not cut the skin, was yet to be developed, and newspaper-reading suggested that acquisitions had started on the lines of products or brands such as Topaz.
- Bajaj Auto Limited, which dominated the scooter market, where there would be a huge wait for the delivery of scooters, and the company would throw up so much of profit that almost every year it announced a bonus.

Having made this list, I had to eliminate Bajaj Auto since the minimum buying size of 100 shares was far beyond the capital I had available. Instead, I travelled around the city to buy what were called fractional or odd lot shares of Indian Shaving Products Ltd (ISPL), Cadbury India and luckily, even Colgate. Not only did I get these, the sellers were happy to offer me 10–15 per cent discount on the prices as, to them, these were 'fractions' and did not have a trade ease as did lots. I found this abnormally a mistake on their part and an opportunity on my part. As I kept getting these odd lots and transferred them to my name, I eventually reached a lot size and was able to sell these and even if they had not moved up in price, which they did, the 15 per cent return in a year was a good buffer for me in my early start. I also discovered another interesting market anomaly. While some investors were interested in selling these odd lots at a discount, others were willing to buy them at a premium to complete their own lots. With my limited capital and understanding, I sandwiched my opportunity.

These, sort of, early buys returned good appreciation commensurate to my capital, and I started reading more on why.

My probe on the 'why' led me to articles by Warren Buffett, but I could not relate everything to India. Thus, I started reading posts written by Mr Chetan Parikh on his blog called capitalideasonline.com (CIO), where I chanced upon some articles written by Mr Parag Parikh and Mr Chandrakant Sampath, both of whom adequately emphasized why consumer companies had competitive advantages that could not be eroded and why, due to this competitive advantage, their profits earned did not require to be deployed back in the business and could be paid out to their respective parents (who were multinationals) as dividends.

I learnt then that in some companies, efficiency was two-fold. One, by top-line growth that came their way by branding power and innovations and second, they cut off leakages in their distribution and doubling of expenses and brought in bottomline gains. Most other companies were only about topline then. They also paid you dividends, often many times a year—as interim 1, interim 2, etc.—and returned cash to you to redeploy without materially impacting their stock price. In fact, markets loved the dividends and increased their confidence in these companies then. The size of market to be addressed by these companies then was huge given their market caps, and to be honest, they would not have been listed had it not been for a government directive that mandated them to list and not own 100 per cent—a reason why Coca-Cola withdrew from India then was this.

It was through reading and absorbing that I learnt that dividends are real cash and when paid out over a period of time, reduce the cost of your capital invested or give you the means to reinvest and build a corpus. There may be times when the dividend yield on the stock is close to or higher than the yield on a savings account or a fixed deposit in businesses that seemed to have high traction. Little can be done by companies who fudge dividend payouts as it involves real transfer of cash from a company to its shareholders.

I learnt that the assets and liabilities of a company may be classified into two categories: those that are authenticated by market forces and hence are true indicators, and the ones that can be played around with in a company's results and thus may be false indicators. For example, a company's claim regarding its bank balance can be authenticated by naming the bank in which the company has an account, and its claim to shareholder capital is authenticated by the Registrar of Companies (ROC) filings. The claim to inter-corporate deposits between one promoter arm of the company and the other may be based upon what is today called not at arm's length or fair pricing and thus, be disguised, just as later, it was discovered in the case of Satyam and Maytas that a lot of wrong can reside in a play of assets that are not fully authenticated and are presented as if.

Having learnt from the example of high returns from consumer companies, it became clear to me that my next step should be in that direction.

Here, the learning is—don't change a winning formula until it becomes outdated.

Instead of exploring buying in other companies, I then mustered up Rs 19,000 to buy fifty shares of Hindustan Lever Limited, as it was then called, which doubled my capital in a few years, way more than market returns.

The mistake many people make is, they do not enter the market thinking their capital is too miniscule, while it is actually the other way around—small leads to big, and big, if not nurtured, becomes small.

At this point, I still had little experience in the market and no access to the wizards who today feature in this book. To get hold of a book recommended by Warren Buffett was beyond my means as—I still recall—that *Poor Charlie's Almanack* was available at Jimmy Book Shop in Mumbai for about Rs 38,000 for a single copy, which was more than my investible capital.

Here begins the hunger search. Do not make the mistake of accepting things as they are and calling yourself somebody not ready for the market. I discovered that on the Bombay Stock Exchange, there were regular roundtables held every year at the Rotunda where some prominent fund managers would come and deliberate on companies, sectors and ideas. Admission was free and I jumped in, as free knowledge from a good source is priceless.

It was not necessary that whatever was discussed by these fund managers was bought by me the next day, a mistake that many make when an idea is discovered. Remember, economics teaches that prices are determined by demand and supply. Therefore, if a recommendation is made at an event attended by many, it is inevitable that demand the next day will outweigh supply to disturb prices. Suddenly, after a week, everyone who had to buy has bought and the price has moved up, causing some to sell and take money home and the principles of return to normal, which are evident in the market in a phenomenon called 'market reverts to mean', applied. Rather than concentrating only on buying basis tips generated by the round table, I tried to concentrate on 'logic'. Hence, I did not participate in some of these ideas but in their learning, and while I did not enrich my portfolio from returns, I enriched my mind by learning the 'why' and 'how' of investing, to whatever extent I could.

Here, I will point out a mistake, which is—all outcomes in the market are wrongly measured in money terms and very few in learning terms. Which brings me to the Japanese proverb 'do not give fish to a man, but teach him how to fish', and he will then not be hungry for the rest of his life. I started, thereafter, attending, as far as possible, presentations made by these fund managers to their investors and prospective investors, only to admire their differentiated thinking and hoping to make a mark. The question you may ask is, what led me towards this apart from the returns that some consumer companies had made.

The answer is that before engaging in this, I would frequently look up databases for sectors that were in vogue in the market, and then try to buy the cheapest stock, thinking that it would inevitably move up. Here lay my mistake, and you will see from the vast number of companies listed on the stock exchanges, that greatness is not qualified by cheapness but by management's vision to become a leader.

Sometimes, companies create complex webs of one acquisition after another, and an unrelated diversification to grow their revenue but partake debt and complex ownership structures that are highly disruptive to wealth creation. The simpler a company, the less the degree of variability in your understanding, and hence the chance of returns.

Realizing that it was not possible for me to be a full-time investor in few companies, some of whose stock I could not afford to buy, I decided to look beyond and diversify. Around this time, the legendary Chandrakant Sampat also went off the market, stating that the competitive advantage of owning shares in a few companies in consumer sectors was being lost to pricing perfection and over-discovery. New sectors were emerging, including technology, which in the years ahead, made less efficient companies more efficient, and hence, more profitable.

I would like to share my take on diversification versus concentration. Consider a class of fifty students of which five always perform in the top five. Based on this, can you accurately predict their success as businessmen and how much each of them will earn? Would you ignore the student who dropped out of school and set up a company in his garage, sacrificing his youth for his passion to build? While you may penalize one of your children for not doing as well as the other, what guarantee is there that this child won't bloom later in life and become a business tycoon?

Just as simple life has uncertainties, investing life has uncertainties, to minimize which, you diversify and then you end up increasing bets over a staggered period of time in the outcomes that are favourable and weeding of unwarranted or poor growth.

Diversification enables you to make mistakes. It enables you to learn across a group of companies rather than being fixated on a few outcomes. In many books where examples are given of concentrated investors, it is overlooked that these are remote examples by randomness, or what Nassim

Conclusion

Taleb calls 'fooled by randomness',[2] rather than examples across a normal staple of people. It is another matter that most books are written on success stories and few on failures, and there is, therefore, little data on failure available to learn from.

Bringing the discussion back to the subject of passion, that is, opportunity cost and the example of a yorker versus a full toss: I believe that even the thought process that all investing is to be done on a single day when money is available at a certain price is a folly. Secondly, many people ask on allocations: for example, if they own ten companies which they believe are good, then they will ask me why I put money on the eleventh.

Price is decided on the day of the decision. The price can make a stock attractive or unattractive. Money has the choice of being invested in stocks, lying in the bank at a certain interest rate, or being spent in the pursuit of luxuries in life. All of this constitute an opportunity cost. If on a day I own ten stocks and none of the ten has fallen or become more attractive in terms of yield, and I find that the eleventh stock is better in opportunity cost than money in the bank at 6–7 per cent, why would I not be pragmatic to buy the eleventh stock and maximize the opportunity cost. Don't forget that you are taking a fresh decision basis the best options and not pre-set options. If you find that you get returns on the eleventh stock, what makes you think that you cannot profit from that and go back to one of your ten if an opportunity arises. What if one of your ten is not ideal and the eleventh replaces the tenth. Here, I'd like to elaborate the mistake of making decisions on biases rather than facts. In the stock market, the principle 'goods once sold will not be taken back' is not applied. They will be taken back whether at a profit or loss depending upon your decision. There is no ego in admitting the widening of your mind to the eleventh idea than trying to become somebody who has scored a ten on ten in Olympics and next year, has to be satisfied with a silver medal. If Kapil Dev won you the 1983 world cup as India's captain, today, he is trying to do well as a golfer—here, Darwin's theory of adaptation for survival applies.

Another mistake I would like to elaborate is that learning is self—facts may be borrowed, but conviction has to be built. Conviction at some point also needs to balance ego, as once you have put your foot in a size nine shoe, it does not mean that a 9.5 or an 8.5 of another company may not be comfortable.

Sometimes, I make the mistake of being influenced by the exit or entry of prominent investors in a stock. You must avoid getting carried away by a me-too attitude without understanding your risk tolerance; your temperament; the logic behind owning certain stocks; exposure to net worth—their exposure might be only 1 per cent of a net worth, so they can afford to lose it, while yours might impact significant decisions, such as your next trip, a car or home purchase; access to the companies' working, factories and competitive advantages or disadvantages that you may not be aware of and hence, any wobble in prices may worry your ability to stay put. Remember, there are examples showing that even the legendary Rakesh Jhunjhunwala made more mistakes in buying stocks of companies than in the few he held long-term, such as Titan, CRISIL or Escorts, and the quantum of money made in the right decisions massively overweighed the mistakes that he would have made in owning companies such as A2Z Engineering.

Thus, in the market, it does not matter whether you are right or wrong—what matters is how much you make when you are right and how much you lose when you are wrong.

I could go on and on, but I shall conclude this chapter by sharing one of my greatest learnings—we live in a world full of volatility, uncertainty, complexity and ambiguity (VUCA). To accept that what my future investing will be based upon past is not entirely correct. For example, it may well be that the next leg of returns comes from an industry that I least understand.

Now if I rewind to the time when I did not even understand a Gillette or a Hindustan Lever, it opens the possibility of new learnings. Most of us are sceptical of new learnings.

We must accept the reality that by being students every day of our lives, we have a greater journey towards becoming teachers, but by being teachers, we create a possible dissection between practical and theoretical. Sometimes, for example, there might be a situation where a technology change, such as electric, is introduced and the whole world goes gaga over electric vehicles and their potential. At the same time, the industry leaders are deliberating on alternate technologies, from hybrid to hydrogen, and being focussed on a newbie in that sector and taking the valuations out of sync with multiple decades of returns, which can mean nothing except digging your own grave.

If you want to take the risk, start small and let the profits of the small—if it was to prove right—be the sponsorship cost of a larger mistake, but do not take the mistake of being the pandit who knows it all.

Till date, despite watching *Nostradamus* multiple times, I am amazed at how almost all predictions relate to a time when they have occurred and very few are relating to the time when they were to occur. Also, do not be the dinosaur who, despite being the largest, could not adapt to changes and today masquerades in amusement parks on musical tunes to remind you that he once existed.

Having explored a series of mistakes and learnings, we understand now that mistakes, when embraced and understood, are your true friends, while success is merely the glitter on the gold that will fade, unless repeated consistently.

Notes and References

Scan this QR code to access the detailed notes and references.

About the Author

Safir Anand is regarded as one of the world's top IP strategists and is a firm believer in behavioural science. With a dynamic career spanning multiple industries, Safir is a sought-after speaker at prestigious platforms such as the London Stock Exchange and the Bombay Stock Exchange, as well as the Festival de Cannes. A thought leader in the market space, his insights on the trends are frequently discussed in India's leading print and electronic media. Ranked among the most innovative lawyers in Asia, Safir boasts over a hundred awards and accolades for his exceptional work.

HarperCollins *Publishers* India

At HarperCollins India, we believe in telling the best stories and finding the widest readership for our books in every format possible. We started publishing in 1992; a great deal has changed since then, but what has remained constant is the passion with which our authors write their books, the love with which readers receive them, and the sheer joy and excitement that we as publishers feel in being a part of the publishing process.

Over the years, we've had the pleasure of publishing some of the finest writing from the subcontinent and around the world, including several award-winning titles and some of the biggest bestsellers in India's publishing history. But nothing has meant more to us than the fact that millions of people have read the books we published, and that somewhere, a book of ours might have made a difference.

As we look to the future, we go back to that one word—a word which has been a driving force for us all these years.

Read.